COOLEST GAME on the ROAD™

A Travel Guide to the NHL®

7.00

COOLEST

GAME

on the

ROAD™

A Travel Guide to the NHL®

with Stuart Hackle

Mike Brehm and Mark Paddock

Published by Total Sports
100 Enterprise Drive
Kingston, NY 12401

For information about permissions to reproduce selections from this book, please write to:
Permissions
Total Sports
100 Enterprise Drive
Kingston, NY 12401

Front phototgraph by Bruce Bennett Studios
Back cover Photograph by C. Andersen/BBS
Permissions appear on page 238.
Stadium diagrams, prices and maps by Aram Song

ISBN: 0-9656949-9-2
Library of Congress Catalog Card Number: 99-69882

Cover and book design by Donna Harris.
Printed and bound by Quebecor World, Tennesse, USA.
Scanning and color correction by Alan Radom, New York.

Visit www.totalsports.net and www.NHL.com

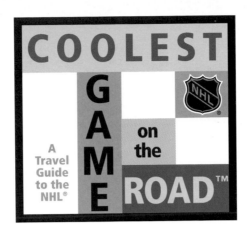

COOLEST
GAME
A Travel Guide to the NHL®
on the
ROAD™
NHL®

Table of Contents

Acknowledgements

Total Sports would like to thank Bruce Bennett Studios for a quick turnaround on images; Alan Radom, for scanning and color correcting all images; fact checker Stuart Hackle and copy editor Ed Dinger; proofreader Mikhail Horowitz; Greg Stangel, for finding numerous copies of the media guides for us; David McConnachie, for keeping a watchful eye out for us at the NHL®; Arthur Pincus, for getting us a quick approval during the holidays; Mike Walters for updating all of the illustrations; Melissa Selvage and Gene Previdi of Quebecor World; and all the teams, players, and people of the National Hockey League® who made the book possible.

Balliett & Fitzgerald Inc. would like to thank John Thorn, Publisher of Total Sports, and David McConnanchie of the NHL.

ANAHEIM

around the town with the Mighty Ducks

Paul Kariya #9

"This place is paradise," proclaims super sniper Teemu Selanne. He's not far wrong. With some of the most beautiful scenery in North America, Orange County and its surrounding area attracts people the way Selanne attracts defensemen. Do you want to see where the rich pass their days? Visit Newport Beach, which has more swanky hotels and houses than most states. Is surfing your passion? Huntington Beach is the unofficial home of the sport and the official home of the US Open surf championships. Or, if you want to get away from the crowds, you can find a place like Crystal Cove State Park (halfway between Corona del Mar and Laguna) and spend an enchanting afternoon in the tide pools.

Athletic types will feel right at home on the paved sidewalks near the Pacific Ocean if they want to take a run, a bike ride or an in-line skate. The mountains are a 90-minute drive away for skiing enthusiasts. During hockey season, in fact, you could ski in the morning, play beach volleyball in the afternoon and watch the Ducks at night. How's that for a full day?

Despite all of the attractions, the County is hardly resting on its laurels. In fact, Anaheim is undergoing a massive renovation of more than one billion dollars: Disneyland is expanding and the working-class neighborhoods are being upgraded. The Mighty Ducks are developing a different look as well. After six seasons in the NHL, the team has assembled a talented group of draft picks and regulars, and names like Ladislav Kohn and Oleg Tverdovsky and Matt Cullen should soon become familiar to hockey fans everywhere. Along with the three stars of Selanne, Paul Kariya and Guy Hebert, they give

Anaheim a bright future. Of course, in Orange County, things are generally bright, for the sun is never far away.

Arrowhead Pond

Where to sit:
The arena has good sightlines everywhere, but the best seats not taken by season-ticket holders are in the Terrace Level, about halfway up the stands. Occasionally, some tickets are available in the lower terrace when visiting teams don't use their allotment.

If it's all you can get:
The rear seats are in the corners and behind the goals and high, but the view is unobstructed. For the budget traveler, there are 500 seats available at $15 in the last four rows. But they go fast.

Special services:
There are about 150 to 200 wheelchair-accessible seats as well as devices for the hearing impaired and a guest services area.

Ticket availability:
During its first five years of existence, the team has sold out 142 of 207 home games. But tickets are actually easier to come by than these figures might suggest. For most games, walk-up tickets are available, although often only standing room or singles. It is best not to wait until the last minute if you want good seats.

Parking:
There are 4,500 official parking spots at $7. But several lower-priced lots are around the arena, starting at about $3. The area is fairly safe.

$175	$120	$75	$44	$32.50
$27	$15	CLUB/PLAZA SEATS		

Capacity: 17,174

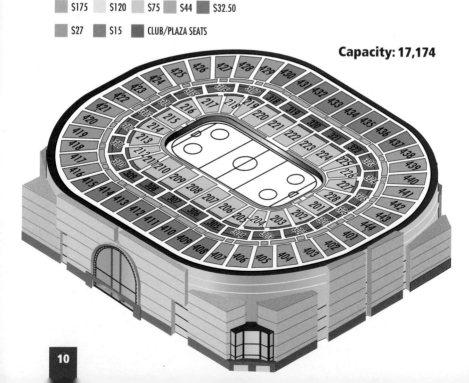

Public transportation:

Orange County Transit has a bus stop in front of the Pond on Katella Avenue. For route information, call 714-636-RIDE. But Orange County is so spread out that renting a car is the best bet.

By car:

Arrowhead Pond is located at 2695 Katella Ave., just east of the 57 Freeway. It's also within five miles of four other major freeways (the 55, 5, 22 and 91). From John Wayne Airport, take Freeway 55 North to Freeway 22 West. Take 22 West to Freeway 57 North. Exit at Katella and the arena is on the right.

Cuisine:

The Pond features a little of everything, from Pizza Hut and

Arrowhead Pond

Carl's Jr. Restaurant (hamburgers) to Chili Pepper's Mexican Stand (try the chicken soft taco) and the Main Street Deli where you can get a garlic clove chicken sandwich.

Home-ice advantage:

Visiting teams often enjoy the sunshine and tend to be just a tad less focused come game time. Some players have even been known to wear themselves out at the golf course before games.

Nightlife

For after the game:

The Ducks often congregate at **The Catch** (1929 S. State College Blvd., Anaheim, 714-634-1829), which is five minutes from the Pond and where the players all know part-owner Don Mayers. "It's a great place to go," ex-Duck Ted Drury says. "It has a bar on one side and a restaurant on the other, so you can go casual or nice. The food is great, too."

For a quiet drink:

Some players go to **Windows on the Bay** (2241 W. Coast Hwy., Newport Beach, 949-722-1400) to unwind after a game. Paul Kariya likes the nice water view from the patio.

To hear live music:

Ted Drury enjoys the blues at **Quiet Woman** (3224 E. Coast Hwy., Corona del Mar, 949-640-7440), and he says the food is even better than the music. If you want a more upbeat scene, visit **Marine Room Tavern** (214 Ocean Ave., Laguna Beach, 949-494-3027).

To watch a game:

The **National Sports Grill & Bar** has several locations in Orange County, but some Ducks hang out at the one just a few minutes from the Pond (450 N. State College Blvd., Orange, 714-935-0300). It's a huge place with pool tables and plenty of TV screens.

Dining

Italian:

Captain Kariya may not notice what adorns the walls of a restaurant, but he is passionate about the menu. "I don't care about ambiance, I care about great food," he says. He suggests either **Da Bianca Trattoria** (7448 E Chapman Ave., Orange, 714-289-1508) or **Barolo Italian Cafe** (13771 Newport Ave., Tustin, 714-734-8882), which he says has "the best chicken parmigiana."

For ethnic:

Excellent Oriental food is the hallmark of **P.F. Chang's China Bistro** (1145 Newport Center Dr., Newport Beach, 949-759-9007). Former Ducks coach Pierre Page loves **Zov's Bistro** (17440 17th St., Tustin, 714-838-8855). For good French cuisine, try La Fayette (12532 Garden Grove Blvd., Garden Grove, 714-537-5011). The specialties include Long Island duck flambe. And, of course, Mexican restaurants are prevalent. **La Casa Garcia** (531 W. Chapman Ave. in Anaheim, 714-740-1108) is a good bet.

Good chow:

Drury is impressed by the cakes at the famous **Cheesecake Factory** (1141 Newport Center Dr., Newport Beach, 949-720-8333). He also loves the cookie dough topping. Steak and salad, and other staples of American fare can be found at **The Barn** (14982 Red Hill Ave., Tustin, 714-259-0115). If you want to dine in a unique setting, go to **Hook's Pointe** (1150 W. Cerritos Ave., Anaheim, 714-956-6404). It is actually built inside the swimming pool of the **Disneyland Hotel**.

Guy Hebert #31

Lodging

Team's favorite:

Drury says visiting players love to stay at the **Westin South Coast Plaza** (686 Anton Blvd., Costa Mesa, 714-540-2500). "Guys like it because there's so much to do around there." The Westin has a walkway to **South Coast Plaza**, a major shopping complex with many shops, theaters, and restaurants.

Close to the arena:

Other teams stay at the **Hilton Hotel Suites** (400 N. State College Blvd., Orange, 714-938-1111), **Embassy Suites** (900 E. Birch St., 714-990-6000) and the **Doubletree Hotel** (100 The City Dr. S., Orange, (714-634-4500), which are minutes from the Pond. And, of course, there's the **Disneyland Hotel** which is walking distance to the theme park.

Down by the boardwalk:

The **Marriott** (900 Newport Center Dr., Newport Beach, 949-640-4000) is popular because it's next to the beach. One hotel that gives you a stunning ocean view is the **Hilton** (21100 Pacific Coast Hwy., Huntington Beach, 714-960-7873). Also in Huntington Beach is the **Sunset Bed and Breakfast** (16401 Pacific Coast Highway, 562-592-1666).

For luxury:

The **Four Seasons Hotel** (690 Newport Center Dr., 949-759-0808, 800-332-3442) in Newport Beach and The **Ritz Carlton Laguna Niguel** (335331 Ritz Carlton Dr., 949-240-2000, 800-287-2706) in Dana Point will treat you right. The Four Seasons has excellent views, a spa, aerobics studio, gym, whirlpool and lighted tennis courts and is next to the lavish Fashion Island Shopping Center.

Shopping & Attractions

Where to start? **Fashion Island Newport Center** (550 Newport Center Dr., 949-721-2022) is set on a bluff overlooking Corona del Mar and Newport Beach. It's trendy and expensive. Ted Drury loves the place because it features a great movie theater. "It's got the biggest screen in the Western United States." **South Coast Plaza** (I-405 at Bristol St., 714-435-2000) has been called the Disneyland for adults. It's actually three shopping centers (there's also **Crystal Court** and **South Coast Plaza Village**).

Teemu Selanne once said the best thing about being a Duck was getting to go to Disneyland for free whenever he wants. "I'm still a kid," he says. **Disneyland** (1313 S. Harbour Blvd., Anaheim, 714-781-4300) is actually several parks in one, with theme sections such

Mighty Ducks

On the Pond
Opened:
6/19/93

First regular-season game:
10/8/93,
7-2 loss to Detroit

First playoff game:
4/16/97,
4-2 win over Phoenix

First goal:
Aaron Ward of Detroit

Address:
2695 Katella Ave., Anaheim

For single-game tickets:
714-704-2701.

Website:
mightyducks.com

as Fantasyland, Tomorrowland and Frontierland.

If you want to hit the links, Paul Kariya and Drury recommend **Pelican Hill** (22651 Pelican Hill Rd., Newport Beach, 949-640-0238). "Even when you play bad, you have fun because of the view right on the ocean," Kariya says. January through March is a good time to go whale watching. Several companies offer outings, including **Newport Bay Harbour Cruise** (400 Main St., Newport Beach, 949-673-5245). and Newport Landing Sportfishing(309 Palm St., Newport Beach, 949-675-0550). For just a good sunset view, Drury recommends the cliffs overhanging the beach at Corona del Mar. Just pick a spot and relax.

Favorite City on the Road

Paul Kariya picks his first home, Vancouver. Family ties are very important to him, and he'll take a home-cooked meal from Mom instead of a gourmet meal at one of the city's many fine restaurants. A lot of Ducks enjoy New York and Chicago for their superb nightlife, while Toronto is a natural choice because many of them have families and friends there or in southern Ontario.

Cool Fact

Steve Rucchin took an unusual path to the NHL. While most top Canadian youngsters go to major junior hockey, he played high school hockey, "which is pretty much for kids who can't skate." He then played at the University of Western Ontario for fun while pursuing a degree. "The last time I had hopes of being in the NHL was when I was a little kid," he says. "I never thought about it until I was drafted by Anaheim (in the 1994 supplemental draft)." By the 1996–97 season, he was centering superstars Paul Kariya and Teemu Selanne.

Franchise History

Which came first: the Ducks or the Pond? Most fans assume

Teemu Selanne #8

ANAHEIM

that the creation of the Disney-owned Mighty Ducks of Anaheim was all part of a grand marketing scheme to capitalize on the success of the 1992 hit Disney movie "The Mighty Ducks." In fact, the arena that became known as the Pond was already under construction before the movie opened. The city of Anaheim, to showcase its community, had decided to build a world-class facility without a major tenant. Lucky for them the head of the Disney Corporation, Michael Eisner, is a hockey fan whose curiosity was piqued by the arena that was located down the street from where his son played hockey. "There was an arena and no team," Eisner said, "and I added two and two together. It came out to about 11 and I went and got the franchise." The Mighty Ducks of Anaheim joined the league on June 15, 1993.

Mighty Ducks

Oleg Tverdovsky #10

Famers

Most Valuable Player (Hart Trophy): None.
Hockey Hall of Fame: None

Records

Games played		Most assists, season		Most goalie wins, career	
Joe Sacco	333	Paul Kariya	62	Guy Hebert	133
Career goals		**Most points, season**		**Most goalie wins, season**	
Paul Kariya	168	Teemu Selanne	109	Guy Hebert	31
Career assists		**Most goals, game**		**Most shutouts, career**	
Paul Kariya	210	Several players	3	Guy Hebert	21
Career points		**Most assists, game**		**Most shutouts, season**	
Paul Kariya	378	Dmitri Mironov	5	Guy Hebert	6
Most goals, season		**Most points, game**		**Stanley Cups:**	
Teemu Selanne	52	several players	5	None	

Thrashers

Kelly Buchberger #16

around
the town with the
Thrashers

It sounds like the perfect nickname for a hockey team, doesn't it? Atlanta hopes to thrash more than a few opponents in the coming years, and with Ted Turner as owner, anything's possible. After all, when Ted decided he was going to start a 24-hour news station, few people thought it would work. Now, the 14-story CNN Center (which includes Philips Arena, the home of the Thrashers) in downtown Atlanta stands as a testament to his foresight and perseverance.

Atlanta is growing rapidly, so it makes sense that hockey should find a place here. The Midtown and Virginia-Highland districts are thriving again after falling on hard times, while downtown is home to such landmarks as Centennial Olympic Park and the Georgia Dome. Upscale Buckhead is the place to find high-quality shops to rival Fifth Avenue and Rodeo Drive.

Actually, major-league hockey has already been tried in Atlanta, so many fans don't even need to be recruited. The Flames played here from 1972 to 1980, and they didn't leave because attendance was poor. New ownership transferred the franchise to Calgary where the team went on to win the Stanley Cup. The Thrashers should capitalize on the puck-starved fans who have been waiting two decades to see another NHL game. In fact, quite a few were so excited that they drove 200 kilometers to Columbus, GA to watch the Thrashers' first exhibition game. With respected general manager Don Waddell at the helm—he worked for the champion Red Wings and also carried minor-league expansion teams to victory—the team is steering a course towards success. For Ted

Turner, nothing less will do.

Philips Arena

Where to sit:
There are no bad seats in this ultra-modern facility, but the best view of the action will be from the Club Seats, which are the first 19 rows next to the ice. The 90 Private Suites also have excellent sightlines. A Private Suite gives you televisions, a fridge, a bar and staff service, while Club Seats offer waiter service and access to three theme restaurants. As well, these seats are extra-large.

Ticket availability:
In the first year of an expansion team, expect the ticket demand to be high, especially on weekends. There are 300 $10 tickets that are released to the

Philips Arena box office two hours before each game. They're high up in the end zone, but you can't beat the price. Be aware that resale of tickets above face value is illegal in Georgia, and both scalper and buyer are subject to prosecution.

Thrashers

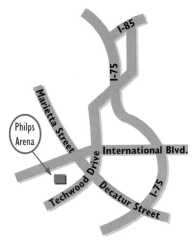

$70	$65	$55	$50
$45	$40	$35	$24
	call for information		

Capacity: 18,750

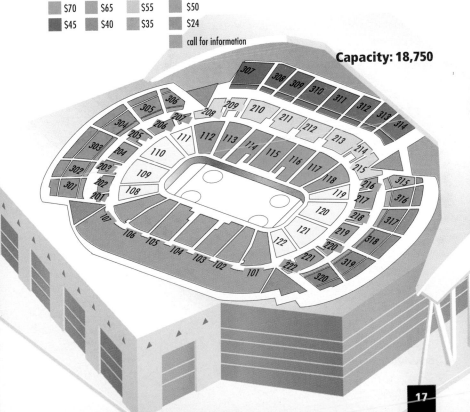

17

Parking:

Premium seatholders receive

VIP parking at the building. Since this is downtown Atlanta, there are also some spots available on nearby streets.

Philips Arena

Public transportation:

You can get to the arena by rail. Get off at the Omni / Dome / GWCC Station.

By car:

From I-75/I-85 South, exit at Williams St. (exit 99). Turn right on International Blvd. and go through Centennial Park. Cross Marietta St. From I-75/I-85 North, exit at Central Ave. Turn left on Decatur St., which turns into Marietta. Turn left on Techwood.

Cuisine:

There are 23 food outlets and four restaurants. The Suite and Club seatholders have access to the restaurants, which will offer seafood, Italian and American Bistro dishes.

Home-ice advantage:

Everyone knows how well the Atlanta Braves have been supported in the 1990s. True, the Thrashers aren't a contender yet, but expect the fans to be enthusiastic and loud.

Nightlife

Most of the action is located just north of Downtown Atlanta in Buckhead, one of the hottest upscale neighbor-

Andrew Brunette #15

hoods in the country. In a very small area you'll find more than 100 clubs and restaurants. Just wander around and you'll discover plenty of possibilities for a good time. Because Atlanta traffic is notoriously congested, consider using mass transit (MARTA) to get there.

If all you're looking for is a quiet drink and cigar try **Beluga** (3115 Piedmont Rd., 404-869-1090) or the **Havana Club** (247 Buckhead Ave., 404-869-8484). For the Boomer with happy feet there's **CJ's Landing** (270 Buckhead Ave., 404-237-7657). Dance music from the 1970s and '80s is featured on Friday and Saturday nights. If you're with a group mixed in ages you can't go wrong with **Mako's Cantina** (3605 Peachtree Rd., NE, 404-846-8096). It's three clubs in one. On the main floor Mardi-Gras is celebrated six nights a week. Underground is where the younger set will find high-voltage dance music. And if you simply care for a drink and a smoke, in the back is a cigar lounge/martini room.

Dining

For New American:

For an excellent dining experience, **Bacchanalia** (3125 Piedmont Rd., 404-365-0410) comes highly recommended. Its prix fixe New American cuisine is served in the charming setting of a Victorian home. It's difficult to get a reservation on weekends, so be sure to call early.

For steak:

If you're looking for a good steak, try **Chops** (370 W. Paces Ferry Rd., 404-262-2675), which also offers a lobster bar for those members of the party not partial to red meat. Although on the pricey side it's well worth it.

For soul food:

Since you're in the South, why not try some soul food? A fun place is **Agnes & Muriel's** (1514 Monroe Dr. NE, 404-885-1000). The food is good, not overly expensive, and the wait staff will keep you amused.

Players' favorites:

For upscale diner food, the **Buckhead Diner** (3073 Piedmont Rd., 404-262-3336) is where locals, out-of-towners and celebrities, including some of your favorite hockey players, go to enjoy such specialties as veal meat loaf, homemade potato chips with Maytag blue cheese and white chocolate banana cream pie. But be prepared to wait to get a table. If you're looking for a bite to eat before the Thrashers' game, or want to

Thrashers

Phillips Pull-ups Opened:
9/18/99

First regular-season game:
10/2/99, 4-1 loss to New Jersey

First goal:
Krzysztof Oliwa of New Jersey.

Ticket Information:
(404) 584-PUCK

Address:
100 Techwood Dr., Atlanta

For single-game tickets:
404-249-6400 or 800-326-4000

For suite rental or club seats
404-878-3000

Website
atlantathrashers.com

watch the game on TV, there's Jocks and Jills sports bar

Thrashers

located in the **CNN Center** (404-873-5405).

Lodging

Metro Atlanta has an abundance of hotel rooms, from luxury to economy. As the community continues to grow, expect even more accommodations to be added.

Closest to the Arena:

The **Omni Hotel** (450 Capitol Ave., SW, 404-554-3000) is part of the new CNN Center that includes Philips Arena. The Omni offers plenty of rooms but a limited number of suites; prices range from $220 to $240 per night.

Luxury Hotels:

There are several high-end hotels located close to the Arena, including the **Marriott Marquis** (265 Peachtree Center Ave., 404-521-000), **Embassy Suites at Centennial Olympic Park** (267 Marietta St., 404-223-2300), the **Hilton Atlanta** (255 Courtland St., NE, 404-659-2000), and the **Hyatt Regency** (265 Peachtree St., NE, 404-577-1234). Prices for suites run upwards of $300.

Mid-priced:

Less expensive hotels include **Courtyard by Marriott** (175 Piedmont Ave., NE, 404-659-2727, **Holiday Inn - Downtown** (101 International Blvd., 404-524-5555), **Howard Johnson Suites** (330 Peachtree St., NE,

404-577-1980), the **Sheraton** (165 Courtland St., 404-659-6500), **Westin Peachtree Plaza** (210 Peachtree St., NW, 404-659-1400), and **Residence Inn by Marriott** (134 Peachtree St., 404-522-0950)

Package Deal:

The **Days Inn Downtown** (300 Spring St., 404-659-2727) offers package deals for hockey fans. For $220 on weekdays and $275 on weekends you receive a pair of 200 Level tickets to a Thrashers game, a night of lodging, plus tokens for the MARTA/Thrashers shuttle. For more information on the package deal call 404-842-000.

Damian Rhodes # 1

Shopping & Attractions

There's no excuse for being bored in Atlanta. If you're staying near Philips Arena you'll be close to many shopping centers, restaurants, theaters and nightclubs. If the weather is inclement, check out **Underground Atlanta** (50 Upper Alabama St., 404-523-2311). This subterranean shopping complex may not be in the same league as the one in Montreal, then again Montreal doesn't get Atlanta's seasonable weather. Underground Atlanta takes up six city blocks in the heart of the city and features a dozen restaurants, more than 100 specialty shops, entertainment emporiums and street-cart merchants.

Upscale shoppers will definitely opt for trendy Buckhead. For a more mainstream experience try **Lennox Square Mall**, at 3393 Peachtree Rd, featuring hundreds of upscale, glitzy shops, anchored by Neiman Marcus, Macy's and Rich's. In addition to the usual food court, Lennox Square offers some nice restaurants as well. And if that's not enough, directly across busy Peachtree Road, and accessible via shuttle, is a twin mall, Phipps Plaza.

If you're more interested in a pleasant outdoor stroll and a chance to browse for antiques, furniture and jewelry, **"2300 Peachtree Road"** (same street address) is a collection of elegant shops not too far from the twin malls. "Gone With the Wind" fans won't be able to resist a visit to the **Margaret Mitchell House and Museum** (990 Peachtree St., 404-249-7012). If you miss it this trip, don't worry—tomorrow is another day.

If you want to get out of the city, there are 54 public parks all within a day's drive of Atlanta. Believe it or not, Georgia has mountains, and the activities aren't limited to the summer variety. During hockey season you can go snow skiing as well.

American History buffs can make day trips to such Civil War battle sites as the Chickamauga and Chattanooga Line **National Military Park** (Fort Oglethorpe, GA, 706-866-9241), our nation's first National Military Park, established in 1890. Located off of U.S. Highway 27, it honors the Civil War soldiers who fought at the Battle of Chickamauga and the battles for Chattanooga, which includes the Battle of Lookout Mountain.

If you prefer a taste of the Civil War without leaving the city visit the **Atlanta Cyclorama** (800-C Cherokee Ave., SE, 404-658-7625). The 1864 Battle of Atlanta is depicted in the world's largest diorama painting that revolves around the viewer. But don't expect to see Rhett or Scarlet.

And, of course, no trip to Atlanta is now complete without a visit to **Stone Mountain Park**, featuring the Confederate Memorial Carving that rivals Mount Rushmore in grandeur and outdoes it in scale. The figures of Confederate President Jefferson Davis, General Robert E. Lee and General "Stonewall" Jackson, all mounted on horseback, cover nearly three acres of the mountain's north face. But there is much more to the park. Stone Mountain Park

Thrashers

also boasts two golf courses, a lake, tennis center, wildlife preserve and petting zoo, and several museums. The Park is located on U.S. Highway 78, 16 miles east of downtown Atlanta. For more information call 770-498-5690.

Cool Fact

Twenty years have passed since the Atlanta Flames left for the cooler climes of Calgary, yet the Atlanta Flames Fan Club soldiers on. To share memories about the Flames, and perhaps other glorious lost Southern causes, check out the web page for the Atlanta Flames Fan Club. (atlflames.freeservers.com/ATLFLMS.HTM).

Franchise History

Atlanta may have been without NHL action since 1980, but that does not mean the area has been

Nelson Emerson #19

bereft of hockey. The Atlanta Knights played in the IHL for four seasons, winning the Turner Cup in 1994. The state also boasts three minor league teams, with rather colorful names: the Augusta Lynx, the Columbus Cottonmouths and, our favorite, the Macon Whoopee.

BOSTON

around the town with the
Bruins

Bruins

Dave Andreychuk #38

If you haven't been to a game in Boston for a while, there's still time—to see Ray Bourque, that is. The greatest defenseman of his generation is playing in his 21st NHL season in 1999–2000, but after that, who knows? Amazingly, Ray was elected to the Second All-Star Team in 1998–99 at age 38, although some people doubt if he's aged a day since he stepped into the league as a teenager.

There's a lot more to the Bruins than their captain, though. In fact, the entire defense looks remarkably solid with names like Kyle McLaren, Hal Gill and Don Sweeney. Up front, Joe Thornton, Sergei Samsonov and Jason Allison give Boston its best offense since the glory days of Cam Neely. Some people think the Bruins would have gone to the Cup finals in '99 if they could have squeezed past Buffalo—and they almost did. Yes, happy days are here again for the fanatics who inhabit the FleetCenter.

The new building lacks the quirks and intimacy of the old Garden, so it doesn't have the latter's wild and intense atmosphere, but it is miles ahead in comfort and service. Moreover, the fans still know when to turn up the noise. Just watch what happens when the Bruins skate in an important playoff game.

It's appropriate that the Bruins have such a rich history, since Boston itself is a historical gem, a 360-year-old matron who has watched local children such as Paul Revere, John Hancock, Samuel Adams, John Fitzgerald Kennedy and many others grow up to change their world. Where else would Bobby Orr—the man who revolutionized defense—go to ply his trade? In Boston, people cherish tradition, and the current crop of Bruins knows it well.

Where to sit:
Unlike the Boston Garden, the FleetCenter has no obstructed-view seats. There really are no bad seats in the house, either. The loge sections and balcony rows 1–2 are sold out with season tickets, but plenty of other prime locations are available. The club seats are excellent and include waiter service.

If it's all you can get:
The Bruins sell tickets on one side of Level 9, the halo where the media sit. While it is high up and a bit back from the ice, it's very comfortable. It is away from the concourse traffic and has its own concession stand and restaurant facilities. It's also near the Bruins' alumni room, so you're likely to get a glimpse of the former greats who pop in to watch the game.

Special services:
If you need special seating, call 617-624-1754. In the FleetCenter, you can find customer service on Level 4, Portal 4. The people in Customer Service can help with a variety of problems. The event line for hearing-impaired fans is 800-943-4327. The arena was designed for the disabled, and all seating configurations reflect that. For disabled patrons who are con-

$77 $140 $57 $46
$41 $27 $20

Capacity: 17,565

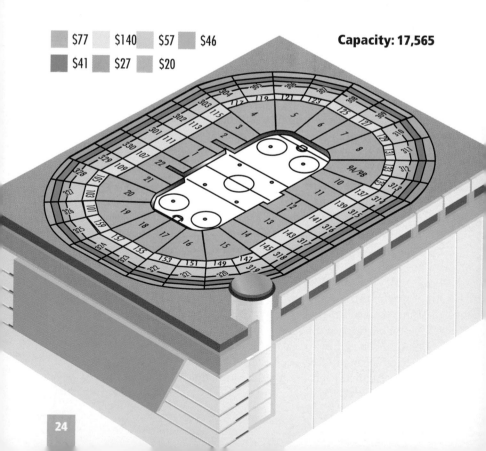

cerned about where to park, the MBTA can answer questions at 617-222-3042.

Ticket availability:
Attendance was up last year, but there are still enough seats available for most games. Games against the New York Rangers sell out fast, and games against other "Original Six" teams and Philadelphia are big draws. For group tickets, call 617-624-BEAR.

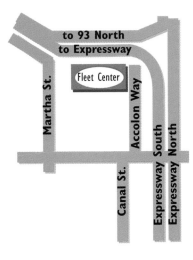

Parking:
The FleetCenter has parking for 1,150 cars and costs $15. The bad news is that if you plan to go out and party after the game, you have to have your car out of the FleetCenter garage by 1 a.m. Otherwise, it's stuck there

until the morning commute.

Public transportation:
The Green and Orange lines drop you right at North Station on the MBTA, which is across the street from the arena. Also, commuter rails run underneath the FleetCenter.

By car:
Because of Boston's tough traffic conditions, driving to the game is not recommended. But if you must bring your own car, the FleetCenter is accessible by taking the Causeway Street exit on I-93 North and then turning left. Bear to the right after that, then take a right at the lights. Another right will take you to the FleetCenter garage. A better way to get to the same garage is to take the Storrow Drive exit off Rt. 93 (going North). Bear right off the exit (don't go through the tunnel) and continue bearing right at the light. At the stop sign, take a left. That will give you the option of parking in the garage you first come to (on the right) or taking a left toward the FleetCenter, which brings

Bruins
FleetCenter Facts
Opened:
9/30/95

First regular-season game:
10/7/95, 4-4 tie with New York Islanders

First playoff game:
4/24/96, 4-2 loss to Florida

First goal:
Sandy Moger of Boston

Address:
One FleetCenter, Boston

For single-game tickets:
617-931-2222 or 508-931-2222.

Website
bostonbruins.com

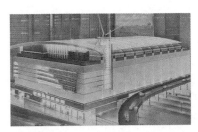
FleetCenter

you right to the FleetCenter garage.

Cuisine:

Legends, located in the Fleet-Center, is a restaurant for season-ticket holders; The Premium Club is for premium seat holders, which includes club seating and skybox patrons. For everyone else, there are 39 permanent concession stands. The fare at the Fleet is pretty basic—pizza, deli sandwiches, nachos, pretzels, popcorn, hot dogs, ice cream, beer and soda.

Home-ice advantage:

Everybody remembers the tight, intimidating confines of the Garden—191 feet by 83. Well, with all the NHL rinks standardized, the Big, Bad Bruins had an adjustment period when they moved to their new home. The crowd, which had been practically on top of the ice surface and was as rabid as any in sports, was no longer the force it once was. The increase in prices forced out some loyal fans and a quieter, more business-oriented fan base took their place.

Nightlife

For after the game:

Players tend to head over to **Harp at the Garden** (200 Portland St., 617-742-1010) across the street from the FleetCenter. "They're good about keeping the kitchen open," says Bruins winger Steve Heinze. "They have

Sergei Samsonov #14

appetizers like chicken fingers. It's American dining. I'd call it upscale bar food." Another attraction is the live music on the weekends, which can be pretty loud. Goaltender Rob Tallas has been known to join his friend, Tim Crandall, onstage for a little guitar playing, but he says he wouldn't be caught dead singing. "Tim doesn't bring an extra microphone for me," says Tallas, laughing. "That's because he's heard me sing. But I love to play the guitar."

Daisy Buchanan's (240 Newbury St., 617-247-8516), draws NHLers from other cities and pro athletes from other sports, though the Bruins tend to stay closer to the FleetCenter. **Dad's Beantown Diner** (911 Boylston St., 617-296-3237) caters to a young just-became-legal crowd that consists mostly of college kids.

For a quiet drink:

No bars immediately around the FleetCenter are particularly quiet because pre- and postgame they're usually packed, but Heinze says if he had friends in from out of town, he'd likely drop by **The Sail Loft** (80 Atlantic Ave., 617-227-7280). "It's pretty relaxing," Heinze says. The food there is decent and during the warmer months, you can get a good look at the wharf.

Two other options, also on Atlantic Ave., are **Tia's on the Waterfront** (200 Atlantic Ave., 617-227-0828), a seasonal restaurant, and **Joe's American Bar and Grill** (100 Atlantic Ave., 617-367-8700). Both are fun

to visit during the summer and are close to the Marriott Long Wharf.

For shooting pool:

A popular place to shoot pool and talk pucks is **The Rack** (24 Clinton, 617-725-1051) at Faneuil Hall. Byron Dafoe likes its roominess, while Heinze praises its food, which he terms "California pizza kitchen." The Bruins have held end-of-season celebrations in another pool hall, **Jillian's** (145 Ipswich St., 617-437-0300), which is in Kenmore Hall and adjacent to Fenway Park.

Bruins

Dining

For Italian:

If you want to find a Bruins player having his pregame meal, postgame meal or meal on a night off, the North End is a terrific bet. The famous Boston neighborhood is full of delightful small restaurants with the best Italian food outside Italy. "You can't go wrong anywhere in the North End," says Bruins winger Steve Heinze. "But I really like **La Cantina Italiana** (346 Hanover St., 617-723-4577). I'm friendly with the owner and most of the people who work there. I like the chicken, broccoli and ziti in a red sauce." On the walls of the restaurant are photos of the famous people who have stopped by for a meal, including many Bruins.

Heinze also recommends the chicken parmigiana at **Mother Anna's** (211 Hanover St., 617-

523-8496). The grilled-vegetable appetizer at **Massimino's** (207 Endicott St., 617-523-5959) is very tasty and could even be an entree if you're a light eater.

Bruins goalie Byron Dafoe swears by **Trattoria Scalinatella** (253 Hanover St., 617-742-8240). "There are only about 10 tables," says Dafoe. "It has a fireplace and it's like eating in your living room. It's very private." Rather than relying on a traditional menu, the chef whips up certain specials of the day.

Backup goalie Rob Tallas says he found his restaurant a couple of years ago when his job situation necessitated he live in a hotel. "The last two years I've had every pregame meal at **Antonio's** (286 Cambridge St., 617-367-3310)," says Tallas. "They know me now. They take great care of me . . . I would eat there before games and after games, they'd keep the kitchen open for me. They even used to send a meal over to the hotel for me." He even has his own dish with chicken, mushrooms and pasta in a lobster/cream sauce that also has some marinara in it.

For steak:
Dafoe recommends **Morton's of Chicago** (1 Exeter Plaza, 617-266-5858). "Usually when I have friends or family come in from Canada we go there," says Dafoe. "They don't have Morton's in Canada. You can't go wrong there. The 48-ounce double porterhouse is unbelieveable." Dafoe says one of his friends actually finished all of it but paid for it afterward anyway.

Fan favorite:
A good pre-game spot is the **Four's Sport's Bar** (166 Canal St., 617-720-4455), across the street from the FleetCenter. The food is delicious and reasonably priced. It's worth a visit just to see the impressive memorabilia on the downstairs and upstairs walls. Reservations on game nights are recommended. There can be a substantial wait if you don't get there early, but the wait-staff, used to feeding fans, can get you in and out quickly. Although. some Bruins stop by after the game, it's more of a post-game media hangout because it serves its full menu until midnight.

Lodging

For luxury:
If you're looking for ultra-posh, check out The **Four Seasons Hotel** (200 Boylston St., 617-338-4400, 800-332-3442). During the holiday season, it's a treat to sit in the lounge, have a drink by the fireplace and take in the festive atmosphere. The hotel is pricey, but it will get you in the holiday spirit faster than standing in line at one of the city's many shopping malls. Close to the arena **Marriott Long Wharf** (296 State St., 617-227-0800) is convenient. In addition to being close to the arena, it's walkable to the Faneuil Hall shops and the restaurants of the North End. It's also next door to the Chart House restaurant and is very close to the outstanding Boston Aquarium.

Location, location:

The **Boston Marriott at Copley** (110 Huntington Ave., 617-236-5800) and The **Westin at Copley** (10 Huntington Ave., 617-262-9600) are next to each other and close to many restaurants on Boylston Street. They are within walking distance of Newbury Street. The mall inside also has some very upscale shopping and a sports bar called **Champion's**, which features a decent menu and good atmosphere, although it tends to be a bit loud at night.

Shopping & Attractions

Newbury Street is the place to go for upscale shopping. There are plenty of good restaurants–**Ciao Bella** (240A Newbury St., 617-536-2626) is one—and it's a fun place to people-watch. There are also plenty of hair salons and designer clothes. "Now that guys are fortunate to be making some money, you see guys there more," says Heinze. "Whether you're looking for art or nice clothes, you can find it there."

Jason Allison travels a little farther north for his clothes. He likes **Giblee's** (85 Andover St., Danvers, 978-774-4080) because he can find high-quality suits and casual wear under one roof.

If you're in the mood for

Bruins

Jason Allison #41

29

something educational, look no further than the three-mile-long Freedom Trail. It will take you past 16 historic sites and starts at the Visitor Information Center in Boston Common.

The North End has historic sites worth noting, including the oldest house in Boston, The **Paul Revere House** (19 North Sq., 617-523-1676). It's closed January to March and there is an admission charge when it's open. The **Old North Church** (617-523-6676), which housed the lanterns for Paul Revere's famous ride is located on 193 Salem St. If you head over into Charlestown, make sure to stop by the USS Constitution, aka Old Ironsides. It's moored in the Navy Yard.

If you want to entertain your kids, you should find an answer at the **Children's Museum** (300 Congress St., 617-426-8855). If that doesn't work, try the **Museum of Science** (617-723-2500) and its **Charles Hayden Planetarium and Mugar Omni Theater**.

Favorite City on the Road

Ask a professional athlete who plays in the winter where his favorite city is and they almost all say, "Anyplace warm." Bruins winger Steve Heinze says while he enjoys Los Angeles because of the abundance of activities, he enjoys Miami, and specifically South Beach, the most. "My favorite restaurant is **Joe's Stone Crab**. The stone crab is unbelieveable. It's like lobster but it's softer, moister and tastier. And you don't need cocktail sauce. It's that good."

Dave Andreychuk has been known to order buckets of Buffalo wings for his teammates from **Frank and Teressa's Anchor Bar** when his team visits Buffalo.

Montreal's restaurants are perennially popular. **Moishe's Steak House** will sometimes host Canadiens and opposing teams like Boston at the same

Ray Bourque #77

time. **Gibby's**, in old Montreal, doesn't know how to serve a bad meal, and **Il Duomo** serves fine pizza for those Bruins who want a simple meal.

Dafoe is one player whose imagination is stirred by the European air of the city. "Montreal reminds me of what it might be like in Paris, even though I haven't been over there. And everyone is dressed up all the time. Everyone looks classy, even at games."

Cool Fact

At the start of his career Ray Bourque wore No. 7, the same as Hall-of-Famer Phil Esposito. When the Bruins retired Phil's number 7, Bourque took off his jersey and handed it to Esposito, revealing his new number, 77, underneath.

Franchise History

As one of the "Original Six," the Boston Bruins history is long and rich. The club was awarded an NHL franchise on November 1, 1924, the first based in the U.S. Fan interest grew rapidly, prompting ownership to construct Boston Madison Square Garden (backed as it was by New York money). The building that became simply known as Boston Garden was an immediate success, as 17,500 fans packed it on opening night to watch the Bruins play the Canadiens on November 20, 1928. Official capacity was only slated at 14,500. The Bruins have remained immensely popular ever since: through the glory years of Eddie Shore; the "Kraut Line" of Schmidt, Dumart and Bauer that finished 1–2–3 in scoring one season; to the golden years of Bobby Orr and Phil Esposito; to Don Cherry's "Lunchpail Team" of overachievers in the late 1970s; to Ray Bourque's illustrious career; and now a young team of emerging stars playing in a new arena that's still too small to hold all the Boston Bruins fans that would like to come to cheer on the five-time Stanley Cup Champions.

Bruins

Famers

Most Valuable Player (Hart Trophy): Eddie Shore, 1933, 1935, 1936, 1938; Bill Cowley, 1941, 1943; Milt Schmidt, 1951; Phil Esposito, 1969; Bobby Orr, 1970, 1971, 1972; Phil Esposito, 1974.

Hockey Hall of Fame: Players: Eddie Shore, Aubrey "Dit" Clapper, 1947; Mickey MacKay, 1952; Frank Fredrickson, Sprague Cleghorn, 1958; Cy Denneny, Cecil "Tiny" Thompson, 1959; Sylvio Mantha, 1960; Milt Schmidt, 1961; Nels Stewart, 1962; Albert "Babe" Siebert, 1964; Marty Barry, 1965; Walter "Babe" Pratt, Frank Brimsek, 1966; Harry Oliver, 1967; Bill Cowley, 1968; Tom Johnson, 1970; Harvey Jackson, Ralph "Cooney" Weiland, Terry Sawchuk, 1971; Reginald "Hooley" Smith, 1972; Billy Burch, 1974; Bill Quackenbush, 1976; Jacques Plante, 1978; Bobby Orr, 1979; Harry Lumley, 1980; Allan Stanley, Johnny Bucyk, 1981; Phil

Esposito, Bernie Parent, 1984; Gerry Cheevers, Jean Ratelle, 1985; Leo Boivin, 1986; Brad Park, 1988; Fern Flaman, 1990; Woody Dumart, 1992; Guy Lapointe, 1993; Roy Conacher, 1998.

Builders: Charles Adams, 1960; Walter Brown, 1962; Weston W. Adams, 1972; Harry Sinden, 1983.

Retired numbers: 2 Eddie Shore, 3 Lionel Hitchman, 4 Bobby Orr, 5 Aubrey "Dit" Clapper, 7 Phil Esposito, 9 John Bucyk, 15 Milt Schmidt.

Bruins

Byron Dafoe #34

BOSTON

Records

Games played		Most points, season		Most goalie wins, career	
Ray Bourque	1453	Phil Esposito	152	Cecil "Tiny"	
Career goals		**Most goals, game**		Thompson	252
John Bucyk	545	Several players with	4	**Most shutouts, career**	
Career assists		**Most assists, game**		Cecil "Tiny"	
Ray Bourque	1083	Bobby Orr		Thompson	74
Career points		Ken Hodge	6	**Most shutouts, season**	
Ray Bourque	1468	**Most points, game**		Hal Winkler	15
Most goals, season		Bobby Orr		**Stanley Cups:**	
Phil Esposito	76	Phil Esposito		1929, 1939, 1941,	
Most assists, season		Barry Pederson		1970, 1972.	
Bobby Orr	102	Cam Neely	7		

BUFFALO

around the town with the
Sabres

Sabres

Miroslav Satan #81

From a simple idea, multi-million dollar results can flow. Two of the most important products of Buffalo are proof of that. As the story goes, the Buffalo wing was invented in the city's Anchor Bar by Teressa, a cook. She took a batch of chicken wings, sliced off the tips and cut them in half. She then deep-fried the lot and served them with celery and bleu cheese dressing. Suddenly, everyone in the city wanted them. Now, a couple of decades later, they provide the North American restaurant industry with millions in profits every year.

Unlike chicken wings, the Buffalo Sabres were the product of two minds: Seymour and Northrup Knox. They knew the city was ripe for an NHL franchise in the 1967 expansion, though they had to wait until 1970 to land a team. Playing in the small and intimate War Memorial Auditorium, the Sabres grew on the locals with their flashy and skilled style. Indeed, throughout most of the 1970s, Buffalo had as much natural talent as any team in the NHL except Montreal. Nowadays, the Sabres win with hard work and defense: not just from their All-Universe goalie, Dominik Hasek, but from the entire roster. It's an approach the blue collar natives appreciate, and it's proven to be even more successful than the old, attack-first mentality.

Not only do the Sabres have a winning team, they have a winning place to call home. Marine Midland is a beautiful, glass-walled stadium with a playoff atmosphere that rivals any in the league. The fans have watched Division and Conference champion flags being raised, and they know there's still space for a Stanley Cup banner to fly alongside Buffalo's wings.

Marine Midland Arena

Sabres

Where to sit:

The Arena has the standard upper bowl/lower bowl configuration, with club-level seats in the middle. The club level has the most expensive tickets, but because of the distance. the lower bowl actually may offer a better view. The best bargain is in the 100 level end zone.

If it's all you can get:

Buffalo will charge $19 for an upper end-zone seat. That's still a pretty good deal, if you don't mind the altitude.

Special services:

There are many areas for wheel-chair seating on every level of the building. Call 716-855-4100 for information.

Ticket availability:

Most games usually aren't sold out in advance, so with a little planning you should have no problem getting into the Arena.

Parking:

It's plentiful and all around the building at a variety of prices. By Boston or New York standards, it's also dirt cheap.

Public transportation:

The subway line goes right down Main Street to the arena, and it's free in the downtown section. You can't beat it for convenience.

$70 $63 $52 $44 $31

$26 $19

Capacity: 18,595

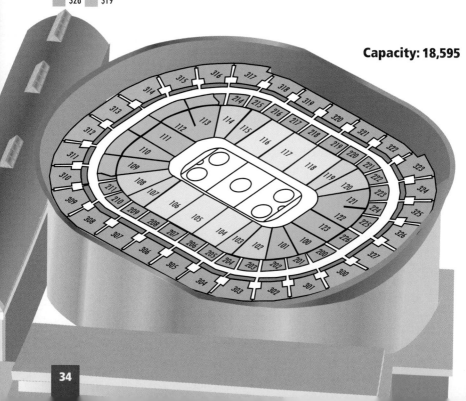

By car:
Take Interstate 190 to downtown Buffalo, and use the Elm Street exit. Take a left on Swan and a left on Washington. The main entrance is essentially at the start of Washington Street on the waterfront. It's relatively easy to get in and out of the area on game nights.

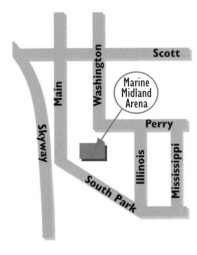

Cuisine:
For most fans, it's pretty standard arena fare these days. But those who have paid to get into the 200 level can order a variety of items directly from their seat. They also can walk to the Harbour Club for dessert or a snack and beverage—all while watching the game.

Marine Midland Arena

Home-ice advantage:
It's not like it was in the good old days of Memorial Auditorium, where visiting teams needed time to adjust to the smaller ice surface. This new Sabres home isn't quite as loud as the old one, as the modern acoustics dampens the noise. Still, Buffalo hockey fans are loud and knowledgeable.

Nightlife

For after the game:
Richard Smehlik likes **Colter Bay Grill** because "It's only five minutes from the arena, and the menu has a lot of things to choose from." Stu Barnes enjoys **Mother's Restaurant** because "They have a very good late-night menu, and when the weather's nice, you can't beat the patio." Wayne Primeau says "My favorite part about the **Buffalo Brew Pub** is the free peanuts and popcorn. And they don't even mind when you throw the shells on the floor."

For live music:
The Lafayette Blues Room in the **Hotel Lafayette** (391 Washing-

Sabres
Marine Midland Marks

Opened:
9/21/96

First regular-season game:
10/12/96,
6–1 loss to Detroit

First playoff game:
4/17/97,
3–1 win over Ottawa

First goal:
Slava Kozlov of Detroit

Address:
One Seymour Knox III Plaza, Buffalo

For single-game tickets:
888-223-6000.

Website:
sabres.com

ton St., 716-855-2587) is a cozy place to take in some 12-bar rhythms, as is the **Lafayette Tap Room** (320 Pearl St., 716-855-8800). Not every place in Buffalo is called Lafayette. The **Tralfamadore Cafe** (100 Theater Pl., 716-851-8725), which

Sabres

takes its unique name from a novel by Kurt Vonnegut, is a local institution. Every conceivable type of band has played there.

For a quiet drink:
Founding Fathers (75 Edward St., 716-855-8944), about 10 minutes from the arena, has been a media hangout for years. The atmosphere is Revolutionary era, and popcorn is free. **The Swannie House** (170 Ohio St., 716-847-2898) is a few blocks from the Arena. It's small, quiet and down-to-earth.

For watching a game:
The specialty at **Damon's Clubhouse** (5483 Sheridan Dr., Williamsville, 716-565-0295) is either ribs or televisions: there are four giant screens on the walls, with speakers provided at each table. Former Sabres Matthew Barnaby and Brad May were fond of this joint.

Dining

Local fare:
If you have tried Buffalo wings in other cities, you'll realize that they are a sad imitation of the real thing when you visit the city where they originated. Chicken wings were first served at **Anchor Bar** (1047 Main St.,

716-886-8920) in Buffalo. The wings fly out of there in huge quantities every night. Of course, other restaurants around town serve them as well. The other local delicacy is beef on weck, a roast beef sandwich served on a special type of salted roll.

Dining with a view:
James Patrick has been in the league for 16 years, so he knows where to go. He says "There is probably no better view of the Buffalo riverfront than **Harry's Harbour Place Grille** (2192 Niagara St., 716-874-5400). I'd recommend the seafood."

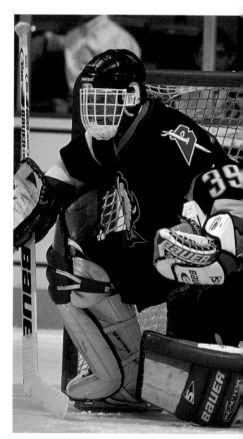

Dominik Hasek #39

For celebrity watching:
Chef's (291 Seneca St., 716-856-9187) is a classic Buffalo place to go. You are likely to see top political figures, business executives and sports stars all within a few tables of each other. Chef's specializes in Italian food, and it's only a few blocks from the Arena.

Lodging

Closest to the arena:
The Adam's Mark (120 Church, 716-845-5100) is a relatively easy walk, and you'll pass the team's old home, Memorial Auditorium, along the way. A majority of the visiting teams stay here, so you might get to see some of your favorite stars in the lobby.

Also downtown:
The other major hotel is The Hyatt (2 Fountain Plaza, 716-856-1234, 800-233-1234). The metro rail on Main Street runs right by it on the way to the Arena, and it's a free ride. If visiting teams aren't at the Adam's Mark, they are at the Hyatt.

There are a couple of other, smaller hotels in the downtown area, such as the Holiday Inn (620 Delaware Ave., 716-886-2121).

For more upscale tastes:
You have to head to the suburbs. Williamsville has the Marriott (1340 Millersport Hwy., 716-689-6900) near the University at Buffalo, while Cheektowaga has the Sheraton (2040 Walden Ave., 716-681-2400) a short ride from the airport.

Both are 15–20 minutes away from the arena by car or taxi.

Shopping & Attractions

If you want to buy something hockey-related, your best bet probably is right in the arena. The Sabres' store is open during the day and on game nights. There are even some game-worn uniforms on sale every so often.

Sabres

Otherwise, Buffalo is like many other cities that have seen retailers flee the central city for the suburbs. The biggest concentration of stores is in the Walden Galleria Mall, which is off Union Road and Walden Avenue in Cheektowaga—15 minutes from the Arena. There is the usual collection of department stores and specialty shops in the mall and in the immediate area.

For attractions, the most obvious for hockey fans will be spotted as you walk to the Arena. You'll ask, "What are those battleships doing in the river?" Buffalo is the home of the only inland naval park in the country, and you can tour the ships when the park is open. Otherwise, the obvious must-see stopping point in the region is Niagara Falls. It's worth an afternoon visit at any time of the year. Be sure to go all-out—take the Maid of the Mist boat ride and walk in the scenic tunnels. For those so inclined, the Canadian side has a relatively new casino that has done a brisk business.

The Albright-Knox Art Gallery in North Buffalo (1285 Elmwood Ave., 716-882-8700) has world-class works. Baseball fans will want to take a look at **Dunn Tire Park** (275 Washington St., 716-846-2033), which is only a few blocks from Marine Midland Arena. It's one of the best minor-league facilities in the country, and you can even go to Pettibone's Grill for a good lunch on gamedays.

Favorite City on the Road

As a former Canuck, Dixon Ward votes for Vancouver. "It's the most beautiful city in the league," he states. Most Sabres grew up watching Stanley Cup parades in Montreal, and now that they play there, it gives them an extra rush. "I always look forward to going to my favorite restaurant there, Da Vinci," says Jason Woolley.

Cool Fact

Buffalo's Dominik Hasek was overlooked early in his career because of his unorthodox style. Stuck behind Ed Belfour in Chicago, he was acquired by the Sabres in 1992 and Buffalo left him unprotected in the 1993 expansion draft. Luckily for the Sabres he wasn't taken. He has since reeled off five Vezina Trophies, two MVP awards and an Olympic gold medal, and is considered the world's top goalie.

Franchise History

For a team that has not yet won a Stanley Cup, the Buffalo Sabres have been extremely successful in their 29 seasons in the NHL. Only six times has the club missed the playoffs, and three of those were within the first four years of its existence. Awarded an NHL franchise on May 22, 1970, the Sabres were quickly competitive and title contenders for many years. The French Connection line of Gilbert Perreault, Rick Martin

Stu Barnes #41

BUFFALO

and Rene Robert was the dominant scoring combination of their day, dazzling fans—and goaltenders—across the league. The Perreault-led teams only managed one Stanley Cup final, losing in six games to the defending champion Philadelphia Flyers, but they'll always be remembered for their stylistic yet gritty play. Almost 25 years later the Sabres returned to the Stanley Cup Finals, this time led by superstar goalie Dominik Hasek, only to lose again. But with a new arena and a roster of rising young stars, the club hopes to be the first professional team in Buffalo to reward the city's loyal sports fans with a championship.

Sabres

Famers

Most Valuable Player (Hart Trophy): Dominik Hasek, 1997, 1998.

Hockey Hall of Fame:

Players: Tim Horton, 1977; Gilbert Perreault, 1990.

Builders: George "Punch" Imlach, 1984; Scotty Bowman, 1991; Seymour H. Knox III, 1993.

Retired numbers: 2 Tim Horton, 7 Rick Martin, 11 Gilbert Perreault, 14 Rene Robert

Curtis Brown #32

Records

Games played		Most points, season		Most goalie wins, career	
Gilbert Perreault	1,191	Pat LaFontaine	148	Dominik Hasek	182
Career goals		**Most goals, game**		**Most goalie wins, season**	
Gilbert Perreault	512	Dave Andreychuk	5	Don Edwards	38
Career assists		**Most assists, game**		**Most shutouts, career**	
Gilbert Perreault	814	Gilbert Perreault		Dominik Hasek	41
Career points		Dale Hawerchuk		**Most shutouts, season**	
Gilbert Perreault	1,326	Pat LaFontaine	5	Dominik Hasek	13
Most goals, season		**Most points, game**		**Stanley Cups:**	
Alexander Mogilny	76	Gilbert Perreault	7	None	
Most assists, season					
Pat La Fontaine	95				

Flames

Valeri Bure #8

CALGARY

around the town with the
Flames

It was an unforgettable day in 1980 when the Flames arrived in Calgary from Atlanta. Frenzied fans bought the entire selection of season tickets before team officials could blink, and support has remained strong ever since. In a city that's small by major-league standards, there's a special relationship between fans and players: the players are truly part of the community. Many former Flames have chosen to stay in Calgary, the most notable being Lanny McDonald, who occupies a prominent place in the team's front office. Lanny is a visible reminder of the team's greatest moment—his last game came in the 1989 Stanley Cup finals, when Calgary defeated Montreal to win its first title.

The Saddledome's roof gives you a reminder of a different sort, for its saddle shape is a tribute to Western culture. Calgary has done its best to honor the past. The diverse collections and exhibitions in the famous Glenbow Museum include one on Western history. Heritage Park, a short drive outside town, is the largest living historical village in the country. Across its 66 acres, the life and times of the old West are recreated in the shadow of the beautiful Rocky Mountains. Downtown Calgary may be a collection of tall, granite and glass office buildings, but in Alberta, the past and the present blend nicely together.

The other outstanding attraction of this area is landscape. Banff and Lake Louise, two of the world's finest ski resorts, are only a moderate drive from Calgary, and there are many parks worth visiting. Flames general manager Al Coates says, "I've never heard people complain about a lack of anything but lakes. Otherwise, you have everything conceivable to do here, plus internationally famous hospitality." If you're a visiting hockey fan, Calgary will never disappoint you.

Canadian Airlines Saddledome

Where to sit:
The President's Club, a 1,700-seat private club that extends halfway around the lower bowl, has a private entrance, waiter-service and access to meeting rooms. One ticket costs $103 with Goods and Services Tax,(GST) but is discounted to $76 for season-ticket holders.

An equally good vantage point, but without the amenities, can be had in the Red-level seats (Sections 101–114), immediately adjacent to the President's Club. The upper bowl behind the goals goes for $66.36 ($53.50 to season ticketholders).

If it's all you can get:
The upper loges are a bargain at $14.72, but put you so high above the action you cannot even see the Jumbotron.

Flames

Special services:
The Saddledome has 65 seats set aside for the disabled, plus an additional 65 places for their attendants. The 1997–98 season featured two new, popular Super Suites located in two of the corners above the upper bowl. Sold on a game-to-game basis and thus perfect for out-

$102.80	$75.47	$66.36	$31.31
$39.25	$23.13	$23.13	$14.72
WC1 $49.07	WC $43.46	WC2 $29.44	$72.43

Capacity: 17,139

of-town groups, it cost $2,995 plus food and beverage for 25 people and can seat up to 36 ($24.75 for every person above 25). In addition, the Flames withhold one skybox (Suite No. 25), which seats 16, for sale on a game-by-game basis for $1,795 plus food and beverage.

Ticket availability:

Flames Just under 19,000 seats are available for each game, and although a handful of teams—Montreal, Toronto, Philadelphia—sell out immediately, there are usually up to 2,000 seats available on game day.

Parking:

As part of their 1995 renovation, the Flames added a parkade for suite and club-seat holders that requires a special pass and costs $450 annually. In addition, there are four other parking lots on the grounds, with 1,069 spaces available, priced at $6. Some residents of nearby Victoria Park will allow you to park on their lawns and in their driveways for $2 to $3.

Canadian Airlines Saddledome

There is a limited amount of street parking available within an easy walking distance, but those spots usually disappear 90 minutes before the game starts.

Public transportation:

The C-Train, the city's light-rail transit system will drop you on the west side of the Stampede Grounds. Exit at the Victoria-Stampede station stop. From downtown, the No. 403 or the No. 24 will drop you at 12th Avenue and 5th Street, three blocks north of the Saddledome. From south Calgary, take the No. 10 bus up MacLeod Trail and exit at 25th Street. For more information, call 403-262-1000.

By car:

The Saddledome is at the intersection of 5th St. SE and Olympic Way. From Calgary International Airport, take Barlow Trail south to Memorial Drive and turn right. After three miles, veer off Memorial onto the City Centre overpass, which turns into 4th Ave. SE. Turn left onto 1st St. SE and head south to 12th Ave. SE. Turn left again onto 12th Ave. SE and follow to 5th St. SE. Turn right and the Saddledome will appear immediately in front of you.

Cuisine:

Apart from the standard concession fare—hamburgers, hot dogs and French fries—a number of fast-food franchises are located on the main concourse including Wendy's, Little Caesar's, Subway and Tim Horton's. Alternatives features a "heart smart" menu.

Home ice advantage:
Despite poor results in recent seasons, attendance remains relatively strong. When they have a reason to get excited, the crowds will respond.

Nightlife.

For after the game:
In his playing days, Brian Sutter would beat a path to **Dusty's Saloon** (1088 Olympic Way SE, 403-263-5343), three blocks from the Saddledome. After a game, proprietor Dusty Woznow will appear on the street corner, in full western regalia, with pistols waving, to lure you into his establishment for beer, peanuts, and live music.

For a quiet drink:
You can't go wrong at the **Wildwood Brewing Company** (2417 4th St. SW, 403-228-0100). Downstairs, the gourmet pub is open until 2 a.m. on weekends, while the upstairs dining room features Rocky Mountain cuisine. The pub, a favorite of hockey broadcasters and writers, has a warm fireplace and five regular homemade brews.

For country/western:
Former Flame Theo Fleury recommends **The Ranchmen's** (9615 Macleod Trail S, 403-253-1100), a sprawling barn of a place that features live country and western music six nights a week, plus a menu with cowboy fare and Texas-style smoked barbecue specialties.

To meet the opposite sex:
A perennial favorite of the hockey crowd is Electric Avenue, a strip of bars on 11th between 4th and 7th. A lot of the young guns like to drop in at **Cowboys Dance Hall** (826 5th St. SW, 403-265-0699), a nightclub that began life as the Alberta Liquor Control Board downtown warehouse. A sign mounted on the front door now modestly suggests, "Through these doors walk the most beautiful women in Alberta," a bold, but frequently accurate assessment. Ex-captain Todd Simpson says **The Palace** (219 8th Ave. SW, 403-263-9980) is reminiscent of a New York nightclub. A large restored historic theater, the Palace includes three bars, a concert stage and a well-stocked humidor. For the 20-something types, Derek Morris names **The Fox and Firkin Tavern** (607 11th Ave. SW, 403-237-6411), one of the hottest places on Electric Avenue.

Flames Saddledome Lowdown

Opened:
10/15/83

First regular-season game:
10/15/83,
4–3 loss to Edmonton

First playoff game:
4/4/84,
5–3 win over Vancouver

First goal:
Jari Kurri of Edmonton

Address:
P.O. Box 1540, Calgary

For single-game tickets:
403-777-0000

Website:
calgaryflames.com

Dining

For pasta:

If you're bringing your family, go to **Luciano's Little Italian Grill** (9223 Macleod Trail S., 403-253-4266). Cale Hulse says "The best place to eat Italian is **Da Paolo** (121 17th Ave. SE, 403-228-5556). Most of the guys usually go there for pre-game meals simply because of the great food and service." Ex-Flame Rick Tabaracci enjoyed the **Stromboli Inn** (1147 Kensington Cr. NW, 403-283-1166) across the Bow River in trendy Kensington. The Inn's deep-dish pizza is inspiring. If he wanted good but inexpensive spaghetti, Tabaracci visited **Chianti Cafe** (1438 17th Ave. SW, 403-229-1600).

Flames

For steak:

Alberta beef is world famous, so it's not surprising that the city boasts a handful of premier steakhouses. Since 1972, **Caesar's** (512 4th Ave. SW, 403-264-1222) has been specializing in steaks and seafood, which makes it popular with Derek Morris. Just about everybody on the team checks out venerable **Hy's** (316 4th Ave. SW, 403-263-2222), which is adjacent to the Westin and, as a result, gets a lot of trade from out-of-town players as well.

For something completely different, Jarome Iginla casts his vote for **Japanese Village** (302 4th Ave. SW, 403-262-2738), a popular steak and seafood house that puts a orien-

tal twist on traditional fare. "Japanese Village has a very unique atmosphere," Hulse declares. "And it is fun to watch the food prepared in front of you. It's entertaining as well as delicious."

Local fare:

At lunchtime, players and coaches frequent **Spolumbo's Fine Foods and Deli** (1308 9th Ave. SE, 403-264-6452), an unassuming place. Spicy, homemade sausage is the house specialty, but when James Patrick and Joel Bouchard were with the Flames, they preferred Mamma's special meatloaf sandwiches.

For something different:

Team owner Harley Hotchkiss has a regular table at **La Chaumiere** (139 17th Ave. SW, 403-228-5690), the home of

Jarome Iginla #12

continental cuisine. Former Flame Ron Stern frequented the bistro called Escoba (513 8th Ave. SW, 403-543-8911) as well as Criterion (121 8th Ave. SW, 403-232-8080), which serves South Pacific dishes. You won't find too many restaurants like this in the heart of beef country.

Lodging

Many NHL teams stay at the **Westin** (4th Ave. and 3rd St. SW, 403-266-1611) which features one of the finest hotel dining rooms in the city, the posh Owl's Nest. In addition, the Westin is the team's training camp headquarters, so if you're there in September, chances are you'll see a steady stream of players passing through the lobby.

If a visiting NHL team isn't staying at the Westin, you can generally find it at the **Palliser Hotel** (133 9th Ave. SW, 403-262-1234), a handsome Canadian Pacific Hotel that adjoins the train station and dates to the turn of the century. Its 405 rooms have been extensively renovated. In recent seasons, Dallas, New Jersey, Vancouver and Washington have made it their home away from home.

The Marriott (110 9th Ave. SW, 403-266-7331) is the latest incarnation of a property that over the years has been a Radisson, a Skyline and a Four Seasons. It is the closest major hotel to the Saddledome and Marriott, a chain that attracts many major-league teams south of the border, was aggressively seeking to com-

pete with the Westin and Palliser for the business of NHL teams.

The International Hotel of Calgary (220 4th Ave. SW, 403-265-9600) is owned by Alvin Libin, a minority owner of the Flames. It is home to any number of Calgary players over the course of the season—rookies who make the team out of training camp or emergency call-ups from the minor leagues. It is an all-suites hotel, with a separate bedroom and living room in each unit. In addition, a handful of suites have kitchenettes, but they are available on a first-come, first-served basis.

Flames

Shopping & Attractions

For hockey memorabilia, stop by the Flames **Fan Attic**, the official supplier of licensed NHL sports-gear. They can supply you with authentic game-worn jerseys, from players past and present, plus autographed pucks, sticks, pictures and jerseys. They feature custom-designed Flames sportswear as well as items from their junior hockey team, the Calgary Hitmen. Apart from their Saddledome location, there are also Fan Attics at the downtown **Eatons' Centre** (510 8 Ave SW, 403-571-9757), **Chinook Centre** and **Northland Village Shoppes** (5111 Northland Dr NW, 403-571-9759), a Christmas-only location.

For shopping: The **Eau Claire Market** (200 Barclay Parade SW, adjacent to Prince's Island Park, 403-264-6450) features something for everyone, including popular watering holes like **Joey Tomatos** and The **Hard Rock Cafe**. There are also specialty stores, where you can outfit yourself in Westernwear for the Stampede, plus an **IMAX Theatre**, a **Cinescape Multi-Media Family Entertainment Centre**, galleries and a series of rotating attractions that include clowns, jesters and street musicians.

Flames

For families: Dinosaurs are popular with children of all ages, which is why family man James Patrick recommends the **Royal Tyrrell Museum of Paleontology** in nearby Drumheller (403-823-7707). Situated within the visually stunning badlands of the Red Deer River Valley, the Royal Tyrrell is one of the largest paleontological museums in the world. Fans of equine athletes will also appreciate a visit to **Spruce Meadows** (403-974-4200). In the midst of cowboy country, Spruce Meadows is the premier show-jumping facility in North America, with three major international competitions over the course of the summer. It also features a country fair, bands, displays and other child-friendly activities. You can reach the Meadows by going south on Mcleod Trail and then west on Highway 22x.

Favorite City on the Road

Derek Morris can't wait to get to L.A. for sun and sightseeing and maybe even the chance to run into his favorite actor, John Travolta. Travolta starred in Morris' favorite movie, "Saturday Night Fever," which was released in 1978, the year Morris was born.

Steve Dubinsky likes the food Vancouver has to offer, not to mention the sparkling weather and exciting nightlife. Cory Stillman chooses Chicago and it isn't because he likes the blues. Stillman's a country-western fan who would sooner hear George Strait than Junior Wells. But Stillman loves sampling the variety of steakhouses like Morton's that made Chicago famous.

Cool Fact

The Calgary Flames were a powerhouse when they captured the Stanley Cup in 1989, boasting players like Al MacInnis, Mike Vernon and Doug Gilmour. But they tied two NHL records in the seasons immediately before and after their championship. In 1987–88, Joe Nieuwendyk, Hakan Loob, Mike Bullard and Joe Mullen all scored 40 goals or more, tying the season record held by Edmonton. In 1989–90, Gilmour and Paul Ranheim scored 4 seconds apart to tie the league mark for fastest goals by one team.

Franchise History

In the past 20 years the Calgary Flames have been such a presence in the NHL that fans no longer think twice about the club's name. You say Flames, you think Calgary. In fact, the name is a holdover from the franchise's original city of Atlanta, where a contest was held before the team began play in the 1972–73 season. Since Atlanta's most famous moment came when General William T. Sherman burned the city to the ground during the American Civil War, what better name than the Flames? When Calgary ownership took over the franchise on June 24, 1980, the flaming "A" was simply changed to a flaming "C."

Fire may not be appropriate to the latitude of Calgary, but it certainly fits the attitude, as the Calgary Flames have consistently burned up the league since 1980. The Flames were the only team to interrupt the Edmonton juggernaut of the 1980s, stunning the two-time defending champs in 1986 by eliminating the Oilers in Game 7 in Edmonton. The team went on to lose to the Montreal Canadiens in the finals that year, but gained revenge in 1989 by accomplishing something that no other team in the history of the league has managed to do: win the Stanley Cup from the Montreal Canadiens on Forum ice. Just another team burned by the Calgary Flames.

Flames

Cory Stillman #16

Famers

Most Valuable Player (Hart Trophy): None.
   Hockey Hall of Fame:
   Player: Lanny McDonald, 1992.
   Builder: Bob Johnson, 1992
   Retired numbers: 9 Lanny McDonald

Records

Games played		Most points, season		Most goalie wins, season	
Al MacInnis	803	Kent Nilsson	131	Mike Vernon	39
Career goals		**Most goals, game**		**Most shutouts, career**	
Theo Fleury	364	Joe Nieuwendyk	5	Dan Bouchard	20
Career assists		**Most assists, game**		**Most shutouts, season**	
Al MacInnis	609	Guy Chouinard		Dan Bouchard	
Career points		Gary Suter	6	Phil Myre	5
Theo Fleury	830	**Most points, game**		**Stanley Cups:**	
Most goals, season		Sergei Makarov	7	1989.	
Lanny McDonald	66	**Most goalie wins, career**			
Most assists, season					
Kent Nilsson	82	Mike Vernon	248		

Hurricanes

Bates Battaglia #13

around the town with the Hurricanes

When Carolina decided to launch an eye-grabbing publicity campaign, it didn't reach into the past and pull out an aging hockey legend: what would be the point in a state where basketball and racing rule? No, the Hurricanes picked NASCAR legend Richard Petty. When local people see his seamed face and rugged charm, they listen, even if he's telling them to watch a sport they've never followed.

It was a clever idea, but one which revealed the challenges that lie ahead. Attendance in Greensboro was poor, although optimists point out that that was a temporary home, and how can you build loyalty when you're going to move?

Surprisingly, there is a hockey tradition in the region. The Greensboro Monarchs once played minor pro, and the Carolinas now have teams in the East Coast Hockey League and the United League. The Hurricanes hope to draw upon the casual fans and turn them into devoted ones, while attracting the type of people who might never think about the Rangers or Flyers if they visited New York or Philadelphia.

The Canes had an encouraging time in 1998–99, winning their division and breaking a streak of six non-playoff seasons. Most importantly, they have a collection of young, no-name players who could develop into something good. They also have two of the smallest and most dynamic players around: 5'8" goalie Arturs Irbe, and 5'10" speedster Sami Kapanen. Irbe bounces around like a bowling ball sometimes, but his outstanding play last year was key to the team's success. Kapanen lives up to the Hurricane logo on his jersey, for he is in perpetual motion. Players like him are just the type to attract novice fans into the arena. Of course, winning would help. The Raleigh area has a reputation for college basketball greatness, and the locals love it when their teams contend for the national title. But hockey is the only major-league game in town, and that should stir some pride too.

Entertainment & Sports Arena

Where to sit:
There are 2000 Club Seats which give access to a restaurant on the Club Level which has very good sightlines. The VIP and Club Ledge seats are oversized, so you won't be uncomfortable there. The most unique seats are the Mezzanine Premier in the front row of the upper level. From there, you will be looking right down on the action.

If it's all you can get:
Don't shy away from seats in the upper deck. You'll have a steep climb, but when you've settled in you'll find that the view is great. Even children will have no trouble seeing over the people in the next row.

Hurricanes

Special services:
There are 183 seats for handicapped patrons and their companions.

$99	$80	$65
$59	$44	$33	$22

Capacity: 18,700

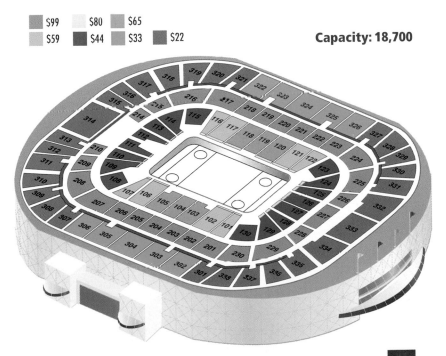

Ticket availability:

The Hurricanes have sold about 6,000 season tickets this season, meaning game-day tickets will be available. "We're officially in our own market for the first year in a non-traditional hockey market," says general manager Jim Rutherford. "This will grow as we go on this year."

Parking:

There are more than 8,000 spots at the arena for $7 each.

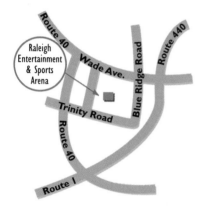

Public transportation:

The Triangle Transit Authority (919-549-9999) runs a bus route in the area.

By car:

The Arena is located next to the North Carolina State Fairgrounds. From Raleigh-Durham Airport, take 40 east and go onto the Wade Avenue exit. Then take the Edwards Mill/Arena exit. Turn left onto Trinity Road and left into the arena.

Cuisine:

There are 18 concession stands. The Arena Club is for VIP and

Entertainment and Sports Arena

Club Ledge seatholders.

Home-ice advantage:

The Triangle is known for its great college basketball teams, and the support they receive is tremendous. If the Hurricanes fans are half as passionate, there will be a definite advantage, especially in the playoffs.

Nightlife

For after the game:

The **Brewery** (3009 Hillsborough St., 919-834-7018) is a 15-year-old nightclub that hosts live bands regularly. You can hear everything from funk to metal here. Nationally renowned acts who pass through Raleigh will play at the Brewery. A quieter time will be had at **Greenshields Brewery and Pub** (214 E. Martin St., 919-829-0214) in the Historic City Market. The pub features homemade ales and lagers, a dining room, and a patio for warm-weather seating. On Saturdays, you can even tour its brewery.

For watching the game:

In Raleigh, try **Jillian's** (117 S. West St., 919-821-7887) where you might spot a Hurricanes fan—or even a player—on a non-game night. But the 'Canes' bar of choice is **Blincos** (5009 Falls of Neuse Rd., 919-790-3882), where the owner is golfing buddies with some management and players.

To meet the opposite sex:

If you have extra time, drive out to Chapel Hill (50 miles east of Greensboro on I-40). Ex-Cane Nelson Emerson found himself in the packed crowds at **Players** (159 1/2 E. Franklin St., 919-929-0101) during the NCAA Final Four playoffs, his first introduction to the basketball-crazed area, home turf of the University of North Carolina Tar Heels. Or, you can boogie down at **Dadio's** in Greensboro (3404 High Point Road, 336-299-6794) or **Wild Magnolia Cafe** (2200 Walker Ave, 336-378-0800), the happening spots for twenty-somethings.

Dining

For local fare:

How would you like to eat solid American dishes at very affordable prices? **Finch's Family Restaurant** (401 W. Peace St., 919-834-7396), which has been open since 1945, is popular with famous and regular people alike. Senator Jesse Helms has been seen enjoying a meal here. If you make it to Durham, do not miss a chance to eat at **Bullocks** (3330 Quebec St., 919-383-3211). The entrance hall is lined with photos of celebrities who have stopped in its famous "family-style dining," where $10 will get you plates filled with

Hurricanes

Arturs Irbe #1

chicken, ribs, barbecue, hush puppies and green beans.

For steak:
As its name indicates, the **Angus Barn** (9401 Glenwood Ave., 919-787-3505) is a rustic, red barn with a roomy interior. It is also one of the best restaurants in Raleigh, one which wins awards for both wine and food. Opened in 1960 and still going strong, the Barn will not disappoint you.

For ethnic:
Kanki (4325 Glenwood Ave, 919-782-9708, and 4500 Old Wake Forest Rd., 919-876-4157) is a Japanese seafood and steak house that has the best sushi in the area. Jean-Claude's French Cafe (919-872-6224) is reasonably priced, and the dishes are cooked with the customer in mind: you don't have to worry about the sauce drowning the food.

Lodging

Location, location:
The Brownestone Hotel (1707 Hillsborough St., 919-828-0811, 800-331-7919) is a short drive from downtown and 15 minutes from the airport. It actually provides free transportation when you want to catch your plane. The **Doubletree Guest Suites** (2515 Meridian Pkwy., Durham, 919-361-4660, 800-222-TREE) are also conveniently situated. The Doubletree has a cute way of welcoming guests: they give you two chocolate chip

cookies when you register.

Players hotel:
Several of the minor-league call-ups stay at the **LaQuinta Inn** (1001 Hospitality Ct, 919-461-1771) in Morrisville, just off exit 284 on I-40.

Shopping & Attractions

The **Four Seasons Town Centre** (High Point Road and I-40, 336-292-0171) has more than 200 stores, including Belk,

Sami Kapanen # 24

Dillard's and JCPenney. It also features The Eye, the best place outside of the arena to get 'Canes goodies. The **Friendly Center** (Friendly Avenue at Wendover, 336-292-2789) has more than 80 specialty stores, services and restaurants.

The top golf courses in the world are in Pinehurst, N.C., home of the 1999 U.S. Open and a short drive from Greensboro. Pack your sticks and call 800-747-7272 for more information. The 'Canes play at the Raleigh Country Club, which is for members only.

The **Guilford Courthouse National Military Park** (2332 New Garden Rd., Greensboro, 336-288-1776) is the site of the decisive Revolutionary War battle fought on March 15, 1781. Surf's up inland at **Emerald Pointe** water theme park (3910 S. Holden Rd., Greensboro, 336-852-972). And just 30 minutes south is the **N.C. Zoological Park** (Asheboro, 800-488-0444), where you can see more than 37,000 plants and nearly 1,400 exotic animals living as they would in the wild.

About three hours east of Greensboro are some of the most beautiful beaches in the country. Head east on I-40 and visit Cape Hatteras Lighthouse. Part of the **Cape Hatteras National Seashore** (919-473-2111), this 208-foot tower was built in 1870. Or, go west and drive the Blue Ridge Parkway. It will take you to George Vanderbilt's country chateau, the 250-room **Biltmore Estate** (off U.S. 25 in Asheville, 828-274-6230).

Favorite City on the Road

Chances are that Raleigh didn't pop up in too many answers around the league. At least not yet. Not surprisingly, Montreal probably did—and that's the top choice for most of the Hurricanes. When in Montreal, coach Paul Maurice likes to go to Bar-B-Barn for ribs. "I imagine for most of the guys who grew up with Hockey Night in Canada, it would be Montreal or Toronto," Maurice said. "For me, it was Montreal. I'd see so many Canadiens games, that was my connection to the NHL."

"It depends on the individual," says Ron Francis. "I've always loved Boston with the atmosphere, the neat little shops, the Italian restaurants. It's great."

At least two Carolina players, wingers Robert Kron and Paul Ranheim, prefer New York City. Center Kent Manderville, who occasionally sneaks off to a museum, likes Chicago and Washington. Defenseman Curtis Leschyshyn likes Denver.

Hurricanes

Arena Observations

Opened:
10/29/99

First regular-season game:
10/29/99, 4–2 loss to New Jersey

First goal:
Andrei Kovalenko of Carolina

Addreess:
1400 Edwards Mill Road, Raleigh

For single-game tickets:
919-834-4000

Website:
caneshockey.com

Leschyshyn is probably biased—he and Colorado center Joe Sakic own an Italian restaurant in town.

Cool Fact

On March 23, 1977, the World Hockey Association's Hartford Whalers outbid other NHL clubs to sign Gordie Howe and his two sons, Mark and Marty, to long-term contracts. When the Whalers **Hurricanes** joined the NHL on June 22, 1979, it marked the first time a father and his two sons played in the NHL. Howe scored his 801st—and final goal—as a Whaler.

Franchise History

When you think of Whalers you think of wanderlust, ships circling the globe in search of great white whales—or at least a port in the storm. That pretty much epitomizes the Hartford Whalers, a team that has since become the Carolina Hurricanes (the franchise transferred on June 25, 1997). Originally a member of the defunct World Hockey Association, the New England Whalers moved from Boston to Springfield to Hartford. Even though the team had trouble competing against the Boston Bruins (which boasted Bobby Orr) during its WHA days, it featured some high-profile players of its own: Bobby Hull, Dave Keon, Gordie Howe and Mark Howe. In June of 1979 the Whalers were granted an NHL franchise. Over the ensuing 20 years the team has been more often out of the playoffs than in, reaching the Division Finals but one time. Prospects, however, are looking brighter in Carolina, for not only has the team found a port in the storm—they've become the storm.

Ron Francis #21

Famers

Most Valuable Player (Hart Trophy): None
    Hockey Hall of Fame:
    Players: Gordie Howe, 1972; Bobby Hull, 1983; Dave Keon, 1986.
    Builder: Emile Francis, 1982.
    Retired numbers: 2 Rick Ley, 9 Gordie Howe, 19 John McKenzie

Hurricanes

Gary Roberts #10

Records

Games played		Most points, season		Most goalie wins,	
Ron Francis	796	Mike Rogers	105	**career**	
Career goals		**Most goals, game**		Mike Liut	115
Ron Francis	285	Jordy Douglas,		**Most goalie wins,**	
Career assists		Ron Francis	4	**season**	
Ron Francis	588	**Most assists, game**		Mike Liut	31
Career points		Ron Francis	6	**Most shutouts, career**	
Ron Francis	873	**Most points, game**		Mike Liut	13
Most goals, season		Ron Francis,		**Most shutouts, season**	
Blaine Stoughton	56	Paul Lawless	6	Arturs Irbe	6
Most assists, season				**Stanley Cups:**	
Ron Francis	69			None	

Blackhawks

around
the town with the
Blackhawks

Doug Gilmour #93

It's the home of the skyscraper. It's a mecca for art, architecture and museum fans. It's also the place where you'll find some of the most enthusiastic hockey followers in America. Chicago is certainly a city for everyone's tastes.

Downtown Chicago is a forest of huge buildings, some post-modern, some traditional in style. Even the Magnificent Mile on Michigan Avenue, once a low-rise section, is growing taller. However, if you pass into the residential neighborhoods, many of them ethnic, the city becomes a series of bungalows and small apartment blocks. No matter where you are, art is never far away. The Daley Plaza holds a Picasso sculpture; a mosaic by Marc Chagall rests in First National Bank Plaza. The Smart Museum of Art holds 8000 works, some priceless creations by the masters.

Chicago has boasted art of a different sort in its hockey rinks. Since 1926, the Blackhawks have given their supporters a lot of memories. There were martyr-like heroics from Charlie Gardiner, who won the 1934 Stanley Cup while dying from a brain sickness. Bobby Hull and Stan Mikita created offensive magic in the 1960s. Tony Esposito did the same in the 1970s with his kick saves. Denis Savard, one of the game's flashiest players, carried the team through the 1980s, while tough Chris Chelios assumed that role in the 1990s. The Hawks have always had a superstar, it seems. Nowadays, Tony Amonte is the center of attention, while up-and-comer J.P. Dumont might be the future leader.

In the old Stadium, the fans were recognized as the loudest in hockey. The United Center doesn't quite equal its predecessor in acoustics, but if you don't get chills down your spine during the national anthem, you may not be alive. Playing for a winning team in any city is great, but it's unique in Chicago because the fans are unique.

United Center

Where to sit:
The 200 club level is complete with waitress service, but there are only 3,000 of these seats. Many of the top-priced $75 seats are terrific. Don't sit too low and near a face-off circle, otherwise you'll miss a lot of the action at the other end of the rink.

If it's all you can get:
The first eight rows of the 300 level provide great viewing of the ice, but any higher things get a little steep. Unlike the old Stadium, there are no obstructed-view seats.

Special services:
Wheelchair areas have easy access to elevators, restrooms and concessions. Services for hearing-impaired fans are also available. For information, call 312-455-7000.

Ticket availability:
It used to be a problem, but with the team rebuilding in recent seasons, it's not difficult to walk up to the box office the day of a game and purchase a

$75 $60 $50
$40 $25 $15

Capacity: 20,500

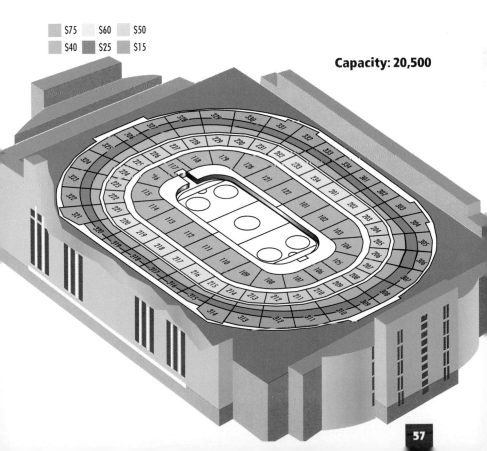

quality ticket. The toughest ticket to get is any game against Detroit or St. Louis. Tickets for games against superstars such as Philadelphia's Eric Lindros—especially on a weekend—are also tough to secure.

Parking:
The official spots cost $10, and there are 5,500 of these within a four-block radius of the United Center. There are also 2,000 spots in nearby lower-priced lots, but security in these lots isn't as tight.

Public transportation:
The No. 20 bus goes to the United Center and operates every 10 minutes from 1½ hours before each game until half an hour after. For more information, call 312-836-7000.

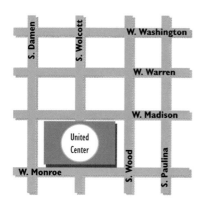

By car:
From O'Hare International Airport, take 1-90 east and exit on Madison Street Travel west on Madison approximately 1½ miles.

Cuisine:
You can still get hot dogs and nachos like the good old days at the Stadium, but the UC has much more to offer, including deli sandwiches, Mexican and Italian specialties and grilled meats, and 25 different beers.

Home-ice advantage:
It isn't what it once was. In fact, the Hawks were under .500 at home in 1996–97 and 1997–98. It was the first time this had happened since 1956–57 and 1957–58. Teams used to fear coming into the stuffy Stadium, but in the cozy UC, they make themselves right at home.

Nightlife

For blues and more:
When he was living in town, Chris Chelios chose **Kingston Mines Chicago Blues** (2548 N. Halsted St., 773-477-4646). **Buddy Guy's Legends** (754 S. Wabash Ave., 312-427-0333) is the right place for those purists seeking an intimate atmosphere. **Blue Chicago on Clark** (536 N. Clark St., 312-661-0100) is another fine nightclub, but there are plenty to choose from in the town that invented electric blues. If alternative music attracts you more, try the

United Center

place that impressed ex-Hawk Jeff Shantz, **Metro** (3730 N. Clark St., 773-549-0203). Lovers of 1970s nostalgia will want to visit **Jilly's Retro Club** (1009 N. Rush St., 312-664-1001).

To watch a game:
Former Blackhawk Steve Dubinsky says you can't go wrong at **Gamekeepers Tavern and Grill** (345 W. Armitage Ave., 773-549-0400), which has close to 40 TV screens. Ethan Moreau is a big fan of **Stanley's** mini-cheeseburgers and its Sunday brunch.

For a quiet drink:
Amonte says **Webster's Wine Bar** (1480 W. Webster Ave., 773-868-0608) is the place to go.

Dining

If the topic is food, hockey players can fill a book with favorite places to eat. Chicago is loaded with choices, but you'll get little argument from Hawk players on the favorites.

For Italian:
Before a game, you might catch Tony Amonte dining at **Maggiano's Little Italy** (516 N. Clark St., 312-644-7700), **Centro** (710 N. Wells St., 312-988-7775), or the **Pompei Bakery** (1455 W. Taylor St., 312-421-5179). Former Hawk Jeff Hackett raves about the knockout pasta with vodka sauce at **Centro**. Chris Chelios and Hackett love **Tuscany** (1014 W. Taylor St., 312-829-1990).

For big appetites:
If it's a first-rate steak you crave, Chelios and Steve Dubinsky recommend **Gibsons** (1028 N. Rush St., 312-266-8999). You'll walk out stuffed from the **Cheesecake Factory**, a Hackett favorite located in the building he used to live in —**The Hancock** (875 N. Michigan Ave., 312-337-1101).

For spicy food:
Chelios would be remiss if he didn't plug his restaurant, **Cheli's Chili Bar** (1137 W. Madison St., 312-455-1237), which is just a few blocks east of the United Center and is a popular hangout for fans before and after Hawks games. When he was Chicago captain, Chelios often ate lunch there with his teammates after practice.

Local flavor:
The new version of the **Billy Goat Tavern** is at 330 S. Wells St. (312-554-0297), or you can stop by the original (430 N. (lower) Michigan Ave., 312-222-1525) for a cheeseburger and Coke, no Pepsi. It has long been a popular hangout for newspaper people, including

the late, great columnist Mike Royko. Chef Hans, who used to wow people with his special creations at the Stadium and later the United Center, is now working his magic at **Smith and Wollensky** (318 N. State St., 312-670-9900).

Lodging

To see the visiting team:
If you want to stay in elegance, near high-quality shopping, and where most opposing NHL teams spend the night, **The Drake** (140 E. Walton St., 312-787-2200) is the place to be.

Location, location:
The Westin Michigan Avenue

(909 N. Michigan Ave., 312-943-7200), like the Drake, is close to great shopping at Water Tower Place, and the **Marriott Chicago Downtown** (540 N. Michigan Ave., 312-836-0100, 800-228-9290) is another staple on the Magnificent Mile.

For luxury:
There's the **Inter-Continental Hotel** (505 N. Michigan Ave., 312-944-4100), restored in 1990 by the Inter-Continental chain. Legend has it that Johnny Weissmuller trained for his role as Tarzan in the pool at the Inter-Continental Hotel, which originally was built as the Medinah Athletic Club in 1929. **The Hyatt Regency** is

Jocelyn Thibault #41

also in the heart of the city at 151 E. Wacker Drive (312-565-1234, 800-233-1234).

Shopping & Attractions

If you can't find something to do in Chicago, you're not looking. The **Lincoln Park Zoo** (2001 N. Clark St., 312-742-2000) is a popular attraction. Then there's the **Adler Planetarium** (1300 S. Lake Shore Dr., 312-922-7827), which was the first of its kind in the Western world when it opened in 1930. The **Art Institute of Chicago** (111 S. Michigan Ave., 312-443-3600) underscores the city's reputation for artistic excellence. There are plenty of museums, too. If you want to climb into a coal mine, try the **Museum of Science and Industry** (5700 S. Lake Shore Dr., 773-684-1414). Naturalists will want to explore the **Field Museum of Natural History** (1200 S. Lake Shore Dr., 312-922-9410). Its Shedd Aquarium is the largest indoor aquarium in the world, and the Oceanarium is simply beautiful.

Is architecture your passion? There are days' worth of exploring, starting with the **Wrigley Building** and **Tribune Tower** on N. Michigan Ave. And don't skip the **Sears Tower**, the tallest building in the United States.

Shop till you drop on Michigan Avenue's Magnificent Mile. There's the **Water Tower Place**, stationed across the street from the historic **Water Tower**, which survived the Great Chicago Fire of 1871. Or visit the house that Michael Jordan built—**Nike-**

town. **Saks Fifth Avenue**, **Neiman Marcus** and **Crate & Barrel** are also Michigan Avenue favorites. For souvenir hunters, **Fandamonium**, located in the United Center, has all of your favorite Blackhawk and Bulls goodies, and for Blackhawks and hockey-only faithful, hit **Hawk Quarters** at 325 N. Michigan Avenue.

Favorite City on the Road

Apart from visiting their hometowns, for some Blackhawks Vancouver is the place to be. Why? "It's not too big," says Tony Amonte, "and there's great shopping and sushi." Bryan McCabe likes Calgary because it's home. For Bob Probert, Los Angeles is a special place, because he can have a casual conversation with the celebrities who visit the dressing room after a game. Amonte, who lived in New York, also rates the Big Apple highly for its nightclubbing.

Cool Fact

The Blackhawks distinctive red and white striped sweater with the logo of Chief Blackhawk on the front was designed by legendary ballroom dancer Irene Castle, who was married to the team's original owner, Major Frederic McLaughlin.

Franchise History

The players that comprised the first members of the Chicago Blackhawks (or "Black Hawks" as they were known at the time) were originally the Portland (Oregon) Rosebuds of the Western Hockey League. The legendary Patrick brothers, Frank and Lester, were unable to compete with the higher-salaried NHL and looking to disband the league. They convinced Major Frederick McLaughlin that he could make money from hockey in Chicago and would have a ready-made team if he bought the Rosebuds. McLaughlin formed a consortium of wealthy Chicago friends and was awarded an NHL franchise on Sept. 25, 1926.

For the first few seasons the team played in the Chicago Coliseum that, because it was home to cattle shows, was better known for its odor than its hockey. Soon the club moved to a plush new arena, the venerable Chicago Stadium, its 18,000 seating capacity making it the largest facility in the NHL. The Blackhawks, despite a stretch of poor seasons after World War II, became consistent winners. Now housed in a new facility, the team looks to return to form in the near future.

Famers

Most Valuable Player (Hart Trophy): Max Bentley, 1946; Al Rollins, 1954; Bobby Hull, 1965, 1966; Stan Mikita, 1967, 1968.

Hockey Hall of Fame:
Players: Chuck Gardiner, Howie Morenz, 1945; Mickey MacKay, 1952; George Hay,

Dick Irvin, Duke Keats, Hugh Lehman, 1958; George Boucher, 1960; Doug Bentley, Earl Seibert, Jack Stewart, 1964; Bill Mosienko, 1965; Max Bentley, Frank Brimsek, Ted Lindsay, 1966; Sid Abel, 1969; Cecil Dye, William Gadsby, 1970; Billy Burch, Arthur Coulter, 1974; Glenn Hall, Pierre Pilote, 1975; Bobby Orr, 1979; Harry Lumley, 1980; Allan Stanley, 1981; Bobby Hull, Stan Mikita, 1983; Phil Esposito, 1984; Bert Olmstead, 1985; Tony Esposito, 1988; Clint Smith, 1991; Lionel Conacher, Harry Watson, 1994; Roy Conacher, Michel Goulet, 1998.

Builders: James D. Norris, 1962; Major Frederic McLaughlin, 1963; Arthur Wirtz, 1971; Thomas Ivan,

Tony Amonte #10

C H I C A G O

1974; Bill Wirtz, 1976; John Mariucci, Rudy Pilous, 1985; Bud Poile, 1990.

Retired numbers: 1 Glenn Hall, 9 Bobby Hull, 18 Denis Savard, 21 Stan Mikita, 35 Tony Esposito

Blackhawks

Eric Daze # 55

Records

Games played			Most points, season			Most goalie wins,		
Stan Mikita	1,394		Denis Savard	131		season		
Career goals			**Most goals, game**			Ed Belfour 43		
Bobby Hull	604		Grant Mulvey	5		**Most shutouts, career**		
Career assists			**Most assists, game**			Tony Esposito	74	
Stan Mikita	926		Pat Stapleton	6		**Most shutouts, season**		
Career points			**Most points, game**			Tony Esposito	15	
Stan Mikita	1,467		Max Bentley,			**Stanley Cups:**		
Most goals, season			Grant Mulvey	7		1934, 1938, 1961.		
Bobby Hull	58		**Most goalie wins,**					
Most assists, season			**career**					
Denis Savard	87		Tony Esposito	418				

Avalanche

Adam Deadmarsh #18

around the town with the **Avalanche**

Denver, sunshine capital. It may not be well known, but it's true: the city boasts over 300 days of sun a year. At the same time, the climate is a mild one, neither too hot, too cold, nor too extreme in its seasonal variations. The exception to this weather rule happens in Avalanche season. This is a hockey team that comes at you in roaring waves: Peter Forsberg, Joe Sakic, Sandis Ozolinsh and others will roll over you in a flash if you aren't careful. Colorado fans proclaim that their team is the fastest and more explosive in the league, and not many would argue with them.

The great and instant success of the club in Denver has resulted in the construction of a new arena, the Pepsi Center. This is a building the team can truly call its own, for the McNichols Sports Arena was actually home to the NHL's Rockies years before the Avalanche arrived. The Rockies couldn't survive in town, but as Don Cherry will tell you, it wasn't because the fans were indifferent. In his final game as coach during the 1979–80 season, almost 12,000 fans traveled through a Denver blizzard to watch the team play, even though it had been eliminated from playoff competition.

Visitors to Denver may want to plan their trip around one of two major, annual celebrations. The first, held in mid-January, is the National Western Stock Show, Rodeo and Horse Show. Cowboy fans can watch expert horsemen riding, roping and penning, to name but three of the many activities that mark this rough and tumble event. In the first weekend of October, the city also hosts the Great American Beer Festival. This is actually a serious competition that draws over 1700 brews and more than 35,000 people. Beer connoisseurs won't want to miss it, but if you arrive in Denver at another time, you can still visit one of the city's fine micro-breweries.

Pepsi Center

Where to sit:
As a new arena, the Center has no obstructed-view seats. However, single-game seats are only available in the lower level. Those who sit in the Premium Seats can enjoy the restaurant and lounge facilities.

If it's all you can get:
There are no bad seats in this ultra-modern new facility.

Special services:
100 parking spots are available for the handicapped. There are handicapped seats on all levels, and the ushers are trained to deal with disabled patrons.

Ticket availability:
Colorado averaged 100% attendance last season, and the introduction of a new arena only makes things more difficult for fans who don't have season tickets.

Parking:
The Center has no lack of it. There are 6300 spots which cost $10 each.

Public transportation:
The RTD line is a bus service that will get you to the game.

By car:
From Denver Airport, take

$165/$116
$94 $80 $73 $50
$47 $36 $33 $20

Capacity: 18,129

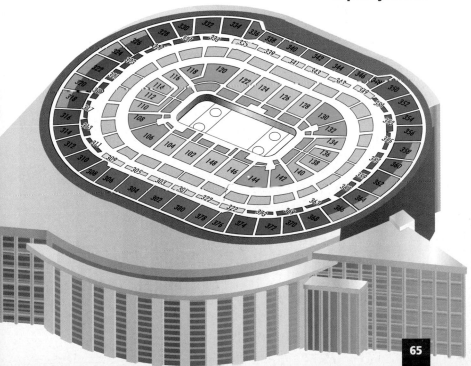

Pena Boulevard to West I-70 and then go south on I-25. Go east on Speer Boulevard and turn right on Chopper Travaglini Boulevard There are arena exits on 7th, 9th, 11th and 12th Streets off Auraria Parkway as well.

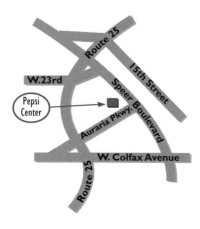

Cuisine:
There are 17 concession stands, each offering its own Rocky Mountain dish. Premium seatholders can enjoy Ridgeline Restaurant and Denver Post Newsroom Lounge.

Home-ice advantage:
The fans make a lot of noise during big games and especially love it when the Red Wings are in town. The Avs' exciting style of play also helps them out.

Nightlife

After the game:
The Avalanche frequently have a good time at **Sing Sing** (1735 19th St., 303-291-0880). In fact, ex-Avs player Claude

Lemieux was known to croon a song to his wife here, accompanied by the pianist. This popular spot is worth visiting even if you don't see any hockey players.

For a quiet drink:
You might see superstar goalie Patrick Roy in **Enoteca** (1730 Wynkoop St., 303-293-2887), which features quiet jazz, lots of oak paneling and fine wines. **The Purple Martini** (1328 15th St., 303-820-0575) has an exotic variety of, yes, martinis and an eclectic mix of people.

Best country bar:
Stampede (2430 S. Havana St., Aurora, 303-337-6909) is a players' favorite. Peter Forsberg and Adam Deadmarsh say "the Stampede is one of many great country-western bars in Denver. The atmosphere can't be beaten."

Stampede features several huge dance floors, lots of twangy music, and plenty of members of the opposite sex. With so many hailing from Western Canada, hockey players love country music, and the whole "Urban Cowboy" lifestyle.

Best nightclub:
Polly Esther's (2301 Blake St.,

Pepsi Center

303-382-1976) is a sprawling multi-level club featuring '70s and '80s music. Inside, you'll find a life-size duplicate of the Partridge Family bus. On weekends, the line to get in sometimes stretches around the block. The Artist Formerly Known as Prince played **The Church** (1160 Lincoln, 303-832-3528) after one of his concerts. The music is more contemporary here, and the club even features a sushi bar.

Best place to play pool:

At **Wynkoop Brewing Company** (1634 18th St., 303-297-2700), you'll often find Stephane Yelle and other teammates playing at one of the many tables at this friendly, relaxed place.

Best bar to watch the game:

Governor's Park (672 Logan, 303-831-8605) has a large screen TV and a staff full of rabid Avs fanatics. When the home team scores, you can win food or drink, and a hat trick by a member of the Avalanche brings a major prize to the lucky customer who chose that player beforehand.

Best live music:

Denver isn't considered a musical mecca, but the **Grizzly Rose** (5450 N. Valley Hwy., 303-295-1330) offers local and national acts most nights. For the grungier set, **Herman's Hideaway** (1578 S. Broadway, 303-777-5840) features some of the city's better local bands. Imagine the bar/club Ethan Hawke sang at in "Reality Bites," and you've got a good picture of what Herman's is like.

Dining

Team favorites:

The boom of the lower downtown area—LoDo, as the locals call it—has spawned dozens and dozens of places to eat, drink, and be merry. You can often find Patrick Roy at **Morton's** downtown (1710 Wynkoop St., 303-825-3353). Morton's steaks are, of course, superb, and hockey players love a good steak. You may find Joe Sakic carving the beef at one of his favorite spots, **Ruth's Chris Steakhouse** (1445 Market St., 303-446-2233).

For ethnic food:

You'll often spot players at **Carmine's on Penn** (92 S. Pennsylvania St., 303-777-6443), which features fine Italian food and a relaxed, upscale atmosphere. The team's brass, including general manager Pierre Lacroix, also come here. Lacroix and some of the team's other French-Canadian personnel on the team like the French cuisine at **Le Central** (112 E. 8th Ave., 303-863-8094). With an affordable yet high-class menu, it has been a Denver favorite for years.

Avalanche

In "the Can"
Opened:
10/1/99.

First regular-season game:
10/13/99, 2–1 win over Boston.

First goal:
Milan Hejduk of Colorado

Address:
1000 Chopper Travaglini Blvd., Denver

For single-game tickets:
303-405-1100 or 303-830-8497

Website:
coloradoavlanche.com

For postgame dinner:

If you really want to see an

Avs player after a game, head over to the **Denver Chop House and Brewery** (1735 19th St., 303-296-0800). The Chop House is a favorite of Adam Foote and Stephane Yelle. Order the Iowa pork chop and garlic mashed potatoes.

For local fare:

If you want to try one of Denver's specialties—Rocky Mountain oysters—do it at the **Denver Buffalo Company** (1109 Lincoln St., 303-832-0880).

Lodging

Most luxurious:

The venerable **Brown Palace Hotel** (321 17th St., 303-297-3111), since it opened in 1892, has never been closed for a single day. Aside from Calvin Coolidge, "The Brown" has hosted every U.S. president since Teddy Roosevelt. The rooms have an elegant Victorian look, yet are modernized to include everything from dual phone lines to Nintendo. The hotel's **Ship Tavern** restaurant offers its own microbrews. In the Wild, Wild West days, the Brown's famous lobby was once the site for a live auction of bulls. Afternoon tea is served there now.

Where the other teams stay:

The Westin Tabor Center's location (1672 Lawrence St., 303-572-9100) makes it a great place for the tourist. It is adjacent to the **16th Street Mall**, and a short walk away from

Joe Sakic #19

lower downtown and **Coors Field**, where the Colorado Rockies baseball team plays. The Westin has 24-hour room service, a health club with indoor and outdoor pools, and a racquetball court. The **Embassy Suites** (1881 Curtis St., 303-297-8888, 800-362-2779) features the chain's renowned large rooms and is near the 16th Street Mall.

Shopping & Attractions

Believe it or not, Denver's No. 1 tourist attraction is a mall—the **Cherry Creek Mall** (303-388-3900). It has more than 1 million square feet and features **Neiman Marcus**, **Lord & Taylor** and **Saks Fifth Avenue**. But if you want to visit more interesting local attractions, try Elitch Gardens (2000 Elitches Circle, 303-595-4386). Many an Avs player has gone on the huge rollercoaster there, and regretted it.

For the best selection of Avalanche merchandise, go to the **Gart Sports** store downtown (1000 Broadway, 303-861-1122).

Of course, if you don't mind a little driving, the skiing in Vail, Aspen, Breckenridge and many others is some of the world's best. Those towns are where you'll see Roy, Forsberg, and Sakic when they have a little time off during the season.

Favorite City on the Road

Patrick Roy likes Boston the best, not only because he has won many games there, but for the city's history. Joe Sakic likes the Vancouver area, where he grew up. You'll often find him at one of the many top-notch seafood restaurants, dining on some plank salmon. Sakic also likes Chicago. In fact, Chicago is a favorite city of several teammates. Avs players say "Chicago is an exciting place. There are so many things to do and places to see, and the people there are really down to earth." Peter Forsberg enjoys Phoenix, where the golfing is

Avalanche

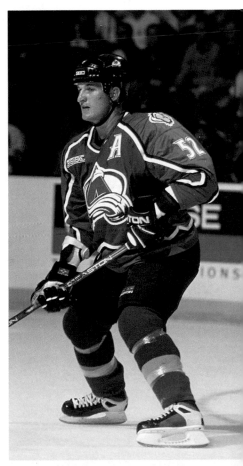

Adam Foote #32

good and the temperature is a tad warmer than in his native Sweden.

Several players on the Avs like the hockey atmosphere of cities such as Montreal, Toronto, and Edmonton, but don't much like the cold weather.

Cool Fact

The franchise has capitalized on trades. The 1992 trade of unhappy No. 1 1991 pick Eric Lindros to Philadelphia for six players, two first-round draft picks, and cash was crucial to the franchise's turnaround and 1996 title. Mike Ricci (hero of Game 1 of the Finals), Peter Forsberg (Game 2 hero), and Chris Simon came from that trade and were still with the 1996 club. Also, 1993 first-round pick Jocelyn Thibault was the key player sent to Montreal to acquire Mike Keane and Patrick Roy.

Franchise History

Colorado sports fans must have been mystified: after suffering through decades of frustration watching their professional teams fail to win the big game, the new kids in town, the Avalanche, won the Stanley Cup their first year in the state. It's not as if Colorado never had an NHL team before; it did, the Rockies. But the Rockies were never a competitive team and eventually moved east to New Jersey. And it's not as if the Avalanche was an expansion team. The franchise was origi-

nally the Quebec Nordiques of the World Hockey Association before joining the NHL in 1979. Always in the shadow of their French Canadian rivals, the Montreal Canadiens, the Nordiques enjoyed early success in the league before a string of years in which the club failed to make the playoffs. The fans in Quebec passionately supported their team, but when the province failed to fund a new arena, the small market Nordiques were forced to move. The franchise was transferred to the COMSAT Entertainment Group on July 1, 1995. Luckily for hockey fans in Colorado, the club was about to harvest the fruits of the Eric Lindros trade to Philadelphia that would lead to a championship and form

Patrick Roy #33

COLORADO

the nucleus of a Stanley Cup contender for years to come.

Famers

Most Valuable Player (Hart Trophy): None
   Hockey Hall of Fame:
   Players: Guy Lafleur, 1988; Michel Goulet, 1998; Peter Stastny, 1998.
      Retired numbers: 3 J.C. Tremblay, 8 Marc Tardif, 16 Michel Goulet

Avalanche

Milan Hejduk #23

Records

Games played		Most points, season		Most goalie wins, season	
Michel Goulet	813	Peter Stastny	139	Patrick Roy	38
Career goals		**Most goals, game**		**Most shutouts, career**	
Michel Goulet	456	several players	5	Patrick Roy 17	
Career assists		**Most assists, game**		**Most shutouts, season**	
Peter Stastny	668	several players	5	Patrick Roy	7
Career points		**Most points, game**		**Stanley Cups:**	
Peter Stastny	1,048	Peter Stastny,		1996	
Most goals, season		Anton Stastny	8		
Michel Goulet	57	**Most goalie wins, career**			
Most assists, season					
Peter Stastny	93	Patrick Roy	123		

Stars

Joe Nieuwendyk #25

DALLAS STARS.

around the town with the Stars

Deep Ellum in Dallas is known as the avant-garde district, but the truth is, the whole city is trendy. Dallas is the place where fashion comes and goes, the place that steals most of the headlines from its twin city, Fort Worth. But Fort Worth has its attractions, and together, they give the visitor the chance to see everything, including pro hockey.

There have been minor-league teams in Texas for quite a while, but the NHL only arrived in 1993. The Stars fit in well with the fast-paced, high-flying business world that is Dallas. They are committed to greatness, as their 1999 championship shows. Their success has made hockey a cool game in this warm city. People know about Ed Belfour's glove hand, Joe Nieuwendyk's wrist shot, Derian Hatcher's toughness and Mike Modano's smoothness. On a team called Stars, there are in truth many of them.

Dallas is known for its modern high-rise downtown; the giant buildings symbolize the huge deals that routinely occur behind their walls. But the city is old and reminders of the past are not hard to find. Built in 1841, the John Neely Bryan Cabin was Dallas' first building, and it still stands in the heart of the city. Fair Park, a National Historic Landmark, has three museums and an unrivaled collection of 1930s architecture. In the more laid-back Fort Worth, there are elegant Victorian buildings. Both cities have Historic Districts: the West End in Dallas, the Stockyards in Fort Worth. This marriage of different eras appeals to the head Star, coach Ken Hitchcock. "What's really great about this area is that it's a mix between the Wild West and the city," he observes. "Anything you want is right here." Including a championship team.

Reunion Arena

Where to sit:
The Stars make up for their lack of luxury boxes with waiter service in their StarsClub and StarsClub Premier sections (mid-ice in the lower level). If you can't work a single-game deal, take the corners down low or, better yet, get in the Executive Terrace, in the upper bowl. With no luxury boxes, you'd be surprised how close you are to the ice.

If it's all you can get:
The Stars have one of the NHL's cheapest seats with their community corner. You're in the last rows of the end zones,

but for $20, you get NHL action. An even better deal is the upper deck corners.

Special services:
The Stars provide excellent services for the handicapped and disabled with convenient parking leading onto lower terrace seating. Call 214-GO-STARS or 972-868-2890 for information.

Stars

Ticket availability:
The Stars are more popular than ever, and only seats in the upper reaches behind the goals are now readily available.

Parking:
There are about 5,000 parking spots within walking distance of Reunion Arena. Most general admission patrons park in a huge lot south of the arena for $6.

$250	$140	$125	$100	$75
$60	$42	$32	$20	

Capacity: 16,962

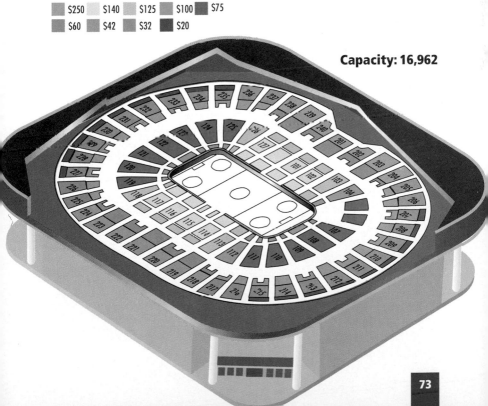

Public transportation:

DART Rail is really beginning to advance in Dallas and can get you from North Dallas or South Dallas to the game, but

you're best off renting a car.

By car:

Reunion Arena is accessible from 35E going north and south and from I-30 going east and west. If you're coming from Dallas-Fort Worth Airport, take 183 East until it dumps into 35E south. Take 35E until you see downtown and start looking for the Reunion Boulevard Exit. Take Reunion Blvd. and follow the signs.

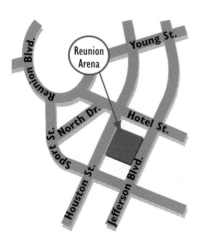

Cuisine:

Reunion Arena is still an old-fashioned barn in that the standard items are the most plentiful. If you're into fine dining, check out the pregame buffet at the StarsClub.

Home-ice advantage:

While much is made of the soft ice at Reunion Arena, players around the league say it has improved greatly the past two years. Now that the Stars are the champs, the fans will be very excited come playoff time.

Nightlife

For after the game:

There's no place to start like the **StarsClub** (972-868-2871). The tent-like structure outside of Reunion Arena is so popular that many fans amble out this way long before the third period is over. Players from both teams often hang out here after the game. It's especially lively after a Stars' win. Even if you're going someplace else, you owe it to yourself to check out the scene. It's reserved for certain ticketholders.

For a quiet drink:

Antares (300 Reunion Blvd. E., 214-712-7145) atop Reunion Tower is a great place for the well-heeled to share a drink. Pomodoro (2520 Cedar Springs, 214-871-1924) gets the nod from Darryl Sydor.

To hang out:

Most of the players live in Valley Ranch, the area of Irving where the Dr. Pepper Star-Center practice facility is located, so many hang out at bars in the area. The hottest of late is the **Cool River Cafe** (1045 Hidden Ridge,

Reunion Arena

972-871-8881). There's good beer and plenty of sports on TV. **Humperdink's Addison** (4021 Belt Line, Addison, 972-934-2612) also is a favorite of fans, with its huge screen TVs and good food. **Big Apple Cafe** (14200 Trinity Blvd., 817-572-7753) is just south of the Dallas-Fort Worth Airport.

To hear live music:
Deep Ellum has the best variety. Ken Hitchcock loves the jazz at **Sambuca's** (2618 Elm, 214-744-0820) and, with its Mediterranean menu, it's one of his favorite dinner spots. Or you can go to **Dallas Alley** (2019 N. Lamar St., 214-880-7420) in the West End, a short walk from Reunion Arena.

Honky tonking:
Former Stars winger Bill Huard loved the cowboy clubs, and a few players like defenseman Richard Matvichuk still stop by. Legendary **Billy Bob's Texas** (2520 Rodeo Plaza, 817-589-1711) is located in Fort Worth's Stockyards. It's a long drive, "but more people are hanging out in Fort Worth than in Dallas," Hitchcock says. Or check out closer country bars at **Cowboys Concert Hall** (2540 E. Abram St., Arlington, 817-265-1535) or **Country 2000** (10707 Finnell St., Dallas, 214-654-9595.)

Dining

Most convenient:
The Reunion Arena's **StarsClub** is quite a boon to the organization, serving a great dinner buffet before the game and offering one of the area's best bars afterward. Reservations are required (call 972-868-2871). Getting to the Arena early and beating the traffic makes the experience that much more relaxing.

Foot-stompin' good:
Any visit to Texas wouldn't be complete without real barbecue. **Sonny Bryan's Smokehouse** (2202 Inwood Rd., 214-357-7120) is the perfect tourist place, but if you want to go off the beaten track, try **The Original Porkie's Bar BQ** (6530 E Northwest Highway, 214-987-0424) for truckstop barbecue.

To be pampered:
If you want to catch team president Jim Lites in a power lunch, visit **The Palm** (701 Ross Ave., 214-698-0470) in the West End. High-grade steak and massive lobsters are the featured items on the menu.

World's greatest pizza:
Who would have thought that the world's best pizza would come from Dallas, but center

Joe Nieuwendyk swears it's so. **Pomodoro Ristorante Italiano** (2520 Cedar Springs Rd., 214-871-1924) has exotic mixes like pesto and goat cheese or just a plain cheese. They also serve fun Italian dishes.

Bring your sunglasses:

If you want to run into Mike Modano or Tom Cruise, check out **Star Canyon** (3102 Oak Lawn Ave., 214-520-7827) at The Centrum on Cedar Springs. It's currently atop the trendy list in Dallas, and the biggest reason is excellent Southwestern cuisine.

Lodging

For luxury:

Crescent Court Hotel (400 Crescent Court, 214-871-3200) is your best chance to meet TV star Robin Leach. But be prepared to pay for this downtown castle ($320–$350 weekdays, $215 weekends), located off McKinney in a trendy area of downtown.

Closest to the arena:

Few NHL cities offer this kind of convenience. **The Hyatt** (300 Reunion Blvd. W., 214-651-1234, 800-233-1234) is across the street from the Reunion Arena and allows you to stay in the city, attend the game, and hang around the West End—all without a car.

To spot players:

Many teams have tired of the autograph dealers that stake out a place between the Hyatt and Reunion Arena, waiting for the players to walk through, so they've moved to the **Wyndham Anatole** (2201 N. Stemmons Freeway, 214-748-1200). It's up 35E a few miles and requires a cab ride or a rental car. The Nana Grill is excellent.

Shopping & Attractions

Dallas is more of a business downtown and isn't known for its central shopping district. One major exception is **Neiman Marcus** (1618 Main St., 214-

Ed Belfour #20

741-6911). You can spend a day at this legendary store. Another branch of Neiman Marcus also highlights the Northpark area (400 Northpark Center, 214-363-8311) near Highland Park. There are plenty of quaint boutiques, too. **The Galleria** (Loop 635 at Dallas Parkway, 972-702-7100) in North Dallas provides miles of indoor shopping along with an indoor ice rink. Aimed at the more affluent shopper, you can find **Tiffany's** and **Saks Fifth** Avenue, along with the normal mall staples.

Team president Jim Lites said a trip to Dallas isn't complete without a visit to the Kennedy exhibit at the **Sixth Floor Museum at Dealy** (411 Elm, 214-747-6660).

If you're a sports fan, you'll likely want to check out **The Ballpark in Arlington** (I-30 on Stadium Drive, 817-273-5100). It rivals Baltimore's Camden Yards for stunning architecture. But if you're in town for the hockey experience, it's pretty hard to pass up the Stars' open practices. The **Dr. Pepper StarCenter** (211 Cowboys Parkway, Irving, 972-868-2890) houses the Stars' offices, locker rooms, and two sheets of practice ice. During the regular season, fans are allowed to stop by and watch.

Favorite City on the Road

Detroit is special for several Stars players. Shawn Chambers and Derian Hatcher grew up in Sterling Heights, Mich., a Detroit suburb. Chambers grew up a Red Wings fan and has family in the area. Hatcher lives in the Detroit area in the offseason—two houses down from his older brother, NHL defenseman Kevin Hatcher—and likes to go boating on Lake St. Clair. Mike Modano also grew up in suburban Detroit, but he was more of a Toronto Maple Leafs and Boston Bruins fan (his dad was from Boston) than a Red Wings fan. Aaron Gavey opts for Miami, a warm weather

Stars

Brett Hull #16

locale. Gavey's preference might stem from the fact that he played his first three seasons in nearby Tampa. It's hard to get the Florida out of the kid once he has spent a full season shivering through a frigid Alberta winter.

Stars

Cool Fact

Tragedy struck the Minnesota North Stars in 1967–68, when Bill Masterton struck his head on the ice after a collision and never regained consciousness, becoming the only NHL player to die from an on-ice accident. He is remembered with the NHL's Bill Masterton Memorial Trophy, awarded annually to the player who best exemplifies the qualities of perseverance, sportsmanship, and dedication to hockey. Only one Minnesota/Dallas player has won the award, Al MacAdam in 1980.

Franchise History

The defending Stanley Cup Champion Dallas Stars may have a brief history in the Lone Star state, but they have a legacy to remember in the North Star state. The Minnesota North Stars were one of six franchises awarded on June 5, 1967 in the first wave of expansion in the NHL that doubled the number of teams from six to 12. In those early years when the best of the "Original Six" played the best of the expansion six for the Stanley Cup, the new clubs were quickly dispatched in four straight games. That didn't

make for a particularly exciting Finals, so the playoffs were rearranged. It was Minnesota that was the first of the expansion teams to test an established team in the playoffs. In 1971 the North Stars gave the eventual Stanley Cup Champion Montreal Canadiens all they could handle before finally losing in six games. The team never quite fulfilled that early promise, and it wasn't until 1981 that the North Stars made their first appearance in the Finals, having the misfortune of going up against the

Mike Modano #9

New York Islander dynasty.

Ten years later Minnesota again made it to the Finals, only to lose this time to the Pittsburgh Penguins and Mario Lemieux at his peak. The Minnesota franchise was then transferred to Dallas for the 1993–94 NHL season. Six seasons later the franchise won its first Stanley Cup Championship, with many of the team's old stars leading the new Stars to victory.

Stars

Derian Hatcher #2

Famers

Most Valuable Player (Hart Trophy): None
   Hockey Hall of Fame:
   Players: Gump Worsley, 1980; Leo Boivin, 1986. Builder: John Mariucci, 1985.
   Retired numbers: 7 Neal Broten, 8 Bill Goldsworthy, 19 Bill Masterton

Records

Games played		Most assists, season		Most goalie wins, career	
Neal Broten	992	Neal Broten	76	Cesare Maniago	144
Career goals		**Most points, season**		**Most goalie wins, season**	
Brian Bellows	342	Bobby Smith	114	Ed Belfour	37
Career assists		**Most goals, game**		**Most shutouts, career**	
Neal Broten	593	Tim Young	5	Cesare Maniago	26
Career points		**Most assists, game**		**Most shutouts, season**	
Neal Broten	867	Murray Oliver, Larry Murphy	5	Ed Belfour	9
Most goals, season		**Most points, game**		**Stanley Cups:**	
Brian Bellows, Dino Ciccarelli	55	Bobby Smith	7	1999	

Red Wings

Sergei Fedorov #91

D E T R O I T

around
the town with the
Red Wings

They don't call it Hockeytown for no reason. Detroit is not only home to one of the NHL's greatest and most storied teams, its population supports hockey at all levels. Red Wings owner Mike Ilitch started the current golden age for his team. After he bought the club in 1982, the season-ticket base eventually multiplied by eight. But the fans didn't need much prompting, not in a state that owns many fine college programs, junior teams and minor pro squads, not to mention living legend Steve Yzerman.

Simply wearing the red wing on your jersey can bring unexpected loyalty from the locals. When Team Russia played Team USA at Joe Louis Arena in a 1996 World Cup of Hockey exhibition, Russia received a warm response because it had three Wings on the ice.

It was a Canadian, Stevie Y, who spurred the Red Wings to the Stanley Cup in 1997 and 1998, but he's hardly alone. Sweden's Nick Lidstrom is almost an ideal defenseman, while Canada's Chris Osgood and Russian Sergei Fedorov rank among the world's best at their positions. These players are reaffirming the tradition that began with names like Syd Howe, Sid Abel, Gordie Howe and Terry Sawchuk.

The Red Wings have been around in different forms since 1926, and Detroit is similarly aged: it is actually the oldest city in the Midwest. In Rivertown, or East Detroit, new businesses exist in refurbished warehouses and carriage houses, some dating back to the late 19th century. The University Cultural Center, spanning 40 blocks, preserves a wide range of local, national and international art and history. In Hockeytown, you have no excuse to be bored between games.

Joe Louis Arena

Where to sit:
Since the Red Wings regularly sell out "The Joe," you sit wherever you can scrape up a ticket if you're not a season-ticket holder.

If it's all you can get:
The seats high up are sometimes available, but it's best to order early. If you want to be closer to the ice surface and don't mind being without a seat, there are standing room tickets that actually offer a better view than many of the seats. This area extends around the concourse level, but it's first-come, first-served as far as position. Again, order early for big games.

Special services:
There are 200 seats in the Concourse level available for fans with disabilities.

Ticket availability:
If you're not already on the never-ending waiting list for season tickets, forget it. Of course, scalpers are available outside of the Joe before games. Be warned though—scalping is illegal in Detroit.

Red Wings

Parking:
Two parking garages serve Joe Louis Arena. They charge $6. If you don't mind a little walk there's also parking on surrounding streets like Fort, Lafayette, and Howard. Many downtown Detroit restaurants and bars also offer shuttle services to and from the game.

Public transportation:
This is the Motor City, so if

$75 $67 $48 $39 $20

Capacity: 19,983

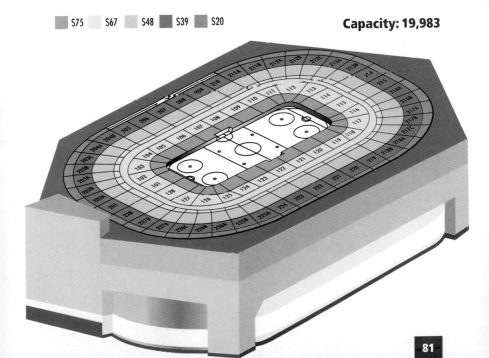

you don't have a car, you're out of luck when it comes to getting around. But there is the People Mover, a raised railway that does a small circuit around downtown Detroit. Call 313-933-1300 for more information.

By car:

Joe Louis Arena is easily accessible from any of the four freeways, Lodge (M-10) from the Northwest, the Chrysler (1-75) from the north, the Fisher (1-75) from the south or the Jefferies (1-96) from the west. All of these freeways empty into downtown Detroit. From Detroit Metropolitan Airport, take The Ford (1-94) East to M-10 South. Take the exit marked for Joe Louis Arena or take Howard Street Exit, which

is just before JLA Exit, for street parking.

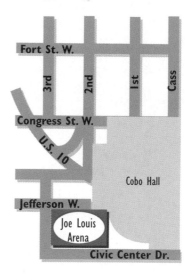

Cuisine:

Since the Ilitchs own the team, there's all the Little Caesar's pizza that anyone could want.

Chris Osgood #30

Joe Louis Arena

There are also hot dogs, bratwurst, sandwiches, popcorn, and giant pretzels. Beer and mixed drinks are also available.

Home-ice advantage:
The Joe Louis Arena crowd can get deafeningly loud, particularly at playoff time. The Red Wings have 13 straight winning records at home.

Nightlife

For after the game:
The best place, by far, is the original **The Post Bar** (408 Congress St., 313-962-1293), across the street from the Cobo Center Parking Garage. Generally packed on weekends and after Red Wings games, the Post is the unofficial downtown party spot for the Red Wings. Chris Osgood, Kris Draper, Darren McCarty, Joe Kocur and others, including the Stanley Cup itself, have been spotted here. Prepare to be pressed up against a lot of people. Another incarnation of The Post has been opened in Ferndale on Woodward Avenue, just north of Nine Mile Road. Osgood, Draper and the Cup have put in

appearances. **The Anchor Bar** (450 W. Fort St., 313-964-9127) is a newspaper hangout and draws Red Wings personnel, though not necessarily players. It offers shuttles to and from the Joe, so there is a good crowd before and after games. **Reedy's Saloon** (1846 Michigan Ave., 313-961-1722) is a gritty, working class bar across from Tiger Stadium. McCarty spends a little bit of time there.

For a quiet drink:
Dunleavy's River Place (267 Joseph Campau St., 313-259-0909) is a good place to have dinner before a game and return for a drink afterward. More of an upscale establishment, Dunleavy's used to be a regular hangout of Wayne Gretzky when his teams visited Detroit. The nearby **Andrews on the Corner** (201 Joseph Campau St., 313-259-8325) has an intimate setting and relaxing atmosphere. Marge's Bar (15300 Mack Ave., Grosse Pointe Park, 313-881-8895) is also a great place to watch a game on TV. It's noisy, of course, but if you stop by after

Red Wings

At "the Joe"
Opened:
12/12/79

First regular-season game:
12/27/79,
3–2 loss to
St. Louis

First playoff game:
4/7/84,
4–3 loss to
St. Louis

First goal:
Brian Sutter of
St. Louis

Address:
600 Civic Center
Dr., Detroit

For single-game tickets:
313-396-7575

Website:
detroitredwings.com

the game, a friendly, homey atmosphere awaits. A longtime hockey hangout, it used to be a favorite party spot for the Jacques Demers-era Red Wings, when many of the players lived in Grosse Pointe or Grosse Pointe Park. But hockey players from beer leaguers to the NHL variety frequent Marge's.

Red Wings

Suburban style:

If you want to hang out in the suburbs after a game, the best choice is **Dick O'Dow's** (160 W. Maple Rd., Birmingham, 248-642-1135), an old-fashioned Irish pub. The atmosphere is warm, thanks partly to the spirited Celtic music. So it's no surprise that it's one of Brendan Shanahan's favorite haunts. Larry Murphy stops by from time to time; Osgood and Draper have also been spotted here.

Dining

Most expensive:
Opus One (565 E. Larned St., 313-961-7766) has one of the best menus in the area. Everything is good, but expensive.

Best ethnic:
The city's Greektown area has outstanding Greek dining—everything from souvlaki to moussaka—at all prices. Tucked in Greektown is an excellent Cajun restaurant: **Fishbone's Rhythm Kitchen Cafe** (400 Monroe St., 313-965-4600). This is the best spicy food in the city. If you like hot, hotter and hottest, Fishbone's is a must.

For pasta:
Intermezzo Italian Ristorante (1435 Randolph St., 313-961-0707) has quickly become one of downtown Detroit's most popular eating spots. It offers quality Italian fare for comparatively low prices.

Good food, good time:
Sinbad's Restaurant and Marina (100 St. Clair, 313-822-7817), on the banks of the Detroit

Steve Yzerman #19

River, is one of Detroit's long-time favorite eating and party spots. Patrons always compliment the meat dishes.

Lodging

Most luxurious:
Atheneum Suite Hotel (1000 Brush St., 313-962-2323), in the heart of Greektown, is the place where many visiting NHL teams stay. It features large, stylish suites. The staff is excellent and the room service menu is outstanding.

Spotting the other team:
Visiting teams also like the **Courtyard by Marriott** (333 E. Jefferson St., 313-222-7700, 800-843-6664) and the **Marriott** (400 Renaissance Center, 313-568-8000). The latter is located in the massive Renaissance complex a short walk from the Joe. At 73 stories and 710 feet, it's one of the tallest hotels in existence. Its Summit Restaurant, on the 71st floor, is a steakhouse with a 360-degree view of the city, Lake St. Clair and Windsor, Ontario. If you don't want to eat anything, you can simply pop in and look down on two countries.

Closest to the arena:
Crowne Plaza (2 Washington Blvd., 313-965-0200, 800-517-3333) houses Red Wings rookies after they are brought up and before they find permanent places to live or are sent back down to the minors. There's a steak and seafood restaurant inside, plus complimentary breakfast.

Shopping & Attractions

Detroit's major stores left long ago, but there are plenty of department stores and malls throughout suburban Detroit. If you want to shop amid history (shopping mall history, that is), try the **Northland Center** (21500 Northwestern Highway, 248-569-1620). It was the first enclosed mall in the United States. If you're looking for a Red Wings jersey, you have many choices. But if you're in the market for used equipment, broken sticks and the like, the best bet is at the Joe.

History is well-preserved in the **Henry Ford Museum and Greenfield Village** (20900 Oakwood Blvd., Dearborn, 313-271-1620). It includes the laboratory of inventor Thomas Edison, who was from the area. The **Museum of African-American History** (315 E. Warren Ave., 313-494-5800), the largest of its kind, is part of the Cultural Center, as is the **Detroit Institute of Arts** (5200 Woodward Ave., 313-833-7900), which has more than 100 galleries and a few ancient treasures to catch your eye. The **Motown Historical Museum** (2648 W. Grand Blvd., 313-875-2264) is the place where Motown records created pop magic.

For those so inclined, Windsor, Ontario, across the river, has casinos.

Favorite City on the Road

When you work and live in the

Red Wings

Midwest, trips to the Sun Belt are always welcome. And when the Red Wings make a swing through Los Angeles, Anaheim, and San Jose, they usually make the Loews Santa Monica hotel their base for about a week and bus or fly to game sites. Over the years, this westward swing has become a great bonding trip. During a California trip in 1996–97, Red Wings members engaged in a legendary paint-ball game at an outdoor facility in Palm Springs. On the same trip, the team's Russian players—Sergei Fedorov, Igor Larionov, Vladimir Konstantinov, Slava Kozlov and Slava Fetisov—took their teammates to a Russian restaurant in Los Angeles. Backup goaltender Kevin Hodson said this experience galvanized them as a team and set the stage for their Stanley Cup run.

Phoenix also holds a recent bit of Red Wings lore. When Fedorov returned after a long holdout late in 1997–98 to sign a six-year, $36 million contract last season, he observed the team tradition of picking up the dinner bill to celebrate his financial windfall. The Red Wings went to Phoenix on the first step of a West Coast swing, so Fedorov took his teammates to the Morton's of Chicago steakhouse there. The bill was reported to be $10,000, although some inside sources say it was much higher.

Cool Fact

Legend has it, at least in one verson, that seafood store-owner

Peter Cusamano started the Red Wings fans' octopus-tossing habit in 1952 because he believed that the eight tentacles represented the eight playoff wins the team needed at the time to win the Stanley Cup. The Red Wings then won three Cups in four years. Decades later, arena supervisor Al Sabotka became locally famous for scooping the octopuses off the ice with his bare hands and

Brendan Shanahan #14

twirling them over his head. Ironically, the Red Wings ended their post-1955 championship drought in 1996–97, the season the NHL banned the throwing of objects onto the ice.

Franchise History

Only Montreal and Toronto have won more than Detroit's nine Stanley Cup Championships. Granted a franchise on September 25, 1926, the Detroit team was originally known as the Cougars, after ownership purchased the roster of the Victoria Cougars of the disbanded Western Hockey League. The team actually played its first NHL season across the Detroit River in Canada while awaiting the completion of its legendary home, Olympia Stadium. The Detroit Cougars became the Falcons in 1930, in an attempt by local sports writers to change the club's luck after failing to make the playoffs the year before.

It wasn't until 1932, when James Norris purchased the franchise, that the team became known as the Red Wings. Norris had played hockey in Canada for a club known as the Winged Wheelers and its winged wheel insignia, modified to incorporate an automobile tire, seemed an appropriate symbol for a franchise representing the Motor City. The fortunes of the team soon improved as well, as it captured three Stanley Cups in the next ten years. With the arrival of Gordie Howe in the late 1940s the Red Wings assembled one of the NHL's great dynasties. The team won a league record seven consecutive regular season titles and four Stanley Cups. Although a drought of championships ensued, fan support never wavered, and the Red Wings rewarded their faithful with another run of success, winning **Red Wings** consecutive Stanley Cups in 1997 and 1998.

Famers

Most Valuable Player (Hart Trophy): Ebbie Goodfellow, 1940; Sid Abel, 1949; Gordie Howe, 1952, 1953, 1957, 1958, 1960, 1963; Sergei Fedorov, 1994.

Hockey Hall of Fame:
Players: Alex Connell, George Hay, Frank Fredrickson, Frank Foyston, Duke Keats, 1958; Cecil "Tiny" Thompson, 1959; Jack Walker, 1960; Charlie Conacher, 1961; Reg Noble, 1962; Ebbie Goodfellow, 1963; Earl Seibert, Jack Stewart, 1964; Syd Howe, Marty Barry, 1965; Ted Lindsay, 1966; Sid Abel, Red Kelly, 1969; Bill Gadsby, 1970; Cooney Weiland, Terry Sawchuk, 1971; Hap Holmes, Gordie Howe, 1972; Doug Harvey, 1973; Glenn Hall, 1975; Bill Quackenbush, 1976; Alex Delvecchio, 1977; Marcel Pronovost, Andy Bathgate, 1978; Harry Lumley, 1980; Johnny Bucyk, Frank Mahovlich, 1981; Norm Ullman, 1982; Leo Boivin, 1986; Eddie Giacomin, 1987; Brad Park, 1988; Darryl Sittler, Herbie Lewis, 1989; Marcel Dionne, 1992; Harry Watson,

1994; Borje Salming, 1996; Roy Conacher, 1998.

Builders: James Norris, 1958; James D. Norris, 1962; Bruce Norris, 1969; Tommy Ivan, Carl Voss, 1974; Bud Poile, 1990.

Retired numbers: 1 Terry Sawchuk, 6 Larry Aurie, 7 Ted Lindsay, 9 Gordie Howe, 10 Alex Delvecchio, 12 Sid Abel

Red Wings

Niklas Lidstrom #5

Records

Games played
Gordie Howe   1,687

Career goals
Gordie Howe   786

Career assists
Gordie Howe   1,023

Career points
Gordie Howe   1,809

Most goals, season
Steve Yzerman   65

Most assists, season
Steve Yzerman   90

Most points, season
Steve Yzerman   155

Most goals, game
Syd Howe   6

Most assists, game
Billy Taylor   7

Most points, game
Don Grosso,
Carl Liscombe,
Billy Taylor   7

Most goalie wins, career
Terry Sawchuk 351

Most goalie wins, season
Terry Sawchuk   44

Most shutouts, career
Terry Sawchuk   85

Most shutouts, season
Terry Sawchuk,
Glenn Hall   12

Stanley Cups:
1936, 1937, 1943,
1950, 1952, 1954, 1955,
1997, 1998.

EDMONTON

around the town with the Oilers

Oilers

Mike Grier #25

It was a proud October day in Edmonton when the Oilers retired Wayne Gretzky's number, kicking off the 1999–2000 campaign. From a small kid who was thought to be too fragile, The Great One grew past all of his peers to hit the clouds and beyond in Edmonton. When they changed the name of the team's arena to Skyreach, they might have been thinking of Gretzky's stature as a player.

Reminders of number 99 are everywhere, most notably in the bronze likeness of him that stands outside the stadium. But the Oilers have continued without him, winning one championship and building a team of fast, exciting young players. Ever since Gretzky appeared, the Oilers have been able to skate with the best opponents. Year after year, you can count on Edmonton to play swift, attacking hockey.

The centerpiece of the Oilers is now Doug Weight, a cunning set-up artist whose style resembles Gretzky's. He is one of those stars who makes a difference whenever he plays. Fans visiting Edmonton will be sure to take away a few memories of Weight from a game. The Skyreach Centre is tailored perfectly for him too, with ice that's known as the fastest in the league. "It's an awesome building, the best," Weight says.

Fans in the city of oil are known for their polite ways, but that doesn't mean they're not rabid fans. Western Canada is a hockey hotbed, and the natives know exactly what's going on during a game.

Moreover, "Any player who has been here for more than a year gets recognized," observes Todd Marchant. "They know their hockey players."

Skyreach Centre

Where to sit:
The Centre was built for hockey. There are no bad seats, just distant ones. Any real fan knows one must be at least seven or eight rows up from the ice to properly take in a game, making the first three rows of the upper tier prime seating.

If it's all you can get:
Like any arena, the nosebleed seats are the last ones to go in Edmonton. There are a handful of seats in the first row of the upper bowl at center ice that are slightly obscured by

television cameras. They're a bit cheaper, and will do just fine in a pinch.

Special services:
The Centre is fully accessible to persons with disabilities, with a special section at the top of the lower bowl in one end.

Ticket availability:
About 13,100 of the 17,100 seats go to season-ticket holders. That leaves about 4,000 a night up for grabs. Scalpers can be found outside the Centre, and they'll make their biggest dollar when Toronto or Montreal is in town.

Parking:
Season ticketholders have access to Skyreach parking. Since cars have trouble starting on cold winter nights, free boosts are available. Northlands Park,

Oilers

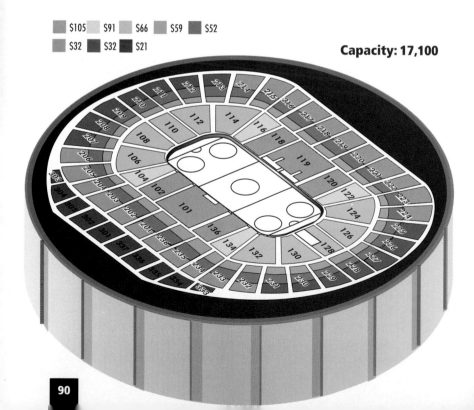

$105 $91 $66 $59 $52
$32 $32 $21

Capacity: 17,100

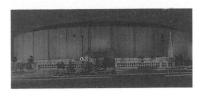

Skyreach Centre

across 188 Ave., has spots going for $5.

Public transportation:

The LRT will leave you downtown after a game, or at the university near the trendy Whyte Avenue district. A smart idea is to find underground heated parking (at the downtown library, perhaps), then hop the train.

By car:

From the International Airport, take Highway 2 north into town, make a right (east) on the Whitemud Freeway, a left (north) on 75th Street and follow it all the way to 118th Avenue (75th becomes Wayne Gretzky Drive). Look for the entrance gates on your left soon after passing over the river on Wayne Gretzky Drive.

Cuisine:

The Centre is in line with most American arenas. The All-Stars Restaurant (780-414-4200) offers pre-game dining. Call ahead to make sure you will have a table.

Home-ice advantage:

Boasting the quickest surface in the league, Skyreach is a good place for the Oilers to play half their season. The fans are not loud, however.

Nightlife

For after the game:

People in search of an active scene prefer these two nightclubs: **Cowboys Country Saloon** (10102 180 St. NW, 780-481-8739) and **Barry T's Grand Central Station** (6111 104 St. NW, 780-438-2582). The Whyte Avenue (82 Ave.) scene can be found just south across the river from downtown, and it's worth the trip. **Big Daddy's** (46th and Calgary Trail North, 780-436-2700) is a cigar and scotch bar on the south side. The best blues room in town can be found at the **Blues on Whyte Pub** (10329 Whyte Ave. NW, 780-439-3981), while pubs like the **Black Dog** (10425 82 Ave. NW, 780-439-1082) and the historic **Strathcona Hotel** (10302 82 Ave. NW, 780-439-1992) are also on the

Oilers

**Skyreach Skinny
Opened:**
11/10/74

First regular-season game:
10/13/79,
3–3 tie with
Detroit

First playoff game:
4/11/80,
3–2 loss to
Philadelphia

First goal:
B.J. MacDonald
of Edmonton

Address:
11230–110 St.,
Edmonton

For single-game tickets:
780-414-4400

Website:
edmontonoilers.com

same Whyte Avenue strip.

For a quiet drink:

A relaxing spot away from the frenzy of nightclubs is the **Manor Cafe** (10109 125th St. NW, 780-482-7577). Other places to have an intimate conversation include **Vi's by the River** (9712-111 St. NW, 780-482-6402) and **Cafe Select** (10018-106 St. NW, 780-423-0419).

Best pub:

There is only one place in Edmonton for the media when it comes time for a post-game drink and snack. That's **Sherlock Holmes** (10012 101A Ave., 780-426-7784) downtown, just across from the Westin. You'll also spot league officials after games, as well as referees and linesmen now and again. The Chicago Blackhawks, as well as members of the Toronto Maple Leafs and Ottawa Senators, favor this pub.

Dining

For steak:

Alberta beef is world-famous, so steak places are plentiful. **Hy's Steak Loft** (10013 101A Ave., 780-424-4444) is Canada's signature steakhouse and a favorite place for many visiting teams. In many Edmontonians' eyes the best steaks can be found at **The Keg** (several locations) and the **Outback Steakhouse** (17118 90 Ave. NW, 780-484-5400).

For pasta and pizza:

For lunch on a game day, try **Sceppas Trattoria** (10923 101 St. NW, 780-425-9241). It has fantastic stuffed peppers and homemade pasta. **Il Portico** (10012 107 St. NW, 780-424-0707) has first-class Italian fare. In the Oilers' dynasty days, **Coliseum Pizza and Steak** (8015-118 Ave., 780-474-1640) was favored by Mark Messier, and remains a favorite spot of fans for a pre-game bite, located just a few blocks west of the Centre. And for the best pizza in town? Try the **Rose Bowl** (10111 117 St. NW, 780-482-5152), a hidden gem for pizza lovers. The Rose Bowl special is noteworthy.

For ethnic:

Bistro Praha (10168 100A St. NW, 780-424-4218) has excellent European cuisine and is favored by Czech and Slovak players. Petr Klima and Zdeno Ciger were sure bets to be seen there during their years in Edmonton. Try a dessert crepe.

Worth the visit:

Cafe Select is equally appropriate for dinner or late-night meetings. It has a wide variety of appetizers, and the brie is recommended. On a Sunday night, when things are slow, try the **Sidetrack Cafe** (10333 112 St., 780-421-1326), which has a wide variety on its menu.

Lodging

For luxury:

The **Hotel MacDonald** (10065 100 St. NW, 780-424-5181) is Edmonton's most stately hotel, an old Canadian Pacific hotel that overlooks the river valley and is situated right downtown.

It's a beauty dating to the beginning of the century, built when the railway made its way across the country.

Players' choice:
For incoming NHL teams, the other two hotels of choice are the **Westin** (10135 100 St. NW, 780-426-3636), where Wayne Gretzky's wedding guests stayed, and the **Sheraton Grande** (10235 101 St. NW,

780-428-7111). They are both downtown, near LRT stations, and next to plenty of shopping and restaurants.

Close to the arena:
A romantic experience is likely at the French style bed and breakfast **La Boheme** (6427 112 Ave., 780-474-5693). It's a quaint spot that's a five-minute drive or 20-minute walk from the Skyreach Centre, a walk that can be nice in spring or fall.

Something special:
Not to be left out is the **Fanta-syland Hotel** (17700 87 Ave. NW, 780-444-3000) at West Edmonton Mall. It's across town from the arena, but North America's biggest mall is right off the lobby.

Shopping & Attractions

Every player's family that comes to Edmonton spends at least one game day at **West Edmonton Mall** (780-444-5200), Edmonton's biggest tourist attraction. And with the exchange rate on the U.S. dollar, it's like a giant discount mall if you're coming from south of the border. You can also find water slides, a wave pool, miniature golf, a driving range, a submarine ride, bars and restaurants inside the mall.

If you asked General Manager Glen Sather, he'd say Edmonton's primary tourist attraction is outside the city limits, hunting and fishing as he does with players from time to time. Former Oilers

Alexander Selivanov #29

Bryan Marchment, Louie DeBrusk and Dave Manson used to practice in the morning and be hunting by 2 in the afternoon. Ice fishing and snowmobiling are other popular pursuits enjoyed by a number of Oilers.

If you come to Edmonton late in the season or during playoffs, you might catch a **Oilers** baseball game at **Telus Field**, where the Triple A Edmonton Trappers (780-414-4450) play. The Canadian Football League's **Edmonton Eskimos'** (780-448-1525) schedule goes from July to November. The Eskimos' natural grass, Commonwealth Stadium is Canada's most beautiful outdoor football stadium.

Favorite City on the Road

Doug Weight enjoys Detroit because he was born and raised in a suburb just outside that city. For most Oilers, a trip to Toronto is the most special because many of them are from Ontario and grew up watching the Maple Leafs on Hockey Night in Canada. Bernie Nicholls, when he played in Edmonton, loved the trips to San Francisco to play the San Jose Sharks, because the shopping there is fantastic and Nicholls' wardrobe never suffered.

Many Oilers pick New York City as their favorite destination, simply because there is so much to do, and Madison Square Garden is a special place to play hockey.

Cool Fact

Wayne Gretzky began his career with Indianapolis of the World Hockey Association in 1978–79 but lasted only eight games and was sold by the cash-strapped team to the Edmonton Oilers. Edmonton joined the NHL the following season, and Gretzky became the dominant player of his era, holding 61 records at retirement, and winning four Stanley Cups. When traded with three other players in the 1988 deal that rocked the hockey world, the Oilers got 50-goal scorer Jimmy Carson, Martin Gelinas, three first-round picks, and $15 million.

Tommy Salo #35

Franchise History

A charter member of the World Hockey Association, the Edmonton Oilers joined the NHL in 1979 and have achieved heights the envy of the hockey world. The four Stanley Cup Championship teams of the 1980s included one of the finest collections of talent ever assembled. Start with Wayne Gretzky and Mark Messier, add Paul Coffey, Grant Fuhr, Jari Kurri and Glenn Anderson, and you have an entire wing of the Hockey Hall of Fame. Even without Gretzky and Coffey, the Messier-led Oilers were able to capture a fifth Stanley Cup in 1990. Championships aside, Edmonton revolutionized the game by incorporating European influences into the North American game—and adding a few twists of their own.

Famers

Most Valuable Player (Hart Trophy): Wayne Gretzky, 1980 through 1987; Mark Messier, 1990.
Hockey Hall of Fame:
Player: Wayne Gretzky, 1999.
Builder: Glen Sather, 1997.
Retired numbers: 3 Al Hamilton: 99 Wayne Gretzky

Oilers

Bill Guerin #9

Records

Games played		Most points, season		Goalie wins, career	
Kevin Lowe	1,037	Wayne Gretzky	215	Grant Fuhr	226
Career goals		**Most goals, game**		**Goalie wins, season**	
Wayne Gretzky	583	Wayne Gretzky,		Grant Fuhr	40
Career assists		Jari Kurri,		**Most shutouts, career**	
Wayne Gretzky	1,086	Pat Hughes	5	Curtis Joseph 14	
Career points		**Most assists, game**		**Most shutouts, season**	
Wayne Gretzky	1,669	Wayne Gretzky 7		Curtis Joseph 8	
Most goals, season		**Most points, game**		**Stanley Cups:**	
Wayne Gretzky	92	Wayne Gretzky,		1984, 1985, 1987,	
Most assists, season		Paul Coffey	8	1988, 1990.	
Wayne Gretzky	163				

around the town with the Panthers

Panthers

Is there a more exciting region than South Florida? Not likely. Apart from the fact you can't play ice hockey outside, you can literally indulge any desire that comes to mind in this humid Atlantic zone. If you're visiting for a Panthers game, don't take a day; take a week. Get the hardest part—shopping—out of the way first and visit Coconut Grove, the oldest community in the district. The streets are packed with shoppers investigating the excellent boutiques, so park on the outskirts and walk the rest of the way. Lincoln Road in Miami is similarly jammed on weekends.

Mark Parrish #21

Once you've bought what you want, you can explore. South Florida keeps your eyes perpetually open because it's so diverse and dazzling. South Beach has Art Deco buildings galore, so many that it became a member of the National Register of Historic Places. Its 50–80 year-old structures can easily fill up a roll of camera film. Coral Gables, boldly named "City Beautiful," was built with Euro-Spanish style while incorporating theme neighborhoods such as French City. Miami Beach—actually a collection of islands in Biscayne Bay—gives you natural beauty instead. With its ever-present palm trees and quiet beaches, this is the area to retreat from the crowds: if you know where to go. Try Bal Harbour.

The team that plays in this exotic area used to thrived on hard work rather than flash. But that changed in January 1999 when the Panthers pulled off a huge trade for superstar Pavel Bure. His speed, slick moves and incredible goals keep fans on the edge of their seats. He scored 13 goals in 11 games before injuring his knee. Fully healed, he's back to his high-scoring ways, and he's locked in for five years. "I think he will get better because he's only 28 and has a lot of hockey ahead of him," President Bill Torrey says.

Fans here are passionate— who can forget Pittsburgh goalie Tom Barrasso crouching in his net as plastic rats rained down on him during the 1995–96 semifinals?—and love a winner. The hope is Bure will bring the team back to the playoffs while raising fans' pulses along the way.

Speaking of crowds, there will be a stream of them in Miami during late January. That's when the Fiesta Tropicale happens, a four-day Carnival with Cajun food and music,

parades and lots of parties. After a long absence, the Fiesta has returned, and it should be louder and more raucous than ever with each year.

Amongst the many activities vying for attention in South Florida, the Panthers have staked a firm claim. The fans have proven to be very passionate; who can forget the sight of Pittsburgh goalie Tom Barrasso crouching in his net as plastic rats showered down on him during the **Panthers** 1995–96 semifinals? During that wonderful run to the Cup final, the Panthers and the people of South Florida forged a bond not likely to be broken.

National Car Rental Center

Where to sit:
The Club Boxes are suites for

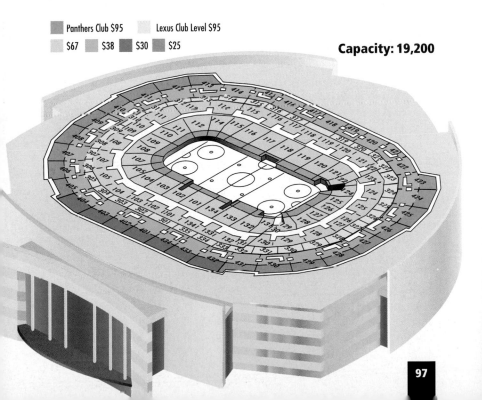

Panthers Club $95   Lexus Club Level $95

$67 $38 $30 $25

Capacity: 19,200

single ticket holders. There are six elevators from your parking spot to the club level. Once there, you'll have a shared bar with the adjacent club box, four televisions with the NHL Center Ice package, a private bathroom for the box, and a private locker for each of the 60 folks in the box.

If it's all you can get:

The 800 Panther Pack tickets are priced at $14. They go on sale at 10 a.m. the day of the games.

Panthers

Special services:

There are 14 elevators, wheelchair-accessible seating for every kind of seat and enhanced sight lines for the wheelchair seating. Assisted hearing devices can be checked out by guests. There are Braille menus and Braille information brochures. For information, call the Panthers at 954-768-1900.

Ticket availability:

Two consecutive playoff no-shows and the uncertainty over Pavel Bure's knee led to a big drop in attendance at the start of the 1999–2000 season to about 15,500. But the Panthers predict that the arrival of the snowbirds and the news that Bure is back to form should boost attendance again. Note: Scalping is illegal and the Panthers will brook no such activity on their property.

Parking:

There are about 7,500 parking spaces in the well-lit, secure lot, which costs $10. No street

National Car Rental Center

parking. Slick trick: park at Sawgrass Mills for afternoon games.

Public transportation:

In South Florida, mass transit means four people in a car. The Broward County Transit No. 22 bus will take you to Sawgrass Mills.

By car:

The least complex, but slower, way is to take the Sawgrass Expressway or Interstate 95, whichever is closest, to Sunrise Blvd. Go east (off Sawgrass) or west (off I-95) until you hit 136th Avenue. Turn north and the road will take you to the arena.

Cuisine:

The sports bar offers typical sports bar food. The six food courts offer fare which reflects South Florida's love for Cuban and Caribbean fare, along with more universal items. And, if you like to grill, you can rent the Skyview Terraces and barbecue with a view of the Everglades.

Home-ice advantage:
The end which the Panthers attack twice is banked to maximize crowd noise. Now that Pavel Bure's in town, he has greatly increased fan excitement, so expect to hear a lot of cheers.

Nightlife

Best nightclub:
The South Beach area of Miami Beach still leads South Florida in chic, and **Liquid** (1439 Washington Ave., 305-532-9154) not only gets the endorsement of some Panthers, but has shown staying power in a scene where clubs come and go quicker than a nervous goalie. If you can't get into Liquid or just don't want to pay the cover charge, swing down to **The Clevelander** (1020 Ocean Dr., Miami Beach, 305-531-3485). It's popular with several Panthers, other players in the NHL and even more NBA and NFL stars.

Where players hang out:
One of the Panthers let slip once that so many of the younger players were hanging out at **Gatsby's Boca** (5970 SW 18th St., Boca Raton, 561-393-3900) that managment had to admonish them. In addition to the Generation X set, some of the veterans have been known to quaff a beer or two here.

Best place to watch the game:
Even before the Panthers, there was the **Penalty Box Lounge** (1921 SW 3rd St., Pompano Beach, 954-971-9694). Owned by former NHL and WHA player Rosaire Paiement with his wife Theresa, this has been a favorite hangout of vacationing Canadians and people from the NHL world. Also, you have the owner on your side if you want to watch the Panthers tangle with the Flyers instead of, say, Monday Night Football.

Dining

Team favorites:
Scott Mellanby, a year-round resident of Coral Springs, just north of the new arena, likes **Chowder's** (1460 University Dr., Pompano Beach, 954-753-7374). "It's American cuisine, steak and seafood, with some Italian dishes," he says. "They serve great appetizers. It's upscale but not stiff, and the owner's a big hockey fan." Ex-Panther Dave Gagner, who lived in Boca Raton, suggests **Maxwell's Chophouse** (501 E. Palmetto Park Rd., Boca Raton, 561-347-7077) for those into steak.

Worth a trip:

One of South Florida's oldest and certainly its most famous restaurant is too far from the arena for a pre- or post-game meal and doesn't take reservations. So, either the night before or the night after, make the pilgrimage to **Joe's Stone Crab** (11 Washington Ave., Miami Beach, 305-673-0365). The side dishes are dirt-cheap and there's steak, chicken, and all sorts of seafood. But it's the Panthers title dish that draws in all manner of sports and entertainment celebrities—and the people who run their lives.

For South Beach chic:

When he was in Florida, Kevin Weekes found a couple of places for the adventurous palate, **China Grill** (404 Washington Ave., Miami Beach, 305-534-2211) and **The Astor Hotel** (956 Washington Ave., Miami Beach, 305-531-8081). The Grill's dishes, a unique combination of Asian-American and South Floridian, are served in very generous portions.

For after the game:

Why not take a drive up to **G.W. Sharkey's** (2388 University Dr., Coral Springs, 954-341-9990)? Scott Mellanby says it's a sports bar where plenty of locals pass their time. To find a knowledgeable hockey crowd, walk through the doors of **Runyon's** (9810 W. Sample Rd., Coral Springs, 954-752-2333), a former haunt of ex-coach Doug MacLean.

Lodging

Luxury without bankruptcy:
The Mayfair House (3000 Florida Ave., Miami, 305-441-0000) attracts visiting basketball teams for good reason. Each bathroom is made from marble, jacuzzis rest on the private verandas of each suite and there's even a rooftop whirlpool. The hotel's Mayfair Grill has a seafood buffet every Friday. Try not to miss it. The Mayfair's prime location in Coconut Grove is another asset.

Highly recommended:
Ex-Panther Kevin Weekes is a big fan of the hip, happenin' Grove, too, but casts his vote for the **Eden Roc Resort and Spa** (4525 Collins Ave., Miami Beach, 305-531-0000), where the Panthers stayed for their 1997 training camp. Once Weekes saw the indoor basketball court, along with the other de rigeur athletic amenities, he

Oleg Kvasha #13

was hooked. "The rooms are excellent, the restaurant is excellent and, with the location, you easily can get to South Beach. The majority of people that come in there can find something they like about it."

To see visiting teams:

Try the **Marriott** (3030 Holiday Dr., Fort Lauderdale, 954-525-4000). Not only is it steps from Fort Lauderdale beach, but you're right on the strip made famous in numerous spring break movies.

Shopping & Attractions

Panthers center Viktor Kozlov came back from **Bal Harbour Shops** (9700 Collins Ave., Miami Beach, 305-866-0311) raving to his teammates. With stores like **Tiffany's**, **Fendi** and **Charles Jourdan**, it's definitely for the upscale.

For those interested in bargains, a pregame trip to **Sawgrass Mills** (12801 W. Sunrise Blvd., Sunrise, 954-846-2350) is in order. The world's largest outlet mall has everything from **Ann Taylor** and **Joan & David** to **The Gap** and a multiplex cinema.

To entertain the kids and yourself, Scott Mellanby suggests **Quiet Waters Park** (401 S. Powerline Rd., Deerfield Beach, 954-360-1315). It boasts a children's water playground, a family beach, cable water skiing and mountain biking. You can camp overnight in your tent.

Dave Gagner recommends **Beach Place**, another something-for-everyone place—bars, clubs, shopping. If you're in the market for Panthers jerseys, tie-tacks, etc., **Home Team Advantage** (17 S. Atlantic Blvd., Fort Lauderdale, 954-463-2582) at Beach Place is your best bet because it's the official store of the Panthers, Dolphins, and Marlins.

And, there's always the ocean!

Favorite City on the Road

Panthers

In an informal 1996 pre-season poll, the Panthers named Montreal as their favorite road city. "It's the mecca of hockey," Scott Mellanby says. "Even though we're not playing in the Forum anymore, it's still the mecca. Hockey is everything there."

Kevin Weekes votes for New York. "I find Toronto to be big and New York's like 10 Torontos in one," he says. "There's always something going on. During the playoffs (in 1997) I would just walk, walk all day and I didn't feel like I'd seen even part of it."

Cool Fact

One rat's misfortune was the Panthers' fortune in 1995–96. Scott Mellanby spotted a rat in Florida's dressing room at the start of the season and sent it to its death with a slap shot. That night, he scored two goals—a "rat trick," a teammate said. The legend stuck and fans began throwing plastic rats after every goal as the Panthers went to the Finals. That summer, though, the NHL instituted a delay-of-game penalty for throwing objects onto the ice.

Franchise History

When it comes to quick success the Florida Panthers could teach a seminar. The idea of locating a hockey team in Miami was ripe for criticism, but almost from the moment the franchise was awarded on June 14, 1993 the Florida Panthers became an example of how to build an expansion franchise. On the ice, management assembled a hardworking club that would force other teams to play their style of hockey. Off the ice, the club marketed the sport to the Sunshine State. Quickly the Panthers became a team to reckon with and the favorite of local sports fans, ending their first season with more points than any first-year team in league history. In only its third season the team shocked the hockey world, and thrilled South Florida, by reaching the Stanley Cup Finals. A few thousand rats on the ice later and you have a franchise firmly entrenched in a state that the critics said would never support a winter sport.

Panthers

Robert Svehla #24

Famers

Most Valuable Player (Hart Trophy): None
  Hockey Hall of Fame:
  Builder: Bill Torrey, 1995.
  Retired numbers: None

Records

Games played		Most assists, season		Goalie wins, career	
Bill Lindsay	443	Robert Svehla	49	John Vanbiesbrouck	106
Career goals		**Most points, season**		**Goalie wins, season**	
Scott Mellanby	135	Scott Mellanby	70	John Vanbiesbrouck	27
Career assists		**Most goals, game**		**Most shutouts, career**	
Scott Mellanby	160	Mark Parrish	4	John Vanbiesbrouck	13
Career points		**Most assists, game**		**Most shutouts, season**	
Scott Mellanby	295	Scott Mellanby	4	John Vanbiesbrouck	4
Most goals, season		**Most points, game**		**Stanley Cups:**	
Scott Mellanby,		Jesse Belanger,		None	
Ray Whitney	32	Scott Mellanby,			
		Ray Whitney	4		

FLORIDA

Kings

Luc Robitaille #20

around the town with the **Kings**

Like many great urban centers, Los Angeles is really a collection of towns—and what a wild and wonderful collection it is. Beverly Hills. Pasadena. Santa Monica, Venice, Malibu. And, of course, Hollywood.

In a city that boasts some of the best architecture on the planet, the LA Kings have kept pace with their new, state-of-the-art home, the Staples Center. Much closer to the heart of the city than the old Forum, the building reaffirms the Kings' place in Tinseltown. Along with the new abode comes a new star, Zigmund Palffy. An electric player who single-handedly creates goals, Palffy is the right man for a town that loves greatness and a team that wants to rediscover it.

Visiting LA can be a problem for those who don't know how to deal with freedom of choice, but since the Staples Center is downtown, why not check out that area? Almost surprisingly, the traveler sometimes overlooks downtown, but it's hardly dull. The Bradbury Building, with its distinctive inner courtyard and glass walls, will be familiar to sharp-eyed movie-goers: it's been in many films. Union Station, built in 1939 but still heavily in use, is Spanish in design and breathtaking in appearance. Then there's the Museum of Neon Art, sure to provoke a chuckle, and the sobering Japanese American National Museum, sure to provoke a few thoughts.

The obvious attractions are in Hollywood and Beverly Hills. The famous Capitol Records Tower in Hollywood looks like a stack of vinyl, while Mann's Chinese Theatre is the place where celebrities go to impress their hand and footprints in cement. Rodeo Drive in

Beverly Hills just might be the most expensive shopping district; it might be better to window shop there or watch others spend their money. Don't forget about Mulholland Drive in the Hollywood Hills. From there, you can look into the San Fernando Valley, an unforgettable view. The Valley is home to Universal Studios and Warner Brothers, two giants of the film industry. Maybe, one day, they'll want Ziggy Palffy to do a cameo appearance. Kings fans would like to think so.

Staples Center

Where to sit:
The Center has 160 Luxury Suites, 32 Party Suites and 2500 Premier Seats. The latter gives you private parking and concessions as well as a concierge service. Sightlines from all seats should be good.

If it's all you can get:
For a bargain, the last eight rows at center ice cost $18 and are still close enough for a fairly good view of the ice.

Special services:
There is disabled parking in eight lots around the arena.

Ticket availability:
Attendance in L.A. has been off recently, but everything from the Premier Seats on up will be in heavy demand now that the team has a new building in a convenient location, not to mention a big star in Palffy. Single-game tickets should be easily available, though.

Parking:
There are 8,900 parking spaces

▇ $300	▇ $90	▇ $70	$50
▇ $40.50	▇ $25.50	$18.50	▇ Premier Seating

Capacity: 18,500

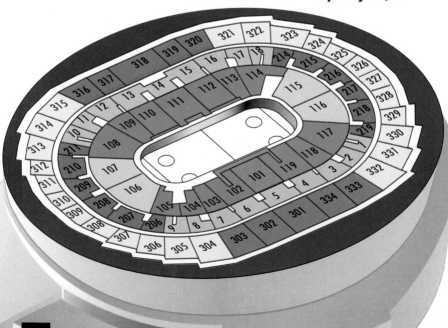

Staples Center

within walking distance of the Center.

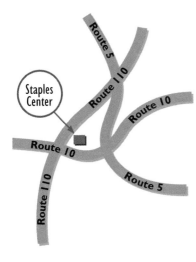

Public transportation:
The Blue Line subway stops just down the road. The MTA also runs a bus service to the immediate area, but in Los Angeles, it might be better to drive to the game.

By car:
The Center is on the corner of 11th Street and S. Figueroa, slightly northeast of the place where the 110 and 10 freeways meet. Both freeways will lead you to the arena.

Cuisine:
There are 23 concession stands and food courts, some of which feature local specialties. There is also a sports bar and restaurant. The Arena Club, reserved for the top tickethold-

ers, has dining before and after the game.

Home-ice advantage:
The major advantage that the Kings have is the nice weather. Many visiting teams like to enjoy the outdoors, and sometimes tire themselves out or lose focus.

Nightlife

For after the game:
All the Kings hang out at one place, **Harry O's** (3600 Highland Ave., Manhattan Beach (310-545-4444). Sean O'Donnell claims "It's our family away from the rink." Steve McKenna says it's usually jammed with people, while Jamie Storr adds that the crowd is usually dancing to the live band.

Best pubs:
The Kings like **Hennessey's Tavern** (313 Manhattan Beach Blvd., Manhattan Beach, 310-546-4813). It's a spot which serves food late and occasionally features bands. Jamie Storr says it's the right place "to have a few drinks, relax and mellow." For a wilder time, Storr suggests going to Pier Avenue in Manhattan Beach, because "they have six or seven places in a row. It gets packed on the weekends."

Kings

Staples Center Samples

Opened:
10/17/99

First regular-season game:
10/20/99,
2–2 tie with Boston

First goal:
Anson Carter of Boston.

Address:
1111 S. Figueroa St., Los Angeles

For single-game tickets:
888-KINGS-LA

Website
lakings.com

To meet the opposite sex:

"Anywhere in South California," McKenna says. But we pinned him down to the **Sky Bar** (8440 W. Sunset Blvd., West Hollywood, 323-848-6025). "You see actors there all the time. I once saw Leonardo Di Caprio there." The view of the L.A. basin is gorgeous. Dress to the max. Weekdays are the best bet. On the weekends, it's hit or miss with doormen selecting the lucky ones to make it inside.

To hear live music:

Try the **Lighthouse** (30 Pier Ave., Hermosa Beach, 310-372-6911), which used to be just a jazz place, but now features an eclectic mix of music.

Dining

Good Italian:

Jamie Storr and Steve McKenna recommend **Mama D's** (1125A Manhattan Ave., Manhattan Beach, 310-546-1492). Storr likes the penne pasta and sauteed chicken in marinara sauce. The **Bottle Inn** (26 22nd St., Hermosa Beach, 310-376-9595) in Redondo Beach also features good pasta dishes. Sean O'Donnell suggests **Mangiamo's Restaurant** (128 Manhattan Beach Blvd., Manhattan Beach, 310-318-3434).

California living:

Storr likes to stop after practice for a bite to eat at **The Beach Hut** (3920 Highland Ave., Manhattan Beach, 310-545-8911). "I really like the teriyaki chicken with white rice, scrambled eggs, and sweet bread." Storr says another good stop, especially for breakfast, is **Uncle Bill's Pancake House** (1305 Highland Ave., Manhattan Beach, 310-545-5177). **Spago** (176 N. Canon Dr., Beverly Hills, 310-385-0880) draws movers and shakers. Hey, the place was opened by Wolfgang Puck. Try to get a table on the patio.

For big appetites:

O'Donnell says he and former teammate Matt Johnson like **Houston's** (1550 Rosecrans Ave., Manhattan Beach, 310-643-7211). O'Donnell says the salmon appetizer is a must. **The Cheesecake Factory** (605 N. Harbor Dr., Redondo Beach, 310-376-0466) "never lets you down," in O'Donnell's opinion.

Jozef Stumpel #15

Good bets:
McCormick & Schmick's (206 N. Rodeo Dr. in Beverly Hills, 310-859-0434) is a big hit with the Kings, who love the huge choice of fresh fish. The oysters are the best. Good Mexican food is actually harder to find than one would think, but **Mi Familia** (8222 ½ W. Third St., Los Angeles, 323-653-2121) is delicious and features a cozy atmosphere. **The Bombay Cafe** (12021 W. Pico Blvd., West Los Angeles, 310-473-3388) has such good Indian food that Meg Ryan and Dennis Quaid are rumoured to fly in the tandoori dishes to their Montana ranch.

Lodging

For luxury:
The Ritz-Carlton Marina del Rey (4375 Admiralty Way, Marina del Rey, 310-823-1700, 800-287-2706) is popular with visiting players. Kings captain Rob Blake had his wedding reception there, just two days after winning his first Norris Trophy. **The Beverly Hills Hotel** (9641 Sunset Blvd., Beverly Hills, 310-276-2251) features the Fountain Coffee Shop, where Lucille Ball ate regularly.

Near the airport:
With time a factor, many teams stay at either the **Westin Los Angeles Airport** (5400 W. Century Blvd., Inglewood, 310-216-5858, 800-228-3000) or **Marriott Los Angeles Airport** (5855 W. Century Blvd., Inglewood, 310-641-5700). Both full-service hotels are just five minutes from the airport.

Better bets:

Players from visiting teams groan a lot if they have to stay near the airport because there are so many great hotels by the beach. Many teams stay at the **Manhattan Beach Marriott** (1400 Park View Ave., Manhattan Beach, 310-546-7511), the **Marina Beach Marriott** (4100 Admiralty Way, Marina del Rey, 310-301-3000, 800-353-6664) or the **Loews Santa Monica** (1700 Ocean Ave., Santa Monica, 310-458-6700). The Loews has a 17-mile bike path outside its doors.

On a budget:
The **Mansion Inn** (327 Washington Blvd., Venice,

Stephane Fiset #35

310-821-2557) is just a few blocks from the always colorful life at Venice Beach. The **Channel Road Inn** (219 W. Channel Rd., Santa Monica, 310-459-1920) is a bed and breakfast near the ocean where bike rentals and horseback riding are available.

Shopping & Attractions

"If I feel like money is burning a hole in my pocket, I'll go to Rodeo Drive in Beverly Hills," Steve McKenna says. A cheaper bet is **Third Street Promenade**, a shopping strip on Third Street between Broadway and Wilshire Boulevard in Santa Monica.

If you want to take advantage of the weather, reserve a round at **Griffiths Park Golf Course** (4730 Crystal Springs Dr., Los Feliz, 323-664-2255). Those of you with an artistic bent and open mind will enjoy the **Museum of Contemporary Art** at **California Plaza** (250 S. Grand Ave., 213-626-6222). Believe it or not, there's a fine place to eat inside the museum. McKenna suggests that a day of people watching at Venice Beach is good entertainment. "You never know what you'll see," he says of the circus atmosphere.

Always good bets:
The **Hollywood Walk of Fame** (Hollywood Boulevard) features the brass stars of more than 1,800 celebrities, including Elvis Presley. And the best part, it's free. **Will Rogers State Historic Park** (1501 Will

Rogers State Park Rd., Pacific Palisades, 310-454-8212) is where writer and entertainer Will Rogers lived in the 1920s and '30s. The park is 186 acres; you can also horseback ride there.

Favorite City on the Road

Jamie Storr always is happy to see Chicago on the schedule. "It's a fun place with a lot of nice restaurants. I always have a good meal there. There's a lot of stuff to do there on off days and we always stay at The Drake. It's a great hotel."

Sean O'Donnell is very fond of the Big Apple, but he mentions Vancouver because of its high-quality restaurants and superior nightlife. He says the city is the right setting to unwind in. The two Florida stops get high praise from him as well.

Cool Fact

Dave Taylor was nearly overlooked as a pro prospect. He was drafted by the Kings in the 15th round in 1975 after coming out of Clarkson College. But he landed a spot on the Triple Crown Line with Marcel Dionne and Charlie Simmer and racked up 1,069 points in 1,111 games. The Kings named him general manager in 1997 and he made a series of trades that ended the team's four-year playoff drought.

Franchise History

Contrary to what some people

may think, hockey in Los Angeles did not begin when Wayne Gretzky joined the Kings in 1988. In fact, minor league hockey had been successful in Southern California since the 1930s. The only major obstacle to Los Angeles obtaining a franchise when the NHL expanded in 1967–68 was the lack of a major league arena in the city. Jack Kent Cooke assured the league that he would build the most beautiful arena in the world and that it would open sometime during the first season of competition. Taken at his word, Cooke got his NHL franchise on June 5, 1967, and Los Angeles would soon receive the "Fabulous Forum," one of the grandest sports palaces ever built. The Kings enjoyed a degree of success in the early years, more often than not earning a berth in the playoffs. And it had its share of star players, most notably Marcel Dionne, who along with Charlie Simmer and Dave Taylor formed the high scoring Triple Crown Line. It wasn't until the arrival of Gretzky, however, that the Kings truly captivated Los Angeles. A town full of stars requires the biggest star of all. As Wayne led the Kings to the 1993 Stanley Cup Finals, the Forum became

Rob Blake #4

Kings

Ziggy Palffy #33

the place to see and be seen for both basketball and hockey. Recent expansion teams to the Sun Belt owe a great deal of their success to what Wayne Gretzky and the Los Angeles Kings did to popularize the sport of hockey.

Famers

Most Valuable Player (Hart Trophy): Wayne Gretzky, 1989

Hockey Hall of Fame:

Players: Terry Sawchuk, 1971; Harry Howell, 1979; Bob Pulford, 1991; Marcel Dionne, 1992; Steve Shutt, Billy Smith, 1993; Larry Robinson, 1995; Wayne Gretzky, 1999.

Retired numbers: 16 Marcel Dionne, 18 Dave Taylor, 30 Rogie Vachon

LOS ANGELES

Records

Games played		**Most points, season**		**Most goalie wins, season**	
Dave Taylor	1,111	Wayne Gretzky	168	Mario Lessard	35
Career goals		**Most goals, game**		**Most shutouts, career**	
Marcel Dionne	550	Several players	4	Rogie Vachon	32
Career assists		**Most assists, game**		**Most shutouts, season**	
Marcel Dionne	757	Bernie Nicholls	6	Rogie Vachon	8
Career points		**Most points, game**		**Stanley Cups:**	
Marcel Dionne	1,307	Bernie Nicholls	8	None	
Most goals, season		**Most goalie wins, career**			
Bernie Nicholls	70	Rogie Vachon	171		
Most assists, season					
Wayne Gretzky	122				

Canadiens

around the town with the Canadiens

Shayne Corson #27

Mark Twain once wrote that you couldn't throw a rock in Montreal without hitting a church window. But in a city renowned for its historic churches, the most famous shrine in Montreal was, for more than 70 years, the Montreal Forum. Montrealers regard hockey as a form of religion and the Forum was a cathedral where the hockey gods rewarded the faithful with 22 of the record 24 Stanley Cup victories.

The Forum was boarded up after an emotional final game on March 11, 1996, and the Canadiens moved into the new Molson Centre five days later. The new building lacks the history of the Forum, but it's brighter, more comfortable, and there's room for more of the faithful. The Canadiens hope they can add a few new chapters to a glorious history that began in 1917, when the NHL was established at a meeting in Montreal and the Canadiens were one of the four original teams. Over the years, the Canadiens have reflected the city's European style. The dynasties of the 1950s, 1960s, and 1970s featured skilled, fast-skating teams which lived up to the nickname the Flying Frenchmen. Though today's team features a multiplicity of nationalities, the emphasis is still on speed, and the atmosphere at games remains decidedly French. And for any true hockey fan life would not be complete without at least one trip to the mecca of the sport.

Montreal's history is as storied as its past in hockey. Earlier this decade, Montreal celebrated its 350th anniversary. While the downtown core is that of a modern, vibrant city, Old Montreal features buildings that date to the 17th Century. There's a hotel and tavern where Charles Dickens wrote about his travels, and American Civil War buffs

can visit the site of Jefferson Davis' post bellum home.

Montrealers are almost as passionate about their food as they are about their hockey. At one point, the best restaurants reflected the city's French heritage. But today the city boasts a variety of fine cuisines from French to Italian, Chinese to Thai, American-style steakhouses to Greek psarotavernas serving the finest in fresh fish.

The sense of style is also evident in clothing. Montrealers are more fashion-conscious than the average North American, and the trendy downtown boutiques offer the latest styles from Europe as well as Quebec's own designers. At hockey games, not all the entertainment is on ice: The Molson Centre is a place to be seen. There's a full complement of fans wearing Canadiens jerseys, but they're likely to be rubbing shoulders with someone wearing a $2,000 designer suit.

Molson Centre

Where to sit:

The best seats in the house are the red seats. These are on the 100, or ice, level behind the first six rows of "prestige" seating. Try for a seat in the corners about 12 rows up. This is where the scouts like to sit in less-crowded junior or college arenas because it affords the best

$116 $125 $82

$47.20 First 6 Rows $33.80 $33.80

$22.70 Rows A B $20.70 Rows C D $15.70 D Corners

Capacity: 21,273

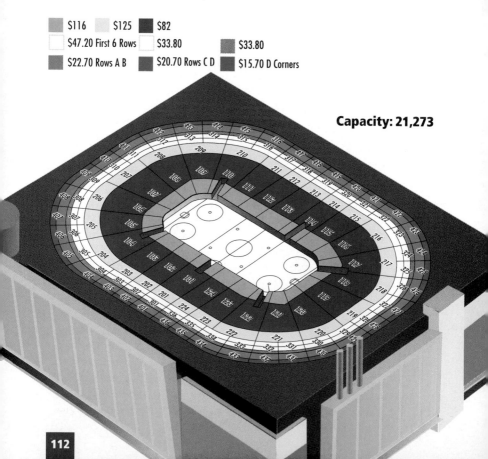

view of the play as it develops. Occasionally, you might find tickets for the Air Canada Club seats on the 200 level. These are the most expensive tickets but shouldn't be confused with the best.

If it's all you can get:

Most of the single-game tickets available through the box office are on the 300 or 400 level. The sight lines are good, but there's a steep pitch to the stands and they can be as far as 150 feet from the ice.

Special services:

58 spaces are available for persons in wheelchairs and their companions. The Molson Centre is wheelchair accessible with entrances on de la Gauchetiere or through the underground parking garage, the best bet when there's snow on the ground.

Ticket availability:

When the Canadiens moved to the Molson Centre, they added 5,000 new seats and promised to make 250 red seats and 250 white seats, available for each game. They've kept the pledge, but tickets for popular teams go quickly. Scalping is illegal in Montreal, but there are dozens of scalpers around.

Parking:

There are 580 parking spots available inside the Molson Centre for $15 and they are filled early. Outdoor lots north and south of the arena charge between $8 and $15. There are 15,000 parking places within a half-mile radius of the arena. Most of them are indoors and connect to the arena through Montreal's "underground city."

Public transportation:

The arena is midway between the Bonaventure and Lucien L'Allier stations on the Metro (subway) Orange line and is connected to both stations by covered walkways. The arena is three blocks from the Peel station on the Green line.

By car:

From Montreal International Airport, take Highway 20 East

Canadiens

Tapping "the Keg" Opened:
3/16/96

First regular-season game:
3/16/96, 4–2 win over New York Rangers

First playoff game:
4/21/96, 2–1 win over Rangers

First goal:
Vincent Damphousse of Montreal

Address:
1260 de la Gauchetiere St. W., Montreal

For single-game tickets:
514-790-1245

Website:
canadiens.com

to the Ville Marie Expressway and exit at de la Montagne.

Molsen Centre

Cuisine:

The Forum hot dogs—grilled wieners on toasted buns—have made the move, and a number of Montreal restaurants provide concessions in the building. The Ovation Resto-Bar, run by former Canadien Yvon Lambert, is a popular place for dinner before the game.

Home-ice advantage:

It's not what it used to be. The Canadiens are known for having impatient fans; one moment they boo, the next they cheer. When times were good, they did a lot of cheering, and the Forum was a tough place for any opponent. This hasn't been the case at the Centre as the Canadiens rebuild their team.

Nightlife

Dance the night away:

Modesty forbids us from translating its name into English, but **Les Foufounes Electriques** (87 Ste. Catherine E., 514-844-5539) is where the adventurous go. It's not wild compared to some Montreal hangouts, but it is uniquely fun. If you can't handle rejection, don't bother joining the lineup outside because while the deejay-driven techno music is the best in the city, appearances do count and only the most beautiful people are granted admis-

Brian Savage #49

sion by the city's most discriminating doormen. Two other evening haunts are the **Sir Winston Churchill Pub** (1459 Crescent, 514-288-0616) and **Thursday's** (1449 Crescent, 514-288-5656). For the under-30 crowd, check out **Edwards' Cheers** (1260 Mackay, 514-932-3138).

Taste of Irish:

When player agent Don Meehan comes to town, he takes clients like Patrice Brisebois and Turner Stevenson for a post-game drink at **Hurley's** (1225 Crescent, 514-861-4111). This authentic Irish pub features live music on two levels and a full complement of imported beers on tap, including the best pint of Guinness in North America. You'll also find one of the city's most extensive selections of single malts from Scotland and Ireland. The noise level in the music rooms is high, but there are several quiet areas where out-of-town fans and visiting scouts can rehash the action.

Cheap and cheerful:

A Mexican restaurant with a Czech-speaking bartender? That's one of the reasons why Martin Rucinsky makes the occasional visit to **Carlos and Pepe's** (1420 Peel, 514-288-3090), a favorite hangout for college students and hockey fans who appreciate a bargain. The pub upstairs has a 2–for–1 happy hour from 4–7 pm. For $10, you can feast on four tacos and a couple of beers and still have enough left over for a generous tip. There are nightly specials and happy hour prices also

apply to the best margaritas and sangria in the city.

Channel surfing:

The best place to watch any sporting event on TV is **Champs** (3956 St. Laurent, 514-987-6444). Eight satellite dishes and more than 40 TV screens provide patrons with action from around the world. Saturday night hockey and Sunday NFL action are the staples but the owners, Carlos and Luis, go out of their way to find Colombian soccer, cricket from India and Formula One auto races from around the globe.

Place your bet:

For action of a different kind, check out the **Casino de Montreal** (1 Ave. de Casino, 514-392-2746) which is housed in the former French pavilion from the 1967 World's Fair. There are no craps tables because dice games are illegal in Canada. There is a first-class restaurant with a strict dress code and a showbar, although the entertainment seldom approaches Vegas levels.

Dining

Old favorite:

When former Canadien Mark Recchi wanted to do something special for his teammates after a big win, he had the folks at **Da Vinci** (1180 Bishop, 514-874-2001) deliver 30 orders of chicken parmagiana to the team's charter flight an hour after the game. The Canadiens have been enjoying the pasta and other Italian specialties since 1960 when the restaurant first opened a few blocks from the Forum as King of the Pizza. The Da Vinci name was adopted in the 1970s and the restaurant moved to roomier and more luxurious quarters in the midtown area a few years before the Canadiens moved. Reservations are a must, and it's so popular with the players that it's not unusual to find the Canadiens and their opponents sharing a pre-game meal in the private salon.

Canadiens

Location, location:

Martin Rucinsky and ex-Canadiens Vinnie Damphousse and Stephane Quintal are also pasta fans. Their favorite postgame hangout is **Buona Notte** (3518 St. Laurent, 514-848-0644). The restaurant is known for its homemade pasta—ask the chef to put together a three-pasta plate if you can't make up your mind—and milk-fed veal. The food is the main attraction, but the restaurant's location in the midst of the city's most fashionable nightclub strip adds to its appeal.

Steak and history:

When Brian Savage and Patrice Brisebois are in the mood for a steak, they head to **Gibby's** (298 Place d'Youville, 514-282-1837) for an opportunity to combine fine dining with a taste of history on the side. The restaurant is in the d'Youville Stables, which date to the late 17th Century. The thick stone walls and blazing hearths offer a respite on cold winter nights and there is

an outdoor courtyard when the weather is warm. Steaks are the specialty, but there's always a selection of fresh fish and seafood. Steak lovers are also directed to **Moishe's Steak House** (3961 St. Laurent, 514-845-3509). Although it lacks the atmosphere of Gibby's, the beef is prime and the french fries are reputed to be the best in the city.

Island retreat:

Former Canadien Marc Bureau also appreciates a bit of history with his dinner and his favorite is **Helene de Champlain** (Ile Ste. Helene, 514-395-2424). The scenic restaurant is on a smaller island in the middle of the St. Lawrence River, housed in a stone building fashioned around 17th Century fortifications. The food is classic French, supplemented by some Quebec specialities such as tourtiere (meat pie), ham baked in maple syrup, and sugar pie.

Local specialties:

Don't leave without trying Montreal smoked meat, a slow smoked beef brisket that is at its best at **Schwartz's**, aka **Montreal Hebrew Delicatessen** (3895 St. Laurent, 514-842-4813). Regulars order their sandwiches medium-fat with french fries and Cott's black cherry cola. Another Montreal treat is poutine, a mixture of french fries and curd cheese topped with hot gravy. It tastes better than it sounds.

Lodging

Players' choice:

Want to rub shoulders with the

players on the visiting team? Then, your destination in Montreal is probably the **Marriott Chateau Champlain** (1 Place du Canada, corner of de la Gauchetiere and Peel, 514-878-9000). This is home away from home for most of the visiting NHL teams, partly because it is the closest major hotel to the Molson Centre and partly because one of the owners is Serge Savard, the Hall of Fame defenseman who once served as general manager of the Canadiens. Savard and his partners renovated the hotel three years ago. The improvements include a state-of-the-art health club.

Jeff Hackett #31

Up on the roof:

If you want to go swimming outdoors on a snowy day in February, try the

Hotel Bonaventure Hilton (Place Bonaventure 514-878-2332). The hotel is perched on the top two floors of Place Bonaventure, a monstrous concrete exhibition hall built during the Expo '67 construction boom. The hotel's rooms mostly look onto the rooftop garden, which features a year-round heated outdoor swimming pool. The hotel is two blocks from the Molson Centre and is connected through the underground city.

Queen of hotels:

The venerable **Queen Elizabeth Hotel** (900 Rene Levesque, Queen Elizabeth, 514-861-3511) was the site of the NHL entry draft 11 times between 1963 and 1979 and for decades was home to most visiting NHL clubs because of its proximity to the train station. It also houses the suite where the late John Lennon and Yoko Ono held their famous "Bed-In for Peace." The Beaver Club is one of the city's finest restaurants and recalls the early days of Montreal when prominent businessmen and trappers passed away the long winters with feasts under the auspices of the Order of Good Cheer. Roast beef and classic French dishes are the highlights and the hotel is justifiably proud of its 4-ounce birdbath martinis and Manhattan cocktails.

Touch of luxury:

The Inter-Continental Montreal

(360 St. Antoine W, 514-987-9900) is a fairly recent addition

Canadiens

to the City's luxury lineup and has an alluring location. It is in the World Trade Centre on the doorstep to Old Montreal. Other choices for the price-is-no-object set include the **Ritz-Carlton** (1228 Sherbrooke W, 514-842-4212) with its Old World charm and service, **Westin Mont-Royal** (1050 Sherbrooke W, 514-284-1100) and the **Loews Hotel Vogue** (1425 de la Montagne, 514-285-5555), where most rooms come complete with a whirlpool bath. Fans on a more moderate budget should check out **Best Western Ville-Marie** (3407 Peel, 514-288-4141) or **Comfort Suites** (1214 Crescent, 514-878-2711). Both are within four blocks of the arena.

Shopping & Attractions

Before you start shopping in Montreal, remember that the U.S. dollar is worth more in Canada. Exchange rates vary widely from store to store, so it's best to change your money at a bank or use a credit card.

For something dressy, the players head across the street to check out the latest European designer suits at **L'Uomo** (1452 Peel, 514-844-1008), **L'Equipe Par Bensussan** (1450 Peel, 514-499-1242) and **Eccetera** (1440 Peel, 514-845-9181). The three stores carry a wide selection from well-known designers such as Hugo Boss, Ferre, Balmain, and Cerutti 1881. For women's fashions, check out the designers boutiques at

Ogilvy (1307 Ste. Catherine W, 514-842-7711) or **Holt Renfrew** (1300 Sherbrooke W, 514-842-5111).

The **Cours Mont Royal** is the westernmost stop in the underground city that winds through five major underground malls, two railroad stations, and one of Canada's largest department stores, **The Bay**. Highlights of a trip underground include Place Montreal Trust with its new Planet Hollywood restaurant and Super Monde des Athletes, the largest athletic shoe store in Canada, and the Galeries de la Cathedrale, a shopping mall that lies under Christ Church Cathedral. Unique Canadian gifts available include Hudson's Bay blankets—there's one in Jerry Seinfeld's TV apart-

Trevor Linden #14

ment—pure maple syrup, and Cuban cigars. Just remember it's illegal to bring those cigars back to the U.S.

Favorite City on the Road

The Canadiens now only make infrequent trips to the West Coast each season but La-La-Land has made a favorable impression of many of the players. Patrice Brisebois, Martin Rucinsky, and Shayne Corson are among the players who list Los Angeles as their favorite city on the road. The team stays in Manhattan Beach and the schedule usually allows for a round of golf, a welcome respite from the harsh Montreal winters. Brian Savage appreciates Vancouver for its mild climate (even if it does rain a lot), spectacular scenery, and seafood restaurants. Another popular warm weather stop is Miami, where the China Grille's steaks and Chinese food get top marks from Shayne Corson and Saku Koivu. Miami provides another opportunity to play golf when the schedule permits, and Brian Savage and Martin Rucinsky have been known to hop a plane to Nassau for an afternoon of casino gambling.

While pasta appears to the favorite fare when the Canadiens are at home, they become carnivores on the road. A favorite eating spot on the road is one of the many's Morton's of Chicago steakhouses and former Canadiens Stephane Quintal and Jocelyn Thibault agree that if you're going to eat at Morton's of Chicago, it might as well be

the original restaurant in the Windy City. The team's Chicago digs are in the Drake Hotel, which is ideally suited for shopping along the city's Magnificent Mile.

Cool Fact

Maurice "Rocket" Richard was the fiery leader of the Montreal Canadiens when they captured a record five consecutive Stanley Cups from 1956–60. He was the first NHL player to score 50 goals in 50 games and the first to score 500 career goals, and still holds the record for most overtime goals in Stanley Cup history. Appropriately, the NHL in 1998–99 began giving the league's top goal scorer a trophy named after Richard.

Franchise History

A full-length book is not long enough to do justice to the storied past of the Montreal Canadiens—you'd need several volumes. To mention that the team has won a record 24 Stanley Cups, almost twice as many as closest rival Toronto, does little to explain the mystique of "The Flying Frenchmen." The club was formed in 1909 to give a French presence to what was then a predominantly English game. The Canadiens won their first Stanley Cup in 1916, defeating the Portland Rosebuds of the Pacific Coast Hockey Association in a five game series. The next year the team became a charter member of the National Hockey

League. In 1919 the Canadiens were poised to win a second Stanley Cup when they were struck down by the Spanish influenza pandemic. The team was unable to put a team on the ice. Defenseman Joe Hall died within a few days, followed later by Manager George Kendall. Tragedy stuck the team again in 1937 when one of the greatest Canadiens of all time, Howie Morenz, broke his leg in a game, and lingered in the hospital for two months before dying of a coronary embolism.

Then came the Rocket. The exploits of Maurice "Rocket" Richard added several chapters to the Canadiens' story. He was hockey's equivalent of Babe Ruth, scoring goals at an unimagined rate. So devoted to him were the Montreal fans that they rioted in 1955 when Richard was suspended for the final three games of the season and the playoffs. Only a radio appeal by the Rocket could restore order. When teammate Boom Boom Geoffrion passed Richard for the scoring title his hometown fans vilified him. And that's just a taste of the legacy of the Montreal Canadiens.

Famers

Most Valuable Player (Hart Trophy): Herb Gardiner, 1927; Howie Morenz, 1928, 1931, 1932; Aurel Joliat, 1934; Albert "Babe" Siebert, 1937; Hector "Toe" Blake, 1939; Elmer Lach, 1945; Maurice Richard, 1947; Jean Beliveau, 1956; Bernie Geoffrion, 1961; Jacques Plante, 1962; Jean Beliveau, 1964; Guy Lafleur, 1977, 1978.

Igor Ulanov #55

MONTREAL

Hockey Hall of Fame:

Players: Howie Morenz, Georges Vezina, 1945; Aurel Joliat, 1947; Joe Malone, Newsy Lalonde, 1950; Sprague Cleghorn, Herb Gardiner, 1958; Sylvio Mantha, 1960; Joe Hall, George Hainsworth, Maurice Richard, 1961; Jimmy Gardner, Jack Laviolette, Didier Pitre, 1962; Bill Durnan, Albert "Babe" Siebert, 1964; Marty Barry, 1965; Hector "Toe" Blake, Emile "Butch" Bouchard, Elmer Lach, Ken Reardon, 1966; Tom Johnson, 1970; Jean Beliveau, Bernie Geoffrion, 1972; Doug Harvey, 1973; Dickie Moore, 1974; Gordon Drillon, 1975; Jacques Plante, 1978; Henri Richard, 1979; Gump Worsley, 1980; Frank Mahovlich, 1981; Yvan Cournoyer, 1982; Ken Dryden, 1983; Jacques Lemaire, 1984; Bert Olmstead, 1985; Serge Savard, 1986; Jacques Laperriere, 1987; Tony Esposito, Guy Lafleur, Buddy O'Connor, 1988; Bob Gainey, 1992; Guy Lapointe, Steve Shutt, 1993; Larry Robinson, 1995.

Canadiens

Saku Koivu #11

Builders: William Northey, 1947; Sen. Donat Raymond, 1958; Frank Selke, 1960; J. Ambrose O'Brien, 1962; Leo Dandurand, Tommy Gorman, 1963; Hon. Hartland de Montarville Molson, 1973; Joe Cattarinich, 1977; Sam Pollock, 1978; Scotty Bowman, 1991.

Retired numbers: 1 Jacques Plante, 2 Doug Harvey, 4 Jean Beliveau, 7 Howie Morenz, 9 Maurice Richard, 10 Guy Lafleur, 16 Henri Richard

Records

Games played		Most goals, game		Most shutouts, career	
Henri Richard	1,256	Newsy Lalonde	6	George Hainsworth	75
Career goals		**Most assists, game**		**Most shutouts, season**	
Maurice Richard	544	Elmer Lach	6	George Hainsworth	22
Career assists		**Most points, game**		**Stanley Cups:**	
Guy Lafleur	728	Maurice Richard,		1916, 1924, 1930,	
Career points		Bert Olmstead	8	1931, 1944, 1946,	
Guy Lafleur	1,246	**Most goalie wins,**		1953, 1956. 1957,	
Most goals, season		**career**		1958, 1959, 1960,	
Guy Lafleur,		Jacques Plante	311	1965, 1966, 1968,	
Steve Shutt	60	**Most goalie wins,**		1969, 1971, 1973,	
Most assists, season		**season**		1976, 1977, 1978,	
Peter Mahovlich	82	Jacques Plante,		1979, 1986, 1993.	
Most points, season		Ken Dryden	42		
Guy Lafleur	136				

Predators

Rob Valicevic #12

NASHVILLE

around the town with the **Predators**

In an unconventional hockey town, the Predators decided to play unconventional expansion hockey: rather than concentrate on defense, the team of small, quick players chose a high-tempo style. It worked. The club recorded 28 wins and earned league-wide respect for its approach and hard work.

Even more importantly, the Predators were unexpectedly popular with Nashville natives. Country stars turned out in droves to watch games and issue public statements of support. The city was enraptured by the game, and attendance averaged 99%.

Yes, it was a season to remember. Now that the team is here to stay, more and more fans will be making the pilgrimage to Nashville, and when they arrive, they'll find it's more than the country music capital of the world. True, the main attraction remains the Grand Ole Opry, which debuted in 1925 and still does live shows on Fridays and Saturdays. But music is only one facet of Nashville's appeal. The city is a bastion of higher learning, and many connections have been drawn between it and Ancient Greece. In tribute, an exact replica of the famous Greek Parthenon was built in Centennial Park and filled with sculptures and paintings. At the Tennessee Performing Arts Center, one of the state's cultural magnets, you can experience art in a more modern vein. And, since this is The South, reminders of Southern history are abundant. At the Belle Meade Plantation—another Greek-style house—bullet holes from the Civil War have been preserved for all to see. Amidst all this, a hockey team might seem strange, but the

Predators have shown that appearances don't count.

Gaylord Entertainment Center

Where to sit:
The 1,800 premium club-level seats, with waiter service and other amenities, are your best bet. Team officials used to joke that for the first few seasons, fans should sit at the south end of the arena. The Predators will defend that goal for two periods, making it the most likely spot for the majority of the action. That's not the case anymore.

If it's all you can get:
The upper balcony seats at the north end of the arena run for $15. One section costs $10 and is sold on a single-game basis.

Special services:
Accessible seating is on all levels. The Southwest elevator goes to all concourses. The East elevator goes to all but the upper concourse. Assistive listening devices are available. For information, call 615-770-2300.

Predators

Ticket availability:
The Predators sold over 12,000 season tickets in their first year. The only games expected to create a great demand for seats, though, are those against teams with premier players, such as Steve Yzerman and Dominik Hasek. Call 1-615-770-PUCK for information.

Parking:
There are about 10,000 spots within walking distance. They rent for around $10. Shuttle

■ $95	$85	$75	■ $60
■ $50	■ $40	■ $30	■ $25
■ $15	■ $10		

Capacity: 17,298

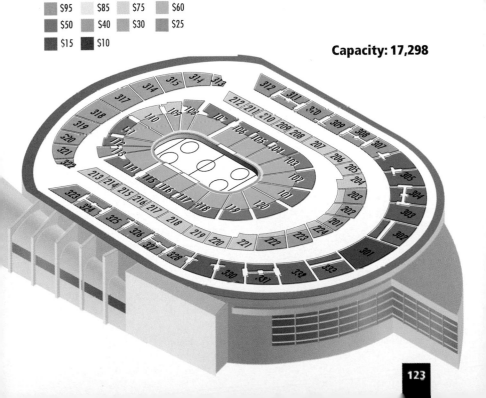

buses run from the more remote downtown lots.

Public transportation:
Metropolitan Transit Authority (615-862-5950) is Nashville's bus system.

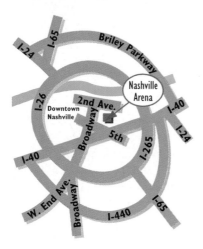

By car:
Exit the airport on I-40 West. Proceed seven miles to the Broadway exit. Turn right on Broadway, go seven blocks. The arena is on the right.

Cuisine:
The arena has a food court for general ticketholders. The Private Club concourse, the Arena Club and the Club Bar and Grille are the other establishments.

Gaylord Entertainment Center

Home-ice advantage:
Despite its losing record in year one, Nashville put on a good show at home, especially early in the season, and the fans were appreciative. This is a surprisingly vocal crowd.

Nightlife

Professional hockey and country music formed an almost immediate partnership in Nashville. Many hockey players come from Western Canada, where country and western is the music of choice. It did not take long for Predators players to find some of the most famous venues in the history of the business. "I'm very impressed with the music that is playing on Broadway, with all the bands that are playing down there," former Predator J.J. Daigneault says. "I knew that Nashville was the mecca of music but I didn't really know it was that big."

Some of the top country places:
Tootsie's Orchid Lounge (422 Broadway, 615-726-0463): Opened in 1960 and never redecorated, Tootsie's is across the alley from the Ryman Auditorium, original home of the Grand Ole Opry. Many Opry members used to frequent this rustic joint between and after performances. Easily recognizable by its exterior lavender paint job, the walls are papered with autographed pictures of those who have performed there. Some made it big, like Willie Nelson and Kris Kristofferson, who wrote songs while sitting in Tootsie's. Many did not.

With two stages, live music plays from 10 a.m.–2 a.m. daily. "You can't build a place like that today," says former Predator Blair Atcheynum. "It has its own character and it has people popping up on stage. Incredible music. It gives you something to do on a Tuesday night when you're tired of going to the movies. You go sit down and listen to some live entertainment. You just don't run into that everywhere."

Legends Corner (428 Broadway, 615-248-6334): Opened in March 1997, this modern facility captures the feel of country music's early days. The name comes from the fact that it rests on the corner fans would round as they lined up for the **Grand Ole Opry**. Live music is heard seven days a week.

Bluebird Cafe (4104 Hillsboro Rd., 615-383-1461): The center of Nashville's songwriting universe, some of the biggest names in the music industry often turn up unannounced at this cozy, unassuming club. It's famous for its "in-the-round" shows, when up-and-comers, as well as established stars, test their material and share the stories that produced the songs.

For blues:
Bourbon Street Blues and Boogie (220 Printers Alley, 615-242-5837) has a smoking house band Wednesday-Sunday, but some real gems can be heard Monday and Tuesday. This joint, in the historic section of downtown, is a "routing stop" for blues bands traveling from Memphis or New Orleans to

weekend dates in the East. Many of these acts are on the rise and the intimate setting is a treat for blues aficionados. A Cajun-American menu helps spice up the evening.

For a quiet drink:
Blackstone Restaurant (1918 West End Ave., 615-327-9969) is the best of Nashville's microbreweries. Six brews are made on site, two of which won awards at the 1998 World Beer Cup at Rio de Janeiro. A wide-ranging menu includes pub food, steak, and chicken.

Dining

All-American fare:
Don't expect a heavy dose of Southern hospitality from the legendary curmudgeon, Mrs. Rotier, as you enter **Rotier's Restaurant** (2413 Elliston Place, 615-327-9892). She is all business, and that mindset has served the family well since Mr. Rotier returned from World War II and opened the eatery in December 1945. Legendary singer Jimmy Buffett has proclaimed Rotier's hamburgers the best in Nashville. All of the classic American fare is offered in a small, relaxed setting across from the Vanderbilt University campus.

Elvis ate here:

Pictures of famous patrons, including Elvis Presley, decorate the walls of the cozy **Varallo's Restaurant** (817 Church St., 615-256-9109), which has been in business since 1907. It's still a favorite among many of the early generation of country music superstars. Although an Italian-American family, the Varallos are noted for their chili, in particular, their three-way chili (chili, spaghetti, and tamales). All of the entrees are served in generous portions at incredibly affordable prices.

For steak:

Morton's of Chicago (625 Church St., 615-259-4558) is the standard for fine dining in the downtown area. The restaurant is within walking distance of the arena.

Standard fare:

For those who enjoy the modern theme restaurants, **Hard Rock Cafe** (100 Broadway, 615-742-9900), **Planet Hollywood** (322 Broadway, 615-313-7827), and **NASCAR Cafe** (305 Broadway, 615-313-7223) are within three blocks of the arena.

Lodging

Grand ole place:

Opryland Hotel (2800 Opryland Dr., 615-889-1000), a tourist attraction in itself, has 2,883 guest rooms and 220 suites on more than nine acres. It features a glass dome that encases lush greenery, walk-ways, and waterfalls. Under Opryland's roof are many specialty shops and 600,000 square feet of convention space, making it the world's largest convention center within a hotel. Opryland has three pools, a fitness center and offers golfing privileges at Springhouse Golf Course. Located minutes from the airport, the hotel is adjacent to the Grand Ole Opry House and The Nashville Network television studios.

For luxury:

Loews Vanderbilt Plaza Hotel (2100 West End Ave., 615-320-1700) was built in 1984 by a group of Vanderbilt University doctors and lawyers as a center for business meetings. The group was relatively unsuccessful at the hotel business, so it sold the place after a few years to Loews. Across the street from Vanderbilt University, the hotel has 340 rooms, 19 meeting rooms, and a fitness center. It stands several blocks from Music Row and is within a mile of the Gaylord Entertainment Center.

Close to the arena:

Renaissance Nashville Hotel (611 Commerce St., 615-255-8400, 800-468-3571) is one block from the arena and is connected by a walking bridge and underground tunnel. Its 673 rooms are housed in one of downtown's tallest buildings.

Something special:

The **Hermitage Suite Hotel** (231 Sixth Ave. North, 615-

244-3121), opened in 1910, is Nashville's only historic suite hotel—120 suites in all. The hotel's Capitol Grille restaurant was named one of the nation's 25 best in 1996. Union Station **Wyndham Grand Heritage** (1001 Broadway, 615-726-1001), originally the city's train station, opened as a hotel on New Year's Eve 1986 and stands five blocks from the arena. An original schedule board hangs behind the front desk, and 127 original Tiffany Panels and many of the original sculptures adorn the lobby. With 124 rooms, the Wyndham Grand Heritage is a National Historic Landmark.

Shopping & Attractions

Much of Nashville's appeal is that it maintains the feel of a small town. Regardless of where you are, you are never far from something you might want to do. "It's a beautiful city," center Greg Johnson says. "I've been in some bigger cities like Chicago and Detroit. I can't believe there's no rush-hour traffic. It's just a beautiful area."

Shoppers will want to head to The Mall at Green Hills (2126 Abbott Martin Rd., 615-298-5478). Department stores **Castner-Knott** and **Dillard's**

Predators

Tomas Voukoun #27

serve as bookends for this collection of upscale specialty shops. Predators merchandise can be found inside the team's pro shop at the arena.

Music Row (16th and 17th Avenues South), the heart of the music industry, is a must-see. Visitors are free to stroll along the streets amid recording studios—including the famous RCA Studio B—label offices, publishing companies, and management companies. Every aspect of the business exists in this rustic area of converted homes. **The Country Music Hall of Fame** (4 Music Sq. E, 615-256-1639), which is relocating in 2000, gives you a guided trolley tour of Music Row. Inside the Hall, you can watch films, learn how records are produced and see some of the instruments the legends used.

The Parthenon Museum (Centennial Park, 615-862-8431), the centerpiece of 1897's Centennial Exposition in Tennessee, serves as Nashville's primary art gallery, a repository of Tennessee history, and a link to the city's reputation as "the Athens of the South." Nashville earned that title in the 1800s when it was home to 30 colleges and universities, many of which centered their curriculum on studies of Greek and Latin languages, architecture, and philosophy.

The Hermitage (4580 Rachel's Lane, Hermitage, 615-889-2941) was the 600-acre plantation home of Andrew Jackson, the seventh president of the United States, from 1804–45. The most authentic early American presidential home in the nation, The Hermitage contains many pieces of furniture used by Jackson and his wife. The Andrew Jackson Center offers a museum and visitor center showcasing many seldom seen artifacts.

Favorite City on the Road

Captain Tom Fitzgerald, a cousin of Phoenix's Keith Tkachuk, grew up in Massachusetts, so Boston is the place he likes to visit best. Bobby Orr was his idol and he's also a huge

Bob Boughner #6

128

Red Sox fan. He often can be found wearing a Red Sox cap in the dressing room. Joel Bouchard likes Montreal and Drake Berehowsky likes Toronto for the same reason. They were born in those cities and have offseason homes there. Berehowsky also used to play for the Maple Leafs.

Cool Fact

Predators

Chosen to represent the Predators as its logo, the saber-toothed tiger was native to the Nashville region in prehistoric times. In fact, 26 years before the Gaylord Entertainment Center opened, a fang and foreleg bone of a saber-toothed tiger was found in a cave just below the site.

Franchise History

The city of Nashville was awarded a franchise on June 25, 1997, and became the first of four new teams (Atlanta, Minnesota and Columbus) to begin league play. On October 10, 1998 the Predators made their regular season debut at home before a sellout crowd, losing to the Florida Panthers, 1–0. On October 27 the team earned its first victory with a 5–4 triumph over the Vancouver Canucks.

Cliff Ronning #7

Famers:

Most Valuable Player (Hart Trophy): None
Hockey Hall of Fame: None
Retired numbers: None

Records

Games played		Most goals, game		Most goalie wins,	
Tom Fitzgerald	80	13 players,	2	season	
Career goals		**Most assists, game**		Mike Dunham	16
Sergei Krivokrasov	25	Sebastien Bordeleau	3	**Most shutouts,**	
Career assists		**Most points, game**		**career**	
Cliff Ronning	35	Sebastien Bordeleau	4	Mike Dunham	
Most goals, season		Sergei Krivokrasov	4	Tomas Vokoun	1
Sergei Krivokrasov	25	**Most goalie wins,**		**Most shutouts, season**	
Most assists, season		**career**		Mike Dunham	
Cliff Ronning	35	Mike Dunham	16	Tomas Vokoun	1
Most points, season				**Stanley Cups:**	
Cliff Ronning	53			None	

Devils

Scott Niedermayer #27

around the town with the
Devils

The state of New Jersey has an image problem, but Devils president and general manager Lou Lamoriello would like to set the record straight. "I look at New Jersey as the best of all worlds. The perception may be something different, but it's got even more than New York. You have all the amenities of New York within 10–15 minutes and you're not in that city environment. You drive a few minutes away and you're in the country without getting on a plane. There's no question in my mind."

The state also has a fine hockey team. Cup champions in 1995, the Devils finish near the top every season, and they have one of the very best crops of young talent in the league. The next decade could be even better than the 1990s for these hell-raisers.

New Jersey plays in East Rutherford, but that's not the town tourists go to see. The state's main attraction is the Jersey Shore, 127 miles of public beaches and waterfronts. The Coastal Heritage Trail will guide you along the route, and most of the trail is accessible by car. Atlantic City is the most popular destination—millions of dollars are gambled there each day—but the city doesn't represent the Shore's quiet charm. Exploring unspoiled Island Beach State Park, you can be alone with the ocean, provided you don't go there on a public holiday. Fishing, windsurfing and sailing can be pursued anywhere on the Shore. Cape May Point State Park draws many bird-watchers in spring and fall, for it is one of the key gathering points for migratory birds. An animal of another type can be found in Margate. Lucy the Elephant is not a real beast but one of the quirkiest architectural attractions you can see: a house built in the form of an elephant. Seriously.

"You have to be around New Jersey to appreciate how beautiful it is," comments Devil Ken Daneyko. Follow his advice and you'll see if he's right.

Continental Airlines Arena

Where to sit:
If you have the money, the ideal place to sit is in the VIP Gold Circle seating at center ice on the lower level. Gold Circle membership includes dining privileges in the Winners Club restaurant before games and access to the Winners Club

lounge during games. You'll also be included in private autograph sessions with Devils players and Gold Circle skates on the arena ice.

If it's all you can get:
Upper-level seats provide a good view for watching plays develop, though it's a steep climb to get there.

Devils

Ticket availability:
With 19,040 seats, tickets are available for most Devils home games and can usually be purchased on game days. However, plan far ahead for games against the New York Rangers and Philadelphia Flyers, as well as weekend giveaways.

Special services:
The building is fully accessible for the disabled, and designated

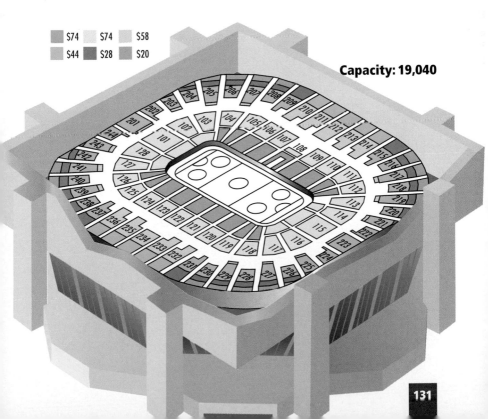

$74	$74	$58
$44	$28	$20

Capacity: 19,040

parking is available in two adjacent lots. Call 201-935-3900 for information.

Parking:
There are 4,000 spaces at the arena and 22,000 spaces by Giants Stadium. The charge is $7.

Public transportation:
Bus service is available from the New York Port Authority Bus Terminal (212-564-8484) and from New Jersey transit (1-800-772-2222).

By car:
You can reach the arena by taking the New Jersey Turnpike to exit 16 W to the Sports Complex or Route 3 to East Rutherford.

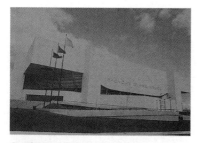

Continental Airlines Arena

Cuisine:
Choices are limited to mostly standard arena fare. The closest you'll find to any gourmet dishes or exotic cuisine inside Continental Airlines Arena are Carvel ice cream and Mrs. Fields cookies.

Home-ice advantage:
The Devils have been the top regular-season team in the East lately, but last year their home record was mediocre compared to their amazing road play. If you look at their track record, that looks like an aberration, so expect the Devils to be dominant again in their barn.

Nightlife

More than food:
When Jacques Lemaire is in town, he frequents **Rascals Comedy Club** (425 Pleasant Valley Way, West Orange, 973-736-2726). For many of the younger players, the hometown spot is the **Verona Inn** (141 Bloomfield Ave., Verona, 973-239-3455). A steak and chops restaurant that ex-Devils winger Bill Guerin has called "my number one place," it has an easy-going casual atmosphere favored by locals and is packed for after-the-game drinks.

For a quiet drink:
You can watch the game or come back afterward to **Stinger's** (413 Paterson Ave., Wallington, 201-933-6016), an out-of-the-way spot for die-hard Devils fans. According to ex-Devil John MacLean, "It's a good spot." So is **The**

Grasshopper (292 Grove Ave., Cedar Grove, 973-239-1189) and **The Grasshopper Also** (645 Washington Avenue, Carlstadt, 201-460-7771), which are known for their generous portions of American and continental fare with an Irish flair. Those seeking an "Original-Six" feel and downtown atmosphere should head to **Monaghan's Tavern** in Jersey City (793 West Side Ave., Jersey City, 201-333-9460).

For live music:

A cross between a supper club and nightclub is the well-known **Club Bene** (State Hwy. 35, South Amboy, 732-727-3000), where a mature audience can have dinner in addition to catching such great bands and singer/songwriters as Kenny Rankin, Loudon Wainwright III, or America. It's a bit of a drive but well worth the trip. The young and adventurous Generation Xers gather at energetic venues such as **The Wreck Room** (551 Main Ave., Wallington, 973-471-8405) or **Connections** (503 Van Houten Ave., Clifton, 973-473-3127) for alternative rock.

Dining

Where the players dine:

No restaurant is better for spotting Devils players in a trendy atmosphere with exceptional food than **Mezzanotte** (115 Bloomfield Ave., Caldwell, 973-403-8500). The fresh fish and pasta rival New York City eateries. Defenseman Ken Daneyko is a co-owner and the place is likely to be packed with players from Lyle Odelein to Scott Niedermayer. "That's the No. 1 place to go for the players and, I think, for a lot of the fans," says ex-Devils winger Bill Guerin. "It's awesome." If goaltender Martin Brodeur isn't at Mezzanotte, he's probably eating sushi at the **Yoshi Sono Japanese Restaurant** (643 Eagle Rock Ave., West Orange, 973-325-2005). Randy McKay is also a sushi lover who recommends the **Mount Fuji Japanese Steak House** (193 State Rte. 17, Hasbrouck Heights, 201-288-2800).

Pasta power play:

General manager Lou Lamoriello's Mercedes can often be seen parked outside **Barelli's** (219 Rt. 3 E, Secaucus, 201-865-2766). Another Italian spot with an elegant atmosphere and great calamari is **Il Villaggio** (650 Rt. 17, Carlstadt, 201-935-7751).

After the game:

Fans and players mix at spots near the arena. For a real taste of New Jersey atmosphere, there is the **Tick-Tock Diner** (281 Allwood Rd. off Rt. 3, Clifton, 973-777-0511). Just as close and more popular with players and reporters is **Chi Chi's Mexican Restaurant** (700 Plaza Dr., Secaucus, 201-348-0407).

Devils

More adventurous fans looking for old-style atmosphere and a touch of Frank Sinatra's New Jersey can head to the **Clam Broth House** (34 Newark St., Hoboken, 201-659-4860).

Lodging

Team favorite:
To get that Stanley Cup feeling, stay at the **Marriott** (100 Frank W. Burr Blvd., Teaneck, 201-836-0600). This is the hotel in which the team stays during the playoffs—under lock and key—and it is also where the team celebrated with the Cup after its 1995 championship.

To spot the other team:
Most visiting NHL teams will stay at the **Radisson Suite Hotel** (350 Mill Creek Dr., Secaucus, 201-863-8700) or the **Embassy Suites Hotel** (455 Plaza Dr., Secaucus, 201-864-7300, 800-362-2779).

Closest to the arena:
If the weather is bad, or to be first in the lot for tailgating parties, the **Sheraton** (2 Meadowlands Plaza, East Rutherford, 201-896-0500) is both close and comfortable. Also nearby is the **Hilton** (2 Harmon Plaza, Secaucus, 201-348-6900).

Rookie heaven:
Located across the street from the Devils' South Mountain Arena practice facility, the **Turtle Brook Inn** (555 Northfield Ave. West Orange, 973-731-5300) is jumping during training camp and many of the team's rookies choose to remain there during the season.

Shopping & Attractions

You may never get to the game if you go on a shopping excursion to the **Outlets** in Secaucus. New Yorkers cross the Hudson to get bargains at **Tommy Hilfiger**, **Bass Shoes**, **Hanes** and dozens of other outlet stores.

Autograph seekers, hockey card collectors and memorabilia

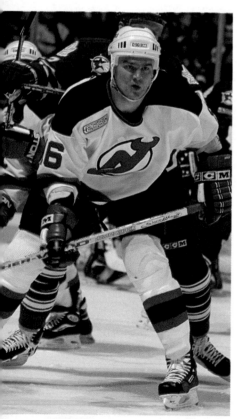

Bobby Holik #16

enthusiasts should check out **T. Wall Sports** (693 State Rte. 23, Pompton Plains, 973-831-7575), where Martin Brodeur has been among the players to appear. In addition to the frequent signings, fans can find unusual plaques and collectibles. Team jerseys can be found at **Modell's** (3 Mill Creek Dr., Secaucus, 201-392-9500).

During the season, especially in the fall and spring, the entire family can watch the Devils practice at **South Mountain Arena** and then visit the **Turtle Back Zoo** (560 Northfield Ave., West Orange, 973-731-5800) right behind the arena.

Favorite City on the Road

Martin Brodeur likes returning to his hometown of Montreal for the Italian restaurants, including Buena Notte, but his favorite eating places on the road are steakhouses. "Every time we go to Miami we always go to Shula's Steakhouse. And if we're not in a Morton's of Chicago, it's Hy's Steakhouse in Canada. Most of our wives, I guess, don't eat that much meat, so we go for steak on the road."

Devils

Lou Lamoriello's favorite hotel is the Ritz-Carlton in Dearborn, Mich., where the team stayed for the 1995 Stanley Cup finals against the Red Wings. His favorite city on the road is Montreal because of its rich history.

Scott Niedermayer's favorite city is Vancouver, where the Cannery is a popular stop for seafood.

Ken Daneyko and Lyle Odelein are partial to steak and

Scott Gomez #23

pasta. "I've always loved Gibson's Steakhouse in Chicago," Daneyko says. "That's one of my favorites. And Montreal has some great Italian places."

Trainer Bill Murray and equipment manager Dave Nichols rarely miss the Bar-B-Barn in Montreal for chicken and ribs. A popular spot for crab is Chicky and Pete's in Philadelphia.

Cool Fact

Martin Brodeur, a dominant goaltender since winning rookie-of-the-year in 1993–94, has a hockey pedigree. His father, Denis, won a bronze medal as goalie for Canada in the 1956 Olympics. Though his father is "a small lefty, and I'm a big righty," Martin says, they share some traits. Says Denis: "Martin first saw me play in a film a guy sent me on (an old-timers) game we played in the Montreal Forum. He said, 'How come you're going out of your net so much?' I said, `I think you're doing the same thing.' I guess he got that from me."

Franchise History

Try telling the Mighty Ducks of Anaheim that there was a time when, if someone called you a "Mickey Mouse operation," it was considered an insult. Before the Devils found their stride in New Jersey, the franchise's only claim to fame was in 1983, when Wayne Gretzky publicly blasted the club's management with a reference to a certain cartoon rodent. Now with one Stanley Cup Championship to

Devils

Claude Lemieux #22

NEW JERSEY

its name, and the team a perennial challenger, the New Jersey Devils command league-wide respect. The franchise was originally awarded to Kansas City and began play as the Kansas City Scouts in 1974. Because the team was unable to compete for talent with other NHL teams and the two-year-old World Hockey Association, the product on the ice suffered. After only two seasons, poor attendance forced the franchise to move to Denver, where the Colorado Rockies were born. The team's losing ways, however, continued. The Rockies fared little better with fans in Colorado than the Scouts had with Kansas City, and on June 30, 1982, the franchise was again transferred, this time to New Jersey. Management urged their new fans to show patience. It would be needed. But after several seasons of failing to make the playoffs the Devils finally broke through in 1988 with a memorable playoff run that ended in the Conference Finals. The team then made steady progress, until finally winning the ultimate prize in 1995: a Stanley Cup Championship.

Devils

Martin Brodeur #30

Famers

Most Valuable Player (Hart Trophy): None
Hockey Hall of Fame:
Players: Lanny McDonald, 1992; Peter Stastny, 1998.
Retired numbers: None

Records

Games played		Most points, season		Most goalie wins, career	
Ken Daneyko	992	Kirk Muller	94	Martin Brodeur	201
Career goals		**Most goals, game**		**Most goalie wins, season**	
John MacLean	347	Pat Verbeek,		Martin Brodeur	43
Career assists		Bobby MacMillan	4	**Most shutouts, career**	
John MacLean	354	**Most assists, game**		Martin Brodeur	36
Career points		Kirk Muller,		**Most shutouts, season**	
John MacLean	701	Greg Adams,		Martin Brodeur	10
Most goals, season		Tom Kurvers	5	**Stanley Cups:**	
Pat Verbeek	46	**Most points, game**		1995	
Most assists, season		Kirk Muller	6		
Scott Stevens	60				

Islanders

Brad Isbister #15

around
the town with the
Islanders

Times aren't what they used to be on Long Island: the team is no longer a contender, but the island itself is more fashionable than it once was. So if you're going there to watch a hockey game, be prepared for more excitement off the ice than on it.

It's true that the Islanders have some wonderful prospects like Roberto Luongo and Jason Krog, not to mention Kenny Jonsson, one of the most reliable and underrated defenders in the league. But, for now, the team is rebuilding through the draft. It's a path the Islanders took with unmatched success in the 1970s and '80s, when Denis Potvin, Mike Bossy, Bryan Trottier and Pat LaFontaine all became cornerstones for what became a perennial contender. In those days, Long Island had the upper hand over Manhattan's Rangers, and the cross-town rivalry was so fierce that it lingers today. Why do you think Ranger fans still chant Potvin's name when they're riled up?

Physically and culturally, there are clear differences between the island and downtown New York. Long Island is more sedate and even pastoral in places. Its North Shore is home to the Gold Coast, a stretch of old mansions built by rich and famous men seeking privacy and relaxed surroundings. Teddy Roosevelt spent his summers on the island, and his house is now part of the Sagamore Hill National Historic Site. Then, of course, there are the Hamptons, those seaside towns turned into summer resorts for the creme-de-la-creme of modern America. But there are beaches for regular people too, places where you can just stop and stroll by the Atlantic, dreaming of the day when the Islanders challenge for the Cup again.

Nassau Veteran's Memorial Coliseum

Where to sit:
The club seating section has the best amenities. It includes waiter service and is near ice-level in Section 227. But there are just 160 of these seats—and, of course, they sell out fast.

If it's all you can get:
Don't worry. Other than home games against the New York Rangers, the Islanders rarely sell out and sightlines at the Coliseum are some of the best in the league, even from the worst seat in the house.

Special services:
There are two sections of accessible seating for persons with disabilities. For more information, call 516-794-4100.

Ticket availability:
The Coliseum seats 16,297. But the team has not sold out the arena on a regular basis since 1994 when it last earned a berth in the **Islanders** Stanley Cup playoffs. Season-ticket sales are among the lowest in the league, so single-game tickets are often available at game time. Scalping is illegal in New York. But, other than for games against the Rangers, there's no reason not to try the box office first.

Parking:
The parking lot is spacious (almost 7,000 spaces) and park-

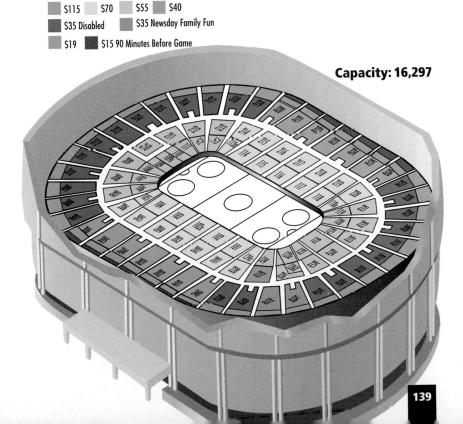

$115　$70　$55　$40
$35 Disabled　　$35 Newsday Family Fun
$19　$15 90 Minutes Before Game

Capacity: 16,297

ing is cheap, just $5. There is little street parking within a half-mile of the arena, so the official lot is really the best option.

Public transportation:
Bus service is available to the Coliseum on the N 70, N 71 and N 72 lines. But you have to travel through the main terminal in Hempstead and this can be an **Islanders** unsavory area late at night. It is an inexpensive cab ride from the Long Island Rail Road stations in Westbury or Hempstead. Call the Metropolitan Suburban Bus Authority (516-766-6722) or the Long Island Rail Road (516-822-5477).

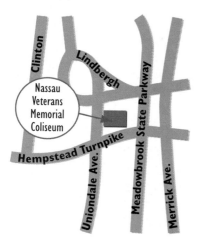

By car:
The Coliseum is on Hempstead Turnpike in Uniondale, adjacent

Nassau Coliseum

to Hofstra University and Nassau Community College. From LaGuardia Airport, take the Grand Central Parkway East—it becomes the Northern State Parkway at the Nassau County border—to Meadowbrook Parkway south and exit at the Hempstead Turnpike (Route 24) exit west. The arena will be on the right. From John F. Kennedy International Airport, take Belt Parkway East—it becomes the Southern State Parkway at the Nassau border—to Meadowbrook Parkway north and exit at the Hempstead Turnpike exit west. The Coliseum will be on the right.

Cuisine:
Don't expect to find a host of gourmet foods, as you would at most modern arenas. The Coliseum is a hot dogs, hamburgers, and fries type of place, though you can purchase grilled sandwiches, Blimpie's heroes, and Sbarro pizza at the concession stands, as well as domestic and foreign beers, cotton candy, and ice cream. There is an arena club, complete with a full-service sit-down menu for pre-game dining, though reservations are suggested.

Home-ice advantage:
Because the building rarely sells out, there is little home-ice advantage for now.

Nightlife

For after the game:
Islanders games are often followed by meals at **Friday's** (829

Merrick Ave., Westbury, 516-832-8320), a chain restaurant with good appetizers. It's a fan hangout and former defenseman Richie Pilon could often be found there. **Chelsea Street** (1900 Hempstead Tpk., East Meadow Plaza, 516-794-3091) is a local hot spot, and **Bogart's Bar and Grill** (1002 Hempstead Turnpike, Uniondale, 516-486-9464) and **Monterey's Bar and Grill** (1166 Hempstead Tpk., Uniondale, 516-538-7881) are often packed with a hip crowd from nearby Hofstra University. **J. Sprats** (737 Merrick Ave., Westbury, 516-832-8060), **Trilogy** (2565 Hempstead Tpk., East Meadow, 516-579-2131), and **Mulcahy's Pub** (3234 Railroad Ave., Wantagh, 516-785-9398) are good places for young crowds to mingle. Former Islander Scott Lachance adds that **Christopher's** (8 Wall St., Huntington, 516-271-0111) is "a hole in the wall, but it's a great little getaway."

For a quiet drink:
Upscale **Carltun on the Park** (Eisenhower Park, East Meadow, 516-542-0700), is no more than a long slapshot from the Coliseum. You can often find Islanders general manager Mike Milbury, as well as staffers and well-heeled business types, in the cigar bar. **Baby Grand's Martini Lounge** (324 Sunrise Hwy., Rockville Centre, 516-763-9664) offers a bit of quiet sophistication.

Best pub:
Chesterfields (330 New York Ave., Huntington, 516-425-1457) is a wonderful, sophisticated, cigar-friendly blues and jazz club, and you can find a number of Islanders there after home games. A terrific upscale club, one loaded with a mix of Long Island's trendiest, not to mention a host of visiting players, is **Dallenger Bar** (45 7th St., New Hyde Park, 516-248-4100).

To hear live music:
Nineteenth-century France meets Hollywood at **Luxe** (2686 Hempstead Tpk., Levittown, 516-520-1332), where a fan can hear some hot local bands. **The Long Island Brewing Company** (111 Jericho Tpk., Jericho, 516-334-2739) is a microbrewery that attracts an eclectic mix against a backdrop of live blues, rock or reggae. Several Islanders and ex-Islanders, like longtime enforcer Mick Vukota, still live in Northport and sometimes catch a live show at **Skipper's Pub** (34 Main St., Northport, 516-261-3589), which is in the town whose main street served as the backdrop for the Kevin Kline movie "In & Out." Many

Islanders
On the Island

Opened: 5/29/72

First regular-season game: 10/7/72, 3–2 loss to Atlanta

First goal: Morris Stefaniw of Atlanta

First playoff game: 4/10/75, 8–3 loss to New York Rangers

Address: Hempstead Turnpike, Uniondale

For single-game tickets: 888-ETM-TIXS

Website: newyorkislanders.com

Islanders like to catch a concert at **Westbury Music Fair** (960 Brush Hollow Rd., Westbury, 516-333-2101).

Dining

For steak:

Peter Luger Steak House (255 Northern Blvd., Great Neck, 516-487-8800) is a New York institution and was heaven to former Islanders Mike Hough and Scott Lachance. "Whenever I have company and I want to take them out for dinner, Peter Luger's is where I take them," says Lachance. "They have great steaks."

For Italian:

Former Islanders stars like Bobby Nystrom often dine at the affordable and underrated **Caffe Baci** (1636 Old Country Rd., Westbury, 516-832-

Islanders

8888). "The food is incredible, the portions are huge and the price is right," says Lachance. "A lot of guys really like the penne riche, a pasta with chicken in a marinara sauce." Not far from the arena, **Borrelli's Italian Restaurant** (1580 Hempstead Tpk., East Meadow, 516-794-0190) has stood for generations.

Local favorites:

Lunchtime often finds a number of Islanders at **The Barefoot Peddler** (37 Glen Cove Rd., Greenvale, 516-621-4840). The kitchen stays open late, so it's also great for a post-game meal. Another popular post-practice stop is **Vincent's Clam Bar** (179 Old Country Rd., Carle Place, 516-742-4577). **The Cheesecake Factory** (1504 Old Country Rd., Westbury, 516-222-5500), famous for its big portions, draws Islanders

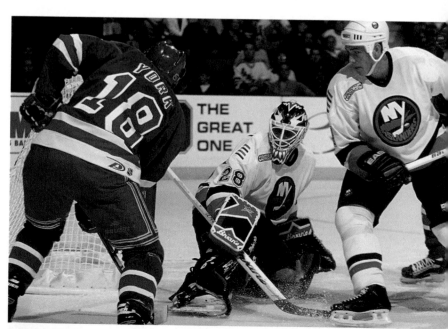

Felix Potvin #28

and New York Jets players, whose training camp is next to the Coliseum at Hofstra University.

For ethnic:
When he was in town, Zigmund Palffy's lone goal when it came to food was to find good Asian cuisine, though you can cross sushi off his list. He often ate at **Benihana** (2105 Northern Blvd., Manhasset, 516-627-3400). "Ziggy eats at those Japanese grill houses, where they cook the food on the table," Lachance says. "He wouldn't be caught dead eating raw fish. But I love the food at **Nagashima Enterprise** (12 Jericho Tpk., Jericho, 516-876-8803). It's clean and fresh and well-prepared. Richie Pilon and I think it's the best sushi we've had anywhere, and we eat sushi all the time when we're on the road, so you know it's pretty good." Want good Cajun cooking? A number of Islanders like **Bayou Restaurant** (2823 Jerusalem Ave., Bellmore, 516-785-9263), a small, cozy Cajun/Creole restaurant and bar with the right ambience.

Lodging

For luxury:
The four-star **Garden City Hotel** (45 7th St., Garden City, 516-747-3000) has Old World charm and is in one of the most regal, upscale towns in Nassau County. The **Wyndham Wind Watch** (1717 Vanderbilt Motor Pkwy., Hauppauge, 516-232-9800) is first-class in every sense, but it's a fair ride from the Coliseum, especially at rush

hour on the Long Island Expressway, which has been dubbed "the world's biggest parking lot."

Close to the arena:
Marriott Long Island (101 James Doolittle Blvd., Uniondale, 516-794-3800, 800-228-9290) shares a parking lot with Nassau Coliseum and is where most visiting teams and recent call-ups stay. Be sure to check out Pitcher's sports bar, where you're likely to spot players after a game.

Islanders

Farther away:
Few other top-notch hotels are close by. More than 20 miles away are the **Radisson** (3635 Expressway Dr. North, Hauppauge, 516-232-3421), **Sheraton** (110 Vanderbilt Motor Pkwy., Hauppauge, 516-231-1100), and **Huntington Hilton** (598 Broadhollow Rd., Melville, 516-845-1000). They all provide excellent service, but 20 miles can mean a 45-minute drive on Long Island.

Shopping & Attractions

Roosevelt Field (Old Country Rd., Garden City, 516-742-8000) is home to the biggest shopping mall on Long Island. It's a mile north of the Coliseum on Meadowbrook Parkway and has Nordstrom's, Macy's, and hundreds of other stores. You can find **Islanders Team Stores** at **Smith Haven Mall** (Rte. 25 and Rte. 347, Lake Grove, 516-724-1433) or at the **Sunrise Mall** (Sunrise Hwy., Massapequa, 516-795-

3550). A wealth of upscale shopping can be found on the so-called Miracle Mile—Billy Joel sang about it in "It's Still Rock and Roll to Me"—along Northern Boulevard in Manhasset on the Long Island Gold Coast. If bargain shopping is your style and you don't mind a drive, **Factory Outlet Center** (1770 W. Main St., Riverhead, 516-369-2724), a huge mall with hundreds of stores, is off exit 73, the last exit on the Long Island Expressway.

The end of the LIE is a good place to start visiting wine country. You can find wonderful vineyards like **Pindar** (Main Rd., Peconic, 516-734-6200),

Paumanok (Main Rd., Aquebogue, 516-722-8800), **Gristina** (Main Rd., Cutchogue, 516-734-7089), **Pellegrini** (Rte. 25, Cutchogue, 516-734-4111), **Bedell Cellars** (Main Rd., Cutchogue, 516-734-7537), and more along a scenic 10-mile stretch of road on the North Fork of eastern Long Island. Or drive Sunrise Highway all the way east to the end of Long Island, see the Montauk Lighthouse and get a bumper sticker that says, "Montauk, the End."

Long Island has some of the world's most spectacular beaches. **Jones Beach** (take the Meadowbrook Parkway or Wantagh Parkway south to the end) has a terrific, quiet boardwalk where you can walk in solitude and listen to the Atlantic crash onto the shore. But it's cold in winter, so bundle up. **The Hamptons**, about an hour's drive east on Sunrise Highway, have funky little shops and wonderful restaurants, but it's a summer spot, so it can be hit or miss during hockey season. "Long Island is great in the summer," Lachance says, "but, it's like Cape Cod. In the summertime, it's the place to be, but who goes to the Cape in winter? It's like a ghost town. They're on Long Island all winter, and there isn't a whole lot to do, except go to New York City. That's why I love to come back in the summer."

Favorite City on the Road

Harry O's, a bar in Manhattan Beach, Calif. is a destination for

Kenny Jonsson #29

most NHL teams in Los Angeles. The nightlife of Yuba City appeals to many Islanders, among them Ray Schultz and Zdeno Chara, when the team visits Tampa. Ted Drury loves his hometown of Boston and its old-fashioned pubs. Former goalie Felix Potvin prefers Chicago. He played his first NHL game there and closed the old Stadium with a playoff shutout.

But most Islanders agree: Nothing tops New York City, an hour's drive to the West. It's the city that never sleeps, remember? Many Islanders like to take in a Broadway show, hit SoHo, TriBeCa, the Village, and Little Italy for some incredible dining, take a trek to the top of the Empire State Building—or, just beat the Rangers.

Cool Fact

Al Arbour, Vice President of Hockey Operations for the Islanders, has his name engraved on the Stanley Cup seven times, three as a player and four as a coach. His involvement in 2,232 games as player and coach is a record and his 781 regular-season wins is second to Scotty Bowman. In 1992, Arbour won the Lester Patrick Trophy for his outstanding service to hockey in the United States, and in 1996, he was inducted into the Hockey Hall of Fame.

Islanders

Franchise History

Awarded a franchise on June 6, 1972, the New York Islanders set the standard for expansion team success. In only its third

Zdeno Chara #3

145

season the team stunned the hockey world with a truly remarkable playoff run. First, they eliminated the established local team, and arch rival, the New York Rangers. That in itself would have been enough glory for a young franchise, but it proved to be just the opening act. In the next round the Isles fell behind the heavily favored Pittsburgh Penguins three games to nothing and became only the second team in major sports history (the other being the 1942 Toronto Maple Leafs) to rally from such a deficit to win a series. If that wasn't enough, the team fell behind the defending Stanley Cup Champion Philadelphia Flyers by three games, and once again it fought back, forcing the series to a seventh game. The Flyers had to rush in their good luck charm, Kate Smith, to stem the tide and finally eliminate the pesky Islanders. But the club had served notice on the league. Several seasons later the Islanders would mature and win four straight Stanley Cup Championships, one of the truly great hockey dynasties in recent years, boasting players the likes of Mike Bossy, Bryan Trottier, Denis Potvin, Clark Gillies and Billy Smith. The four stripes on the team's sweater symbolize that great era in New York Islander hockey.

Islanders

Mariusz Czerkawski #21

NEW YORK

Famers

Most Valuable Player (Hart Trophy): Bryan Trottier, 1979

Hockey Hall of Fame:

Players: Mike Bossy, Denis Potvin, 1991; Billy Smith, 1993; Bryan Trottier, 1997.

Builders: Bill Torrey, 1995; Al Arbour, 1996

Retired numbers: 5 Denis Potvin, 9 Clark Gillies, 22 Mike Bossy, 23 Bob Nystrom, 31 Billy Smith

Records

Games played		Most points, season		Most goalie wins, season	
Bryan Trottier	1,123	Mike Bossy	147		
Career goals		**Most goals, game**		Billy Smith	32
Mike Bossy	573	John Tonelli,		**Most shutouts, career**	
Career assists		Bryan Trottier	5	Glenn Resch	25
Bryan Trottier	853	**Most assists, game**		**Most shutouts, season**	
Career points		Mike Bossy	6	Glenn Resch	7
Bryan Trottier	1,353	**Most points, game**		**Stanley Cups:**	
Most goals, season		Bryan Trottier	8	1980, 1981, 1982,	
Mike Bossy	69	**Most goalie wins, career**		1983.	
Most assists, season					
Bryan Trottier	87	Billy Smith	304		

around the town with the Rangers

Brian Leetch #2

In their very first NHL game in 1926, the New York Rangers defeated the defending champion Montreal Maroons, thanks in part to a raucous crowd urging them on. In New York, spectacular debuts are the norm, of course, but this one still resonates three-quarters of a century later. With fans like these, it's no wonder that the team has rarely suffered from poor attendance.

It's true that New York fans are swift to voice their unhappiness when the game is going wrong, but they won't desert the team. On the contrary, their strong feelings reflect their passion for the game. When the team broke its Stanley Cup jinx in 1994, one fan became famous for the sentiment he displayed on his sign: "Now I Can Die in Peace." Before the drought was broken, former goalie John Vanbiesbrouck suggested fans might start leaping from one skyscraper to another if the team finally won a title again. That didn't quite happen, but the celebration in the streets was long and loud.

Now that New York has become a cleaner and safer place, it is more of a prime tourist destination than ever. Its attractions are well-known: a fistful of pro sports teams, Broadway shows, more art galleries and museums than you can visit in a month, and just about anything else. New York never stands still, and its multi-ethnic makeup has been shifting. Once dominated by French and Italian restaurants, now Austrian, Jamaican and Brazilian establishments, among others, have assumed a higher profile thanks to new immigrants. Still, the city's heartbeat sounds much the same: frenetic, funny, rough and real. When Vanbiesbrouck was a Ranger, he commented, "I like the people here. They have a special identity and they love their hometown. My son is going to be just like these people. They have soul." That, perhaps more than anything, is what defines New Yorkers.

Madison Square Garden

Where to sit:

The penalty box might be the best seat. The Garden's circular shape yields lengthy penalty boxes which were partitioned two years ago to create extra seats for well-heeled fans. They're ideal—if you don't mind hearing a profanity or two or, as Wayne Gretzky's wife, Janet, can attest, getting hit in the head by the odd pane of glass.

If it's all you can get:

The farthest seats house the closest fans to the team—the famous (infamous?) Blue-seaters, so named because the 400-level seats used to be blue. Wear a rival jersey up there or applaud an opponent's goal at your own peril. Seriously. Unused tickets often become available on game day. They are sold on a first-come first-served basis to a line that forms in the lobby late in the afternoon. Scalpers are also quite prevalent in the streets surrounding the Garden.

Special services:

The Garden makes arrange-

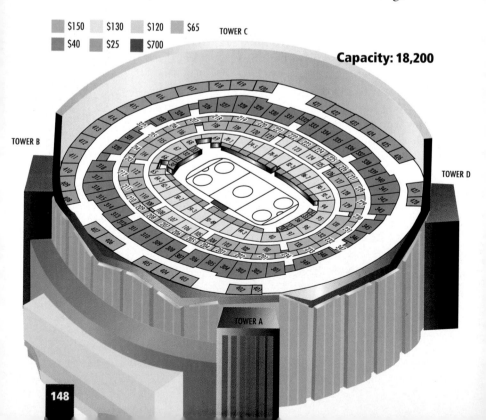

$150 $130 $120 $65   TOWER C
$40 $25 $700

Capacity: 18,200

TOWER B

TOWER D

TOWER A

148

ments for fans with disabilities but has no designated wheelchair locations. Elevators stop at every seating level.

Tickets:

Most of the Garden is sold out for the season, and virtually every Rangers game sells out. Single-game tickets go on sale in early September.

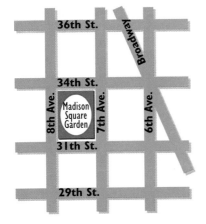

Parking:

Nearby lots are plentiful—and painfully expensive. If you're adventurous, you can scour surrounding blocks for free street parking, but check regulations. Some spots are off-limits until fairly close to game time.

Public transportation:

With nearly a dozen subway lines stopping at Penn Station or within a two-block walk, the Garden is widely accessible, so leave the car at home.

Rangers

By car:

You'll have to battle major traffic, especially weeknights. From LaGuardia or JFK airports, get to the Queens-Midtown Tunnel and then take any westbound street in the 30s across town. From Newark Airport, go through the Lincoln Tunnel,

Adam Graves #9

Madison Square Garden

which dumps you in the Garden's neighborhood.

Rangers

Cuisine:
The Play-by-Play, a glorified sports bar, is the Garden's most upscale restaurant. Dozens of recently upgraded concession stands are around the two main promenades. The beautiful people sitting close to the ice receive waiter service.

Home-ice advantage:
The Garden used to be one of the league's most intimidating buildings. Cheers drowned out the national anthem, though a poor Rangers performance could quickly turn the populace against the home side. In recent years, the crowd has become more skeptical. Still, it's one of the most knowledgeable fandoms in the NHL.

Nightlife

Hot spots:
Studio 54 might now be the stuff of VH-1 documentaries and feature films, but New York remains an unmatched haven for nightbirds seeking a place to dance, drink or just hang out until dawn. The **Jet Lounge** (286 Spring St., 212-929-

4780) in SoHo, with its dark decor and comfy couches, has become a favorite spot to socialize, meet people and listen to music. **Life** (158 Bleecker St., 212-420-1999) in SoHo is currently among the hottest dance clubs. In keeping with the recent cigar craze, **Club Macanudo** (26 E. 63rd St., 212-752-8200) has also become a local hot spot for its cigar lounge and extensive martini menu. And for great people-watching with a parade of the celebrity who's who, the upscale **57–57** bar/restaurant of the Four Seasons Hotel (57 E. 57th St., 212-758-5700) can't be beaten.

For a quiet drink:
Uptown, downtown or in midtown, your best choice is Bar and Books, a mini-chain of elegant bar/restaurants with library motifs. There are three across the city.

Dining

"Great" recommendations:
"One of the best things about living in New York is that you don't have to go out to eat if you don't want—you can order almost anything to be delivered," goaltender Mike Richter says. "I like **Isabella's** (359 Columbus Ave., 212-724-2100) on the West Side because it's in my neighborhood, open late and the food is good."

Ex-Ranger great Wayne Gretzky can go anywhere he wants at any time—no one tells The Great One he can't get a table. But he is a family man first and foremost and recommends places where he's comfortable. "I've been going to **Il Vagabondo** (351 E. 62nd St., 212-832-9221) for 20 years," Gretzky says of the Northern Italian restaurant with the step-down front you could walk right past, the bocce court inside and some of the best gnocchi in town. "The people there are such big Rangers fans and you can go with 13 guys and eat or take the family and get a nice meal. After games, a lot of the players and our wives go to **Campagnola** (1382 1st Ave., 212-861-1102, an Italian restaurant on the Upper East Side). And when we go down to SoHo, we like to go to **Nobu** (105 Hudson St., 212-219-0500) for Japanese."

For steak:

Winger Adam Graves likes a quiet, family-oriented place where he can go with his wife Violet and daughter Madison (yes, she's named after the Garden). But when his dad was in town on a special occasion, "I took him to **Peter Luger's** (178 Broadway, Brooklyn, 718-387-7400). He's never had a steak like that." Gretzky says **Post House Restaurant** (28 E. 63rd St., 212-935-2888) is where players like to go on the night before a game.

Celebrity watching:

The best place to see stars is the restaurant Gretzky co-owns. The **Official All Star Cafe** (1540 Broadway, 212-840-8326) in Times Square has about 20 televisions broadcasting every sporting event imagi-

nable and hundreds of pieces of memorabilia that make you feel like you're in a sports museum.

Lodging

For luxury:

Some of the most famous and opulent hotels in the world are part of the Manhattan skyline—and within walking distance of the Garden. The **Plaza Hotel** (5th Ave. and 59th St., 212-759-3000), which opened in 1907, and **The Waldorf Astoria** (301 Park Ave., 212-355-3000), which opened in 1893, are among the most storied hotels on the globe and qualify as sight-seeing spots as well as elegant places to eat and sleep. The **St. Regis** (2 E. 55th St., 212-753-4500) and **Four Seasons** (57 E. 57th St., 212-758-5700) are among the most beautifully appointed and impeccably serviced.

Trendy:

The **Royalton** (44 W. 44th St., 212-869-4400), **Paramount Hotel** (235 W. 46th St., 212-764-

5500) and **Morgan's Hotel** (237 Madison Ave., 212-686-0300), all in and around the nearby Theatre District, are somewhat more affordably priced and definitely among the trendier places to stay, have a drink, and see and be seen.

More affordable:

If you're seeking more bang for your buck, the **Marriott** (1535 Broadway, 212-398-1900, 800-228-9290) is a good spot, complete with a rooftop rotating restaurant, **The View**, that looks down on Times Square. The **Southgate Tower Suite Hotel** (371 7th Ave., 212-563-1800) is where many Rangers who live near the Westchester County practice rink take their afternoon naps on gamedays.

Shopping & Attractions

Just as with eating and sleeping, New York possesses an unsurpassed array of shopping options, from the sublime to the ridiculous.

In the former category, one must begin with **Tiffany and Co.** (727 5th Ave., 212-755-8000), the world-renowned jewelry store that produced the Rangers' 1994 championship rings. A couple of blocks from the Garden is **Macy's** (151 W. 34th St., 212-695-4400), which calls itself The World's Largest Store. And because the Garden borders the Garment District and its lobby opens onto Fashion Avenue (Seventh), it should come as no surprise that the latest fashions abound in the city's countless clothing stores.

Rangers

Theo Fleury #14

More interested in culture and sightseeing? You've come to the right place. From the **American Museum of Natural History** to **The Guggenheim**, from the **Statue of Liberty** to the **Bronx Zoo** and from **Broadway Theater** to the street "theater" of **Greenwich Village**, New York has something to tickle anyone's particular fancy.

"We've done so much in the city since we've been here," says Wayne Gretzky. "But going to the ballet was probably the most interesting for me, because I didn't know anything about it by any means. But my wife is a dancer and my daughter is now in the School of American Ballet."

Says Mike Richter: "To me, one of the best things you can do anywhere is just spend a summer day in Central Park. . . It's just a great show going by."

Defenseman Brian Leetch, who often accompanies Richter, agrees that one of the best things for somebody used to performing in front of 18,200 people is to turn the tables and become a spectator. "People-watching is the best thing in New York," Leetch says. "I love to walk around, grab a newspaper and something to drink and just people-watch."

Favorite City on the Road

For Gretzky, it was always Toronto. "I don't think there's even a second choice." Defenseman Sylvain Lefebvre loves Montreal.

Adam Graves lists Los Angeles as his favorite. "But my favorite hotel is the Drake in Chicago. I always thought it was like something out of a movie, with the ladies sitting on benches working the elevators and two washrooms in every room."

Cool Fact

The Rangers have two enduring playoff legends. In Game 2 of the 1928 Stanley Cup Finals, general manager Lester Patrick, 44, donned the pads when goalie Lorne Chabot was hurt. The Rangers won in overtime and captured the Stanley Cup a few days later. In 1994, Mark Messier guaranteed a victory in must-win Game 6 of the conference final. He backed it up with a third-period hat trick. The Rangers then went on to oust New Jersey and beat Vancouver in the Finals for their first championship since 1940.

Franchise History

The Rangers were not the first NHL team to locate in Manhattan. The New York Americans hold that honor. Then the league granted Madison Square Garden a franchise to operate a team for 1926–27 and the Rangers were born. A fierce rivalry ensued between the Americans and the Rangers, but it was the Rangers that enjoyed success. In only its second season the team won the Stanley Cup. The Rangers won it again in 1933 and 1940. Two years later the Americans were forced to disband and the Rangers had the city to themselves, yet the

Rangers

team was about to enter a period of frustration, more often finishing out of the playoffs than in them. The team was supposedly cursed. It took 54 years and Mark Messier to break the jinx as the team's long-suffering faithful were finally rewarded with another Stanley Cup in 1994.

Famers

Most Valuable Player (Hart Trophy): Buddy O'Connor, 1948; Chuck Rayner, 1950; Andy Bathgate, 1959; Mark Messier, 1992.

Hockey Hall of Fame:

Players: Howie Morenz, 1945; Lester Patrick, 1947; Bill Cook, 1952; Frank Boucher, Ching Johnson, 1958; Earl Seibert, 1963; Doug Bentley, Albert "Babe" Siebert, 1964; Max Bentley, Walter "Babe" Pratt, 1966; Neil Colville, 1967; Bryan Hextall, 1969; Bill Gadsby, 1970; Terry Sawchuk, 1971; Bernie Geoffrion, 1972; Doug Harvey, Chuck Rayner, 1973; Art Coulter, 1974; Johnny Bower, 1976; Tim Horton, 1977; Andy Bathgate, Jacques Plante, 1978; Harry Howell, 1979; Harry Lumley, Lynn Patrick, Gump Worsley, 1980; Allan Stanley, 1981; Rod Gilbert, 1982; Phil Esposito, 1984; Jean Ratelle, 1985; Ed Giacomin, 1987; Guy Lafleur, Buddy O'Connor, Brad Park, 1988; Clint Smith, 1991; Marcel Dionne, 1992; Edgar Laprade, 1993; Fred Cook, 1995; Wayne Gretzky, 1999.

Retired numbers: 1 Ed Giacomin, 7 Rod Gilbert

Rangers

Mike Richter #35

Records

Games played		Most points, season		Most goalie wins, season	
Harry Howell	1,160	Jean Ratelle	109	Mike Richter	42
Career goals		**Most goals, game**		**Most shutouts, career**	
Rod Gilbert	406	Don Murdoch,		Ed Giacomin	49
Career assists		Mark Pavelich	5	**Most shutouts, season**	
Rod Gilbert	615	**Most assists, game**		John Ross Roach	13
Career points		five tied with	5	**Stanley Cups:**	
Rod Gilbert	1,021	**Most points, game**		1928, 1933, 1940,	
Most goals, season		Steve Vickers	7	1994	
Adam Graves	52	**Most goalie wins, career**			
Most assists, season					
Brian Leetch	80	Ed Giacomin	266		

OTTAWA

around the town with the Senators

Radek Bonk #14

In the middle of winter, Ottawa is the quintessential hockey town. With skaters dotting its Rideau Canal Skateway—even the Senators go there—and snow piled high on the sidewalks, the city looks like an old-fashioned hockey painting. And it should, for it was in Ottawa that Lord Stanley, the Canadian Governor General, had seven sons who formed a hockey team called The Rebels in the late 1800s. By 1892, they had convinced Dad to award a trophy to the hockey champions of Canada. The Stanley Cup was born.

Despite Ottawa's special history, the city had to endure six decades outside the NHL mainstream. From the mid-1930s to the 1990s, it had no team, but the new Senators are trying to compensate for lost time. After an unpromising start, the team found respectability in 1996–97, then made a great leap in 1998–99 to the elite level. Armed with a young and deep defense, the Senators have impressed opponents who once dismissed them.

A small town by major-league standards, Ottawa is a quiet place. Its twin city, Hull, located across the provincial border in Quebec, is the spot where many natives travel to find exciting nightlife. By contrast, the loudest sounds in Ottawa come from inside the Canadian Parliament when MPs debate important or divisive issues. Built in the 1800s and remodeled in 1916, the Gothic-style Parliament is undergoing another renovation for 2000. The National Gallery of Canada is another prime attraction, a glass tower with art galore and a Gothic ceiling that's the only one of its kind in North America. If you want to learn about Canadian culture, this is the place, for the city also holds the Canadian Museums of Nature and Civilization.

The one time Ottawa really lets loose is Winterlude, the three-weekend festival starting in February. If you're booking a trip to see a game, that's the time to go.

Corel Centre

Where to sit:

There really isn't a bad seat in the Corel Centre. Many fans are surprised at the intimacy of its seating. For $125, you can get ice level seating between the face-off circles.

If it's all you can get:

Besides special $19 seats, which are available only well in advance of game day, the Sens' cheapest ticket is a $19 seat located in the top few rows of the upper bowl. Still not a bad spot, especially when the place is full.

Special services:

The Corel Centre has six elevators, and all floors are accessible and equipped for persons with disabilities. For information, call the Senators' box office at 613-599-0300.

Ticket availability:

Tickets in most price ranges are available for most Senators home games, although games with the Toronto Maple Leafs or Montreal Canadiens sell out well in advance. Tickets also tend to be tougher to come by around Christmas. Every Senators playoff game has sold out. The Senators had 16 sellouts in 1998–99.

Parking:

With 6,500 spaces, there is plenty of available parking at the Corel Centre for $9 and up. If you're going in mid-winter,

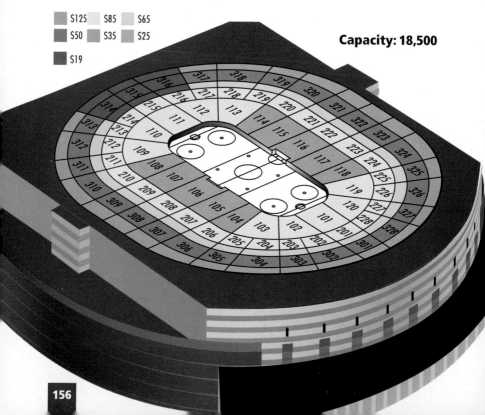

$125 $85 $65
$50 $35 $25
$19

Capacity: 18,500

Corel Centre

it's best to arrive early and park close to the arena to avoid a long walk. After the game, traffic moves slowly for 45 minutes to an hour, longer on sellouts or if weather is poor.

Public transportation:
OC Transpo express "connection 400" buses leave from all areas of the city with departures beginning approximately 1 ½ hours before game time up to an hour beforehand. To check departure times and locations call 613-741-4390. Buses depart immediately after the game and run until roughly one half-hour afterward.

By car:
Head west on Highway 417, the main route in and out of the city, until you see the Corel Centre on your left. Either the Terry Fox or Palladium exits

will direct you toward the arena. Traffic out of the city begins to jam up around 5 p.m. and stays slow until game time. If coming from downtown, leave yourself at least 45 minutes.

Cuisine:
Before or after the game, try **Marshy's**, located on the south side of the building, operated by one of the original Senators, defenseman Brad Marsh. The **Hard Rock Cafe** at the Corel Centre is open seven days a week. Those looking for a high-end meal before a game might want to try the **Air Canada Club**.

Home-ice advantage:
The Senators became a force at home for the first time last season. During the playoffs the atmosphere at the Corel Centre is electric as fans all wear white and are among the loudest in the league.

Nightlife

Close to the arena:
Marshy's (at the Corel Centre, 613-599-0282). is a good place for a pregame meal and a

Senators

Corel Corral
Opened:
1/15/96

First regular-season game:
1/17/96,
3–0 loss to Montreal

First goal:
Andrei Kovalenko of Montreal

First playoff game:
4/21/97,
3–2 loss to Buffalo

Address:
1000 Palladium Dr., Kanata

For single-game tickets:
613-755-1166.

Website:
ottawasenators.com

postgame party. Long lines aren't uncommon, but if you get in, there's a good chance you'll find yourself standing next to one of the players. "My wife and I like to eat there," says one-time Senator Chris Murray, a big fan of the ribs. "My son is two, and I took him to Marshy's and it was the first meal I got him to sit through because he was looking at all the pictures of hockey players."

Downtown scene:

Three bars attract both the Senators and their visiting counterparts. They are the Bulldog Pub, Big Daddy's

Crab Shack, and Nescalaros, all located on Elgin Street. **The Bulldog** (380 Elgin St., 613-567-0921) attracts a young pool hall/tavern crowd, with plenty of contemporary rock music blasting away. **Big Daddy's** (339 Elgin St. 613-569-5200) is a busy, noisy stand-up bar that caters to young, affluent patrons, as does **Nescalaro's** (located above The Bulldog at 380 Elgin St. 613-234-0537). As the night moves on, many who attend those three clubs head upstairs across from Big Daddy's to **Maxwell's Bistro** (340 Elgin St., 613-232-5771), an extremely popular dance bar.

For live music:

Ottawa's home of the blues is the **Rainbow Bistro** (76 Murray St., 613-241-5123), a casual, comfortable live music bar with mostly an early-30s crowd. If a more modern sound suits your taste, try **Zaphod Beeblebrox** (27 York St., 613-562-1010) in the Byward Market, just a couple blocks south of the Rainbow. **Lucky Rons** (209 Rideau St., 613-241-0947) features acts ranging from country to punk. Ottawa's showcase club for live music is **Barrymores** (323 Bank St., 613-233-0307), originally built in the early 1900s as a theatre. Acts that have taken the stage there include REM, U2, Tina Turner, James Brown, and the Allman Brothers. A jazz option is the **After Eight Jazz Club** (101 Sparks St., 613-237-5200). If a more quiet, intimate setting is what you're after, there is

Marian Hossa #18

Rasputin's (696 Bronson Ave., 613-230-5102), which features mostly folk music. "If you want a real Ottawa bar go to the **Bytown Tavern**," (292 Elgin St., 613-233-0057) says Ottawa native Jason York of the downstairs Elgin Street pub that's always rocking. "I used to go there a lot and my friends still go there."

Dining

Franchise favorite:

No doubt about this one. It's **Capones** (2369 Carling Ave., 613-828-8366), an Italian restaurant in the city's west end. "We don't even use the menus when we go there," defense-man Jason York says. Adds former Senator Bruce Gardiner: "All the guys eat there. The owner stays open extra hours for us if we're running behind. They've got a little sports bar so we can watch games on TV or golf if it's the afternoon. A lot of guys eat two meals a day there."

Local favorites:

Hy's Steak House (170 Queen St., 613-234-4545) is recommended for "good service and good food" by coach Jacques Martin. In the Byward Market area, York suggests **Cafe Mezzanotte** (47 Clarence St., 613-562-3978) for fine Italian food and excellent red wine.

For ethnic food:

Ottawa has a fabulous selection of ethnic restaurants, no matter your taste. If it's Italian you fancy, head to Preston Street just west of downtown and choose from any of the restaurants along the city's Little Italy strip. For Asian food, follow Somerset Street west from downtown and take your pick from a variety of Chinese, Vietnamese, and Thai restaurants. The players' choice is the **East Japanese Village** (170 Laurier Ave. W., 613-236-9519), where your food is cooked at the table in front of you. Says Gardiner. "It's fun when they let one of us flip the food around."

Hockey theme:

Don Cherry's (117 Centrepointe Dr., Nepean, 613-226-6647) was founded by the famous Hockey Night in Canada commentator. It's about halfway between the Corel Centre and downtown.

Lodging

For luxury:

The downtown **Chateau Laurier** (1 Rideau St., 613-241-1414) is one of the most famous hotels in Canada. Just east of the Parliament Buildings, it has housed everyone from rock stars to prime ministers. "When I was in Colorado or Quebec, that was where I always stayed," says Senators coach Jacques Martin. "It's unique and has a lot of history and character and it's right in the center of town close to restaurants and stores. It's out of the ordinary from your regular hotel." Adds ex-Senator Chris Murray, "The lobby's beautiful and the ambience is wonderful."

Players' favorite:

Many players also like the **Albert at Bay Suite Hotel** (435 Albert St. 613-238-8858). "It's right down in the center of things and close to the market area and with good access to the highways," says Bruce Gardiner. "The Parliament buildings are one street away and it's easy to get to the casino in Hull if you're into that." Chris Murray lived at the hotel for three weeks when he was traded from Carolina and recommends it for folks who want to eat in because the suites include kitchens.

Closest to the arena:

Not much lodging is available in Kanata because most visitors prefer to stay downtown. In a pinch try, the **Comfort Inn West** (222 Hearst Way, Kanata, 613-592-2200), east of the stadium as you take the highway toward downtown.

Shopping & Attractions

Ottawa's Byward Market features a host of restaurants and souvenir opportunities. It backs onto the city's largest mall, the **Rideau Centre** (50 Rideau St., 613-236-6565), where former Sens goaltender Damian Rhodes got his now-famous bleach blonde hairdo for the '98 playoffs.

As Canada's capital, Ottawa has plenty of attractions, especially the **Parliament Buildings**, located at the north end of downtown on the banks of the Ottawa River, a number of national museums, and the Royal Canadian mint. "I think the Parliament Buildings are the biggest characteristic of our city," says coach Jacques Martin.

Perhaps the biggest attraction during winter is the **Rideau Canal**, which winds from Parliament Hill to the south end of the city and creates the world's largest skating rink. You never know who might be winging past you. Stop, grab a hot drink and one of Ottawa's world-famous Beaver Tail pastries. "I like to go down to the canal in spring or fall and in winter I love putting on a pair of skates and grabbing a cup of hot chocolate," says Bruce Gardiner. "You have to bundle up a lot, so it's hard for people to recognize you. But it's one of the first things I do when we have company: to show people all along the canal."

During the three weeks of Winterlude, the canal is packed with ice sculptures and skating shows. "It's a great attraction," says Martin. "I've had friends that have come for it and really enjoyed being out on the canal."

If you want to see the NHL stars of tomorrow, check out the area's two major junior hockey teams. The Ottawa '67s play at the **Civic Centre** on Bank Street and the Hull Olympiques play across the river at the **Robert Guertin Arena**.

For the really adventurous, there is the opportunity to go ice fishing in the nearby towns of Arnprior and Almonte. "I like to go early in the morning and stay out all day," says Gardiner. "You catch a bunch of perch, but it's tough to convince some of the guys to go with me so I usually end up going alone."

For upscale tastes, check out the calendar for the **National Arts Centre** (55 Elgin St., 613-232-5713), Ottawa's high-culture mecca located in the heart of downtown.

Favorite City on the Road

As you might guess about a team located in the snowy North, many Senators players look forward to that trip to Miami or other southern locales that gives them a bit of sun during the long hockey season. "To be walking around in shorts, it's always nice to get to relax a bit," says Bruce Gardiner.

Coach Jacques Martin says Anaheim is his favorite southern getaway, although he finds the shops and restaurants of Chicago appealing.

Rob Zamuner picks Washington. He loves the tours of the White House (especially the special ones given to NHL celebrities).

Chris Murray, who hails from Port Hardy, British Columbia, says playing in the east for Carolina and Ottawa has taught him he's still a westerner at heart. "Vancouver is my favorite city, but I'm a little biased," he says, laughing. "Growing up in that area, I think I took it for granted and never realized the beauty of it."

Daniel Alfredsson #11

O
T
T
A
W
A

Cool Fact

The Ottawa Senators are one of the original "Original Six." The Senators, along with the Montreal Canadiens, were one of six teams that comprised the National Hockey Association, the predecessor of the National Hockey League. In honor of the team's heritage, old-time Senator Frank Finnigan's number 8 jersey hangs in the rafters of the Corel Centre, retired for all time.

Franchise History

How can the Ottawa Senators have nine Stanley Cups Championships to its name? The original Senators left the city in 1934 after dominating the National Hockey League, winning four Stanley Cups, and another five before the league was born. Story has it that in 1989, after a morning of playing hockey, Bruce Firestone,

Shawn McEachern #15

Randy Sexton and Cyril Leeder of Terrace Investments were inspired to bring the legendary Senators back to life. On December 16, 1991 a franchise was awarded to Ottawa, and on October 8, 1992 the Senators once again played a regular season game in the National Hockey League. It was fitting that they played the Montreal Canadiens. A 5–3 victory made it even more of a dream come true.

Famers:

Most Valuable Player (Hart Trophy): None
Hockey Hall of Fame: None
Retired numbers: 8 Frank Finnigan

Records

Games played		Most points, season		Most goalie wins,	
Alexei Yashin	422	Alexei Yashin	94	season	
Career goals		**Most goals, game**		Damian Rhodes	
Alexei Yashin	178	Several players	3	Ron Tugnutt	22
Career assists		**Most assists, game**		**Most shutouts, career**	
Alexei Yashin	225	Alexei Yashin	4	Damian Rhodes	11
Career points		**Most points, game**		**Most shutouts, season**	
Alexei Yashin	403	Dan Quinn	6	Damian Rhodes	5
Most goals, season		**Most goalie wins,**		**Stanley Cups:**	
Alexei Yashin	44	career		None	
Most assists, season		Damian Rhodes	65		
Alexei Yashin	50				

Flyers

around the town with the
Flyers

John LeClair #10

When the Flyers returned home from their first-ever road trip in 1967, they were welcomed by more than a score of fans during a parade. When the Flyers won the Stanley Cup in 1974, two million crazed people swarmed the team as it paraded through Philadelphia. Yes, in seven years, the City of Brotherly Love had indeed learned to love its hockey. In fact, Philly fans had developed a reputation for rambunctiousness that rivaled that of Ranger crowds. The Flyers were close to unbeatable in the Spectrum in the mid-70s, and the crowd was one reason why. One fan even gained fame through his inventive signs like "START YOUR BUS" (used when the Flyers were assured victory) and "NEXT GOALIE" (when the Flyers had riddled the starting netminder).

Though the team has lost its last five Cup finals, the city has not lost its joy for the game. Attendance in 1998–99 was 100%. Part of the reason for this is owner Ed Snider, who is dedicated to icing a perennially competitive team. Except for a stretch in the early 1990s, he has. Snider is an owner who deeply cares about his players, and the Flyers are known for having a special organization as a result.

Despite all the evidence, there was a long-standing myth that the city had only 17,000 hockey fans, all of which attended the games. The opening of the First Union Center in 1996 put that idea to rest. "The whole city wanted to see it," says general manager and team president Bob Clarke. "We proved what we already knew—

Flyers

that there are a lot more than 17,000 fans in this city. Detroit calls itself Hockeytown, but I like to think hockey is just as big here, maybe bigger." The fact that the Flyers' American Hockey League farm team, The Phantoms, plays across the street to huge crowds at the old Spectrum is testament to Clarke's contention.

First Union Center

Where to sit:

For the ultimate viewing and dining pleasure, there's Victors Club, a private, glass-walled restaurant on the club box level. Patrons can enjoy gourmet dining while watching the action from their table. Included is a beautiful view of the Philadelphia skyline.

If it's all you can get:

For $23, you can watch the game from the upper deck, but your seats are limited to behind each goal. The other upper deck seats that circle the rink are $34, but they, too, are high above the action. The first 10 rows of the second level are probably the best bang for your buck.

Special services:

There are wheelchair areas on all five levels designated for easy access to elevators, rest rooms and concessions. For more information, call (215) 336-3600.

Ticket availability:

Day-of-game tickets are hard to come by, but a limited

$75 $45 $34 $23

Capacity: 19,519

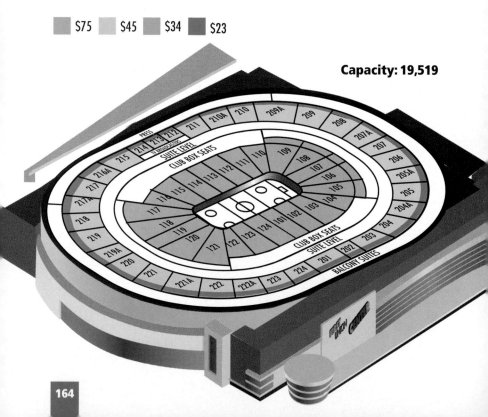

amount might be available for the general public. Although scalping is prohibited on arena property, you will find scalpers on the exit ramps of I-95 and outside the arena parking lots.

Parking:
There are about 6,000 parking spaces in the First Union Center and another 5,000 across the street at Veterans Stadium. Parking in the First Union Center is $8. Surrounding lots can be as low as $5.

Public transportation:
From the city and its surrounding Pennsylvania suburbs, underground rail service is provided on the Broad Street Line and leaves you on the corner of Broad Street and Pattison Avenue. From South Jersey the PATCO Speedline can get you to the Broad Street Line. For more information, call SEPTA at 215-580-7800.

First Union Center

By car:
Take Interstate 95 to the Broad Street Exit. Traveling north from Philadelphia International Airport, it's about a five-mile drive. The Center rests at the bottom of the exit ramp on the right.

Flyers

Cuisine:
You can't leave Philadelphia without wolfing down a cheesesteak with fried onions. It is one of the specialties that can be found among the 30 concession stands in the arena. A popular between-periods hangout is the Red Bell Brewery and Pub located on the first concourse.

Home-ice advantage:
The Flyers used to be tough to beat at the Spectrum, and that carried over to the new Center. They went 47–23–12 in their first two years, and last season, they were 12 games over .500 in the Center.

Nightlife

For after the game:
Fans like to get rowdy at **Philly Rock** (1400 S. Columbus Blvd., 215-463-5771) on the Delaware Riverfront. The walls are adorned with guitars autographed by Eric Clapton and Bruce Springsteen. Eric Lindros likes to hit **Champps Americana** (25 Rte. 73 S, Marlton, N.J., 609-985-9333) for a sandwich, a beverage and all the sports highlights. "It's got a great sports atmosphere and it's got a lot of big-screen TVs," said defenseman Chris Therien.

Champps also has outdoor dining in the spring, summer and fall. Old-time

Flyers

Flyers are fond of **Rexy's Bar** (700 Black Horse Pk., Mt. Ephraim, NJ, 609-456-7911), a rustic shot-and-a-beer bar with great roast beef sandwiches.

For a quiet drink:

Several Flyers go to **Library II Restaurant and Lounge** (306 Rte. 73, Voorhees, N.J., 609-424-0198). Aptly named, the Library is filled with hundreds of books that may be withdrawn by patrons and returned at a later date.

For watching a game:

The **Philly Legends** sports bar in the **Stadium Holiday Inn** (900 Packer Ave., 215-755-9500) is a spacious bar/restaurant with more than a dozen televisions and autographed sports memorabilia.

For live music:

Ex-Flyers Shjon Podein, Alexandre Daigle, and Dainius Zubrus liked to hit the **First Union Center** or the indoor-outdoor E-Center in Camden, N.J., for concerts. At the **E-Center**, fans can bring a lawn chair and watch their favorite acts from the grass while getting a perfect view of Philadelphia.

Mark Recchi #8

Dining

Team favorite:

Because all of the Flyers live across the Walt Whitman Bridge in South Jersey, you'll find most of their favorite restaurants in the Garden State. Longtime Flyer goalie Ron Hextall, now a scout, likes **Library II**, a steakhouse in which patrons order directly from the kitchen window. It also is known for its 22-foot salad bar.

In the city:

When in Philly, Eric Lindros likes to visit the **Palm** (200 S. Broad St., 215-985-9977) and **Ruth's Chris Steak House** (260 South Broad St., 215-790-1515). The Palm has an old-fashioned ambience with original hardwood floors and caricatures of regular patrons and such famous visitors as John Travolta and Frank Sinatra. Ruth's Chris Steak House, across from the Wilma Theatre, is an upscale, dimly lit romantic restaurant great for couples.

For seafood and history:

Old-time Flyers such as Bob Clarke like to eat at the **Bookbinders Old Original Gift** (125 Walnut St., 215-925-7027). Established in 1865, it is the oldest continuing seafood house in the city and is known for its large lobster pots and oyster bar.

Lodging

For luxury:

The ritzy **Sheraton** (1 Dock St., 215-238-6000) is popular for opposing teams who like to tour historic Philadelphia and walk its cobblestone streets past Independence Hall and the Liberty Bell. Located in one of Philadelphia's more upscale neighborhoods, it has a nice restaurant, bar and lounge with entertainment. There's also a pool, fitness center and 24-hour room service.

For convenience:

The **Marriott** (Arrivals Rd., 215-492-9000) is favored by teams who want to stay close to the airport. It's just a 15-minute drive from the First Union Center. Good for quick-in-and-quick out trips, it's connected to Philadelphia International Airport's Terminal B by a skywalk. About 70% of the rooms are designed with the business traveler in mind.

Closest to the arena:

The **Stadium Holiday Inn** (900 Packer Ave., 215-755-9500) is a 10-minute walk from Philadelphia's sports complex, which includes Veterans Stadium, the First Union Center and the First Union Spectrum.

Before and after games, fans fill the **Philly Legends** sports bar,

which is packed with team memorabilia.

Shopping & Attractions

Players' wives like to shop at the **Echelon Mall** in Voorhees, N.J. (609-772-1950), which is anchored by **JC Penney** and regional stores **Strawbridge & Clothier** and **Boscov's**, or take a drive up to the expansive **Franklin Mills Mall** (1455 Franklin Mills Circle Philadelphia, 215-632-1500), where they can walk for miles through food courts and specialty shops. The discount mall has more than 220 stores. Flyers paraphernalia can be found at any of the **Modell's Sporting Goods** stores in the area. Modell's provided the huge Flyers jersey that adorned the William Penn statue on City Hall during the team's 1997 appearance in the Stanley Cup Finals.

Ron Hextall and his four kids visit **Sesame Place** (100 Sesame Rd., Langhorne, Pa., 215-752-7070), about 30 miles north of Philadelphia. The amusement/water ride park features characters from PBS' Sesame Street show.

Former Flyers Bob Clarke, Tim Kerr, Mark Howe and Brian Propp all have places down the Jersey Shore and you can often find them on the Ocean City boardwalk in the summer. Big spenders sometimes wander into Atlantic City for the casinos, about an hour's drive from their homes in Voorhees, N.J.

History buffs should visit the **Independence National Historical Park** (the Visitor Center is at 3rd and Chestnut, 215-597-8974). It includes Independence Hall, where the Declaration of Independence was signed, the Liberty Bell and Franklin Court, a museum on the site of Benjamin Franklin's home.

Speaking of **Franklin, the Franklin Institute Science Museum** (20th and Benjamin Franklin Pkwy., 215-448-1200) celebrates the scientific side of the famed 18th century inventor/statesman. It has a 30-foot-high statue of Franklin, a walkthrough model of a heart—15,000 times life size, complete with thumping sound—a planetarium and plenty of interactive exhibits for children. At the end of the Franklin Parkway is the **Philadelphia Museum of Art** (215-763-8100), which resembles a Greek temple. Climb the steps made famous in the "Rocky" movies and turn around for one of the most spectacular views of the Philadelphia skyline. Then go inside to view more than 300,000 works of art.

Favorite City on the Road

Eric Lindros loves visiting his hometown of Toronto (he grew up in the nearby suburb of London), while teammate John LeClair prefers Montreal, about 40 miles north of his hometown of St. Albans, Vt. LeClair played for the Canadiens for three-plus seasons, scoring two overtime goals on the way to that team's 1993 Stanley Cup championship.

Mark Recchi's favorite city on the road is Vancouver, which is not surprising because he played junior hockey in suburban Burnaby. So did Craig Berube, who says "It's just a beautiful city. There's lots of things to do and I always have a good time. I have plenty of friends to see and have fun with." Ron Hextall likes Chicago for its restaurants and atmosphere.

For the Flyers' favorite eateries on the road, two are at the top of the list: **Hy's Steakhouse** in Edmonton and **Bern's Steakhouse** in Tampa, where they can gather in the downstairs dining room.

Cool Fact

Bobby Clarke, a high-scoring center from Flin Flon, Manitoba, fell to the second round (17th overall) of the 1969 draft because some scouts were concerned about his diabetes. He quickly became

the most important person in Flyers history, their all-time leading scorer, and a three-time league MVP. As a player, he led Philadelphia to two Stanley Cups and two other appearances in the Finals. Under his term as general manager, the team has reached the Finals three times.

Franchise History

Of the six teams awarded franchises on June 5, 1967, the Philadelphia Flyers have proven to be the most successful. The club won the Clarence Campbell Bowl for most regular season points in the Western Division during the inaugural

John Vanbiesbrouck #34

year for the expansion teams. Then, in only their seventh year in the league, the Flyers stunned the mighty Boston

Flyers

Bruins by winning the first of back-to-back Stanley Cups. The "Broad Street Bullies" were known for their rough brand of play but offered plenty of style as well, with skilled players such as Bobby Clarke, Rick MacLeish, Bill Barber, and Reggie Leach. And for several seasons goalie Bernie Parent was the best the league had to offer. The Flyers have been back to the Stanley Cup Finals five more times without winning, but have lost to some of the greatest teams in the modern era (the Canadiens who won four in a row; the Islanders who won four in a row; twice to the Edmonton Oilers who won five out of seven, and most recently to the back-to-back Cup winning Detroit Red Wings).

Famers

Most Valuable Player (Hart Trophy): Bobby Clarke, 1973, 1975, 1976; Eric Lindros, 1995.

Eric Desjardins #37

Hockey Hall of Fame:
Players: Allan Stanley, 1981; Bernie Parent, 1984; Bobby Clarke, 1987; Darryl Sittler, 1989; Bill Barber, 1990.
Builders: Ed Snider, 1988, Keith Allen, 1992.
Retired numbers: 1 Bernie Parent, 4 Barry Ashbee, 7 Bill Barber, 16 Bobby Clarke

Records

Games played		Most points, season		Most goalie wins, season	
Bobby Clarke	1,144	Mark Recchi	123		
Career goals		**Most goals, game**		Bernie Parent	47
Bill Barber	420	several players with	4	**Most shutouts, career**	
Career assists		**Most assists, game**		Bernie Parent	50
Bobby Clarke	852	Eric Lindros	6	**Most shutouts, season**	
Career points		**Most points, game**		Bernie Parent	12
Bobby Clarke	1,210	Tom Bladon	8	**Stanley Cups:**	
Most goals, season		**Most goalie wins, career**		1974, 1975.	
Reggie Leach	61				
Most assists, season		Ron Hextall	240		
Bobby Clarke	89				

P H O E N I X

around
the town with the
Coyotes

Coyotes

Jyrki Lumme #21

They're not in Winnipeg anymore and they aren't called the Jets, but some traditions remain. When the Coyotes play in the post-season, their fans dress in white and wave white towels, creating the "white-out" that characterized Winnipeg playoff drives. The Coyotes haven't rewarded this dedication with many big-game victories yet, but the talent is certainly there. Keith Tkachuk is the first player to get 50 goals and 200 penalty minutes in one season. Jeremy Roenick is a human ball of fire, while Teppo Numminen is one the most underrated defensemen in the league.

The Coyotes have been in Phoenix for four seasons, and the adjustment from frigid Winnipeg to the Valley of the Sun was difficult in the beginning. "It was really a rookie team, regardless of how many years the guys had played," says Roenick. "Everyone had to adapt to living in Phoenix and the distractions that a warm climate has."

There are many of those. The Valley boasts almost 200 golf courses and about 20 four- or five-star resorts. The landscape is widely varied. A 2 ½-hour drive north takes you from 1,000 feet above sea level to 7,200 feet up and skiing among the pine forests. If you drive the same amount of time eastward, you enter the high chaparral of the desert. Go south and you will hit the Sea of Cortez. How many regions combine ocean, desert and forest?

The Coyotes were all over the map in their first season because they had no practice site, but two seasons ago, the team found one in the Ice Den in Scottsdale. It's only 30 minutes from the Phoenix arena, and the club is hoping to build a new stadium in Scottsdale as well. They already know they have the fans to fill it.

America West Arena

Where to sit:
Except for the north-side balcony, all viewing angles are superb. There are $215 seats along the glass, but a better bet is the $54–$80 seats at center ice between five and 25 rows up. Season-ticket holders take up many of these seats, but some are available on a game-by-game basis.

If it's all you can get:
Because the Arena was built with only basketball in mind,

there are 4,283 obstructed-view seats in the north balcony. Fans can see about three-quarters of the ice before having to catch the action on the video screens.

Special services:
America West Arena can accommodate 120 persons with disabilities on the upper level at center ice and on the north and south ends, as well as in the corners of the lower level.

Ticket availability:
The Coyotes averaged 96% in attendance last season, which has been the norm since they arrived in Phoenix. The Rangers were an especially big draw while Gretzky was playing. Also because many Phoenix residents are transplanted Midwesterners, it's best to order early for Detroit and Chicago.

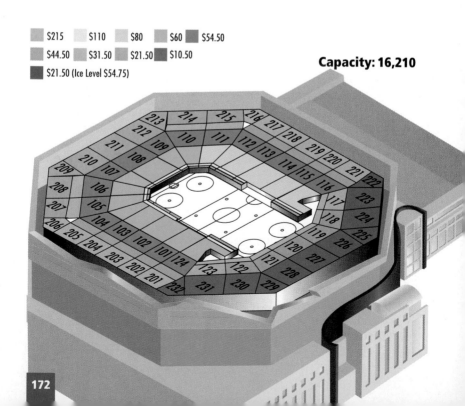

$215 $110 $80 $60 $54.50
$44.50 $31.50 $21.50 $10.50
$21.50 (Ice Level $54.75)

Capacity: 16,210

Parking:

The Arena has a 900-space attached parking garage, a 1,500-space garage next door and more than 11,000 parking spaces within an eight-minute walk. Bank One Ballpark, one block away, makes available three more garages within a five-minute walk.

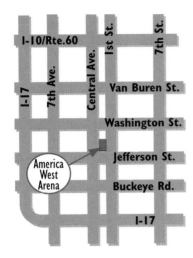

Public transportation:

Numerous bus lines stop at or within several blocks of the arena. Call 602-253-5000 for information.

By car:

Exit the airport via I-10 West to the Washington Street exit. Take Washington Street west to Third Street and make a left. The Arena is one block ahead on the right.

America West Arena

Cuisine:

The main entrance to America West Arena has a food gallery, where patrons can buy tacos, hamburgers, chicken, and the like.

Home-ice advantage:

While the "whiteout" is a big asset in the playoffs, these fans are hardly the passive type. It doesn't take much to get them to do their trademark Coyote howl.

Nightlife

For after the game:

Arizonans drink more beer per capita than residents of any other state, so a good watering hole is never far away. Several places are within a couple blocks of the Arena and you're likely to rub elbows with a player or two. **Majerle's** (24 N. 2nd St., 602-253-9004) is owned by former Suns great Dan Majerle and is often visited by players from Phoenix's various sports teams. **Coyote Springs** (122 E. Washington St., 602-256-6645) is a micro-brewery featuring live music. Both are big pre-game and post-game meeting spots for fans.

Player favorites:

For the most part, the Coyotes like to hang out in Scottsdale, where most of them live. Their favorite haunts there are **Acme Bar and Grill** (4245 N. Craftsman Ct., 480-990-7111), a small pub good for a quiet beer with the guys, **Madison's** (7108 E. Stetson Dr., 480-949-8453) and the **Cajun House of Blues** (7117 E. 3rd Ave., 480-945-5150).

For watching a game:

With the area now represented by all four major sports and Arizona State a national contender in nearly every collegiate sport, the Valley has developed into a sports bar haven. Some of the more noteworthy establishments are the **America's Original Sports Bar** (455 N. 3rd St., 602-252-2502), which has 62 TV sets and more than 10 big-screen TVs inside the Arizona Center Complex; **Philly's** (9301 E. Shea Blvd., Scottsdale, 480-860-6600); **Max's** (6727 N. 47th Ave., Glendale, 623-937-1671); and **The Vine Tavern and Eatery**, which has locations throughout the Valley.

Dining

For Italian:

Rick Tocchet's favorite is **La Locanda** (10201 N. Scottsdale Rd., Scottsdale, 480-998-2822), which features Northern Italian cuisine. "They have a fantastic veal dish that I love called Osso Buco," he says. He also frequents **Il Forno** (4225 E. Camelback Rd., 602-952-1522), as does Jeremy Roenick,

who calls it "a classic Italian restaurant with great dishes."

For steak:

Roenick ate at the original **Morton's of Chicago** during his days with the Blackhawks and enjoys the Phoenix version (2501 E. Camelback Rd., 602-955-9577). Nikolai Khabibulin prefers **Ruth's Chris Steak House** (2201 E. Camelback Rd., 602-957-9600, or 7001 N. Scottsdale Rd., Scottsdale, 480-991-5988), which he calls "the best in Phoenix and nationwide." Another favorite is **Monti's La Casa Vieja** (3 W. 1st St., Tempe, 480-967-7594), located in a historic 19th century home. **Rustler's Rooste** (7777 S. Pointe Pkwy. W, 602-431-6474), a country-western eatery, sits high atop a hill on the grounds of the Pointe-Hilton Resort on South Mountain and offers live music.

For ethnic:

Tocchet loves **P.F. Chang's China Bistro** (7014 E. Camelback Rd., Scottsdale, 480-949-2610) a trendy establishment featuring Chinese fare. "It's a great restaurant with a good atmosphere," he says. "They have a wide variety of dishes, and everything on their menu is great." Khabibulin says **Mancuso's** (6166 N. Scottsdale Rd., Scottsdale, 480-948-9988) "has a unique blend of French and Italian," and **Marco Polo** (8608 E. Shea Blvd., 480-483-1900) "has a great mixture of Chinese and Italian." Team president Shawn Hunter recommends **Tee Pee** (4144 E.

Indian School Rd., 602-956-0178) for its excellent Mexican food.

Other favorites:
General manager Bobby Smith likes **Earls** (15784 N. Pima Rd., Scottsdale, 480-607-1941) "It's casual, also owned by Canadians." **Bandera** (3821 N. Scottsdale Rd., Scottsdale, 480-994-3524) in Old Scottsdale and **Z Tejas Grill** (7014 E. Camelback Rd., Scottsdale, 480-946-4171), feature Southwestern cuisine. Players also frequent **Don & Charlie's** (7501 E. Camelback Rd., Scottsdale, 480-990-0900), which is a little bit of Chicago in Arizona, and **Eddie's Grill** (4747 N. 7th St., 602-241-1188).

Lodging

For luxury:
The Valley is loaded with five- and four-star resorts. **The Phoenician** (6000 E. Camelback Rd., Scottsdale, 480-423-2530) features a fair but demanding 10-hole golf course, the **Camelback Inn Resort** (5402 E. Lincoln Dr., Scottsdale, 480-948-1700, 800-228-9290), also has golf privileges, and the **Wigwam Resort** (300 Wigwam Blvd., 623-935-3811) boasts three excellent golf courses, as well as tennis and swimming.

Something special:
The **Scottsdale Princess Resort** (7575 E. Princess Dr., 480-585-4848) is next to the PGA Tournament Players Course, the home of the Phoenix Open. As well as its 531 rooms, the

resort has 119 casitas and 68 villas, all with private terraces that offer a mountain view. There are tennis and spa facilities, three swimming pools and five restaurants. If that isn't enough, it has the only four-star, four-diamond Mexican restaurant in North America.

Coyotes

Close to the arena:
Two high-rise hotels are within two blocks of the Arena in a

Rick Tocchet #22

revitalized area of downtown: The **Hyatt** (122 N. 2nd St., 602-252-1234, 800-233-1234), and the **Crowne Plaza** (100 N 1st St., 602-333-0000).

Also, a refurbished **Ramada Inn** (401 N. 1st St., 602-258-3411), which features a courtyard and large swimming pool, is four blocks away.

Shopping & Attractions

Arizonans love to shop. There are several malls in Scottsdale, Tempe, and Phoenix, featuring such well-known department stores as **Saks Fifth Avenue**, **Nieman-Marcus**, and **Dillard's**. If you're looking for Coyotes jerseys, try the **Team Shops** inside America West Arena, which also carries merchandise from the Suns, Rattlers, Mercury, and Diamondbacks. Old downtown Scottsdale is filled with top-dollar boutiques, such as the **Borgata of Scottsdale** (6166 N. Scottsdale Rd., Scottsdale, 480-998-1822).

If recreation or sightseeing interests you more, the Valley offers a lot of choices. There are three lakes—Saguaro, Canyon, and Lake Pleasant—within 60 miles for water skiing or fishing, and the beautiful redrock country around Sedona is a two-hour drive by freeway.

Favorite City on the Road

Until the 100-degree-plus temperatures of summer roll around, you won't get a Coyotes player to say he'd rather be elsewhere. But during the season, three places tend to grab their hearts.

Rick Tocchet, Jeremy Roenick, and general manager Bobby Smith all vote for Chicago. Roenick played seven full seasons there and says, "The fans are great, there are great restaurants and the nightlife is good. It's a big, clean city with nice people and a lot of character."

Boston also receives several votes, and not only because Coyotes players Keith Tkachuk, Roenick, Keith Carney, and Deron Quint are from the area. Nikolai Khabibulin, from Sverdlovsk, Russia, also is a big fan. "Boston is a great city," he says. "It's a nice old-style city with a European flavor."

Cool Fact

Bobby Hull was the first NHL superstar to jump to the World Hockey Association in 1972. Hull signed a $2.75 million contract with the Winnipeg Jets.

Franchise History

Before moving to Phoenix on July 1, 1996 the Coyotes' franchise played in Winnipeg for 25 years as the Jets. Originally the team played in the World Hockey Association, three times winning a championship, led by the Golden Jet himself, Bobby Hull. Bobby was back in the NHL for one final season when Winnipeg joined the League in 1979. Unfortunately, the Jets had little success on the ice and eventually a poor eco-

PHOENIX

nomic climate forced the club to transfer to Phoenix. Fortunately for its new city and fans the club's rebuilding efforts were about to pay dividends, and the Coyotes now look to return to the franchise's glory days of winning hockey championships.

Famers

Most Valuable Player (Hart Trophy): None
   Hockey Hall of Fame:
   Players: Bobby Hull, 1983, Serge Savard, 1986.
   Retired numbers: 9 Bobby Hull, 25 Thomas Steen

Coyotes

Keith Tkachuk #7

Records

Games played		Most points, season		Most goalie wins, career	
Thomas Steen	950	Teemu Selanne	132	Nikolai Khabibulin	126
Career goals		**Most goals, game**		**Most goalie wins, season**	
Dale Hawerchuk	379	Willy Lindstrom,		Bob Essensa,	
Career assists		Alexei Zhamnov	5	Brian Hayward	33
Thomas Steen	553	**Most assists, game**		**Most shutouts, career**	
Career points		Dale Hawerchuk,		Nikolai Khabibulin	21
Dale Hawerchuk	929	Phil Housley	5	**Most shutouts, season**	
Most goals, season		**Most points, game**		Nikolai Khabibulin	8
Teemu Selanne	76	Willy Lindstrom,		**Stanley Cups:**	
Most assists, season		Dale Hawerchuk,		None	
Phil Housley	79	Thomas Steen,			
		Ed Olczyk	6		

Penguins

Jaromir Jagr #68

around
the town with the
Penguins

"Without Mario Lemieux," declared Wayne Gretzky, "there would be no NHL team in Pittsburgh today." That's certainly true, but no longer in the way The Great One intended, for he said it well before the fall of 1999. Mario first saved the team in the 1980s. With him in the lineup, attendance rose by almost 50% in one year and stayed high, preventing the team from moving to another town. When the team was in danger of folding completely in 1999, Mario just said no to that as well, leading an ownership group that bought—and saved—it. In the process, he made Gretzky's words doubly true.

His fellow owners were so thrilled by Lemieux's purchase that he received a standing ovation at the Board of Governors meeting after the sale was finalized. Edmonton President and General Manager Glen Sather commented that Lemieux had the right personality for the role: intelligent, respectful, with an aura that in turn commands respect. Already a folk hero in the Steel City, Lemieux instantly became the most popular owner in sports, as well as the only one to have his jersey hanging from the building he oversees. He won't have trouble remembering the stadium's address either: 66 Mario Lemieux Place.

It would have been a deep shame if hockey had left Pittsburgh, for this is a sports town through and through. Former Pens coach Kevin Constantine says, "Pittsburgh people love their sports. It's a joy and a challenge to work in an atmosphere like this." The fans are loyal but critical, the media tough but enthusiastic. In a city that doesn't own many well-known attractions, its major-league teams have become the center of civic pride. At the same time, Pittsburgh is a better place to live than it once was. Pollution levels have dropped, an urban rebirth has been successful, and corporate America has found that Pittsburgh is not a bad place to be. Having come so close to leaving, the Penguins can agree whole-heartedly with the latter.

Mellon Arena

Where to sit:
The best seats in the house are called Igloo seats. They are the first 21 rows between the face-off circles. About 100 seats are available on an individual, game-by-game basis. They include access to a private lounge. The second-best seats are A-level, which form a horseshoe seven rows behind each goal.

If it's all you can get:
The F-level balcony seats go for about $25 each, and the last three rows of the E-level are priced at about $20. An hour before faceoff there is a Student Rush Hour, where all the unsold, non-premium seats go on sale at a discount rate for anyone with a college ID. Look for youth and senior citizen discounts.

Special services:
About 10 percent of the club seating is reserved for people

| $125 | $85 | $70 | $60 | $38 |
| $34 | $30 | $20 | $25 | $25 parents $10 kids |

Capacity: 16,958

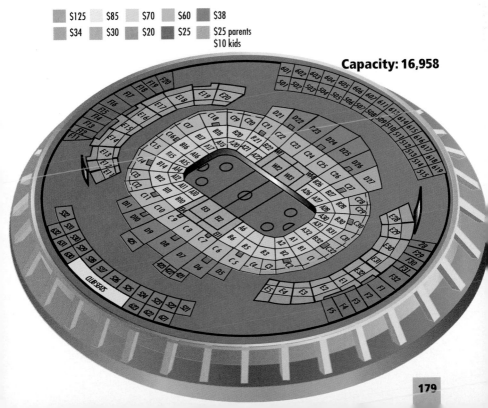

with disabilities. Special seating also is available on the B and C levels.

Ticket availability:

A Penguins game used to be a tough ticket. But attendance has dropped since Mario Lemieux's retirement. Scalpers are readily available outside the arena. Note that it's against the law to scalp a ticket for more than face value in Pittsburgh.

Parking:

There are about 2,700 individual spaces at the Mellon Arena. Of those, 1,300 are open to the public. The nearby Chatham Center is a popular parking spot, and the area surrounding the Arena is rich with public and private parking opportunities.

Mellon Arena

Public transportation:

You can park at Station Square, take the incline up to scenic Mt. Washington, enjoy a meal overlooking the city, then take the incline back down and hop the subway—known as the "T"—from Station Square to the Mellon Arena. Or you can eat at one of Station Square's popular restaurants and take the T over to the game. Station Square also provides a free shuttle service before and after games.

By car:

The centrally-located Mellon Arena is easily accessible from Pittsburgh's main arteries and interstate highways. From the airport, it takes about a half-hour. Take Route 60 toward Pittsburgh and follow until it merges with Route 279. Follow Route 279 through the Ft. Pitt Tunnel, which upon exiting affords one of the finest skyline views in North America. Stay in the right lane as you cross the Ft. Pitt Bridge, bear to your right and take the first exit on the right. Once off the bridge, get into the left lane and take the Grant Street exit (first on the left). Follow Grant Street until you reach the traffic light at Sixth Avenue. Go right, and turn left at first light onto Bigelow Bouvelard. Look for signs to Arena.

Cuisine:

The Igloo lounges, available only to those seated in the club seats, offer upscale concessions. Those in the Igloo seats have access to the Igloo club, which offers a pre-game buffet and finger foods between periods.

Elsewhere in the arena, you can find regular concession fare. Try the locals' favorite brew—Iron City—which is readily available.

Home-ice advantage:

The Igloo is one of the last arenas in the NHL with true balconies that allow fans a closer glimpse of the action. Its design also makes it one of the more intimate buildings in the league.

Nightlife

For after the game:

Rough-and-tumble defenseman Darius Kasparaitis hits **A Top of the Triangle** (USX Tower, 600 Grant St., 412-471-4100) whenever he can. It's 62 floors and 840 feet up in the USX Tower, the largest building between Chicago and Philadelphia. The Top of the Triangle hosts live music and affords an incredible view of Pittsburgh. It's a short walk from the Mellon Arena. Watch for handouts before the game advertising food specials. Open until 1 a.m. on weekends, a little earlier on week nights. Or head over to **Houlihan's** (15 Station Sq. E, 412-232-0302), where the post-game party rages until 2 a.m. and sometimes features a Penguin or two.

For a quiet night:

Walk from the Mellon Arena to the **Tap Room** at the Westin William Penn (530 William Penn Way, 412-281-7100) and sip a Penn Pilsner, brewed fresh at the **Allegheny Brewery** on Pittsburgh's North Side. Players from the visiting team often hang out at the Tap Room, which features single-malt scotches, beers from all over the world, and quiet tunes ranging from jazz to pop hits. Another option is the **Harvest Bar** inside the Doubletree Hotel (1000 Penn Ave., 412-281-3700). Formerly a fine-dining restaurant, the Harvest Bar features comfy wing-back chairs, speciality wines, an extensive martini list and a daily happy hour.

For live music:

Hit the **Rosebud** (1650 Smallman St., 412-261-2199) in the hopping Strip District, or its neighboring club, the **Metropol** (1600 Smallman St., 412-261-4512). Both are a slap shot away from the Mellon Arena. Ex-Penguin Alex Hicks brought his eclectic musical tastes there, and he brought some of his fellow forwards with him. Pittsburgh's athletes can't pass up the **James Street Restaurant** (422 Foreland St., 412-323-2222), where some of the city's best live jazz plays Tuesday through Saturday. Penguins general manager Craig Patrick,

Penguins

Under the Igloo

Opened:
9/17/61

First regular-season game:
10/11/67,
2–1 loss to Montreal

First goal:
Gilles Tremblay of Montreal

First playoff game:
4/23/70,
3–2 win over St. Louis

Address:
66 Mario Lemieux Place, Pittsburgh

For single-game tickets:
412-323-1919

Website:
pittsburghpenguins.com

Hall of Famer Bryan Trottier and ex-Penguins such as Jay Caufield stop by to enjoy the Cajun and Creole cooking and the hot tunes.

Best pub:

For a real taste of Pittsburgh, check out the

Park House (403 East Ohio St., 412-231-0551), where local entertainers like to hang out. Legendary Penguins announcer Mike Lange ("Scratch my back with a hacksaw; Elvis has just left the building.") has been known to stop in, as has his long-time color commentator (now radio voice), Paul Steigerwald. "It's one of those places where there's sports on the tube, great music on the juke box, peanuts on the floor, and lots of cold beer in the refrigerator," Steigerwald says. "You always run into somebody in there. Great conversation." Plenty of imports and micro-brews are available." Across the Monongahela River from the Mellon Arena, bars line the South Side of Pittsburgh along E. Carson Street, stretching from **Margaritaville** (2200 E. Carson St., 412-431-2200) all the way to Station Square. Every once in a while, former Penguin tough guy Tyler Wright popped up in one of these joints, sometimes with a few friends.

To meet the opposite sex:

Nearly all the Penguins are married, so you won't find them at the singles joints, but that shouldn't stop you from going. You'll find plenty of action at **Froggy's** (100 Market St., 412-471-3764) during Happy Hour on Fridays and at the **Grandview Saloon** (1212 Grandview Ave., 412-431-1400) on Mt. Washington. Pittsburgh fixture Froggy Morris has owned Froggy's for two decades. "For 20 years the champions of Pittsburgh have had their drinks here," Morris says. "You name a Penguin, they've been here." When they were single, of

German Titov #9

course. Friday Happy Hour is an absolute butt-kicker, starting at 4:30 p.m. and winding down sometime after midnight. If you're drinking mixed drinks at Froggy's, call a cab. The Grandview Saloon overlooks the magnificent Pittsburgh skyline and features a Happy Hour 6–8 p.m. Monday through Friday with free appetizers. Every now and then a Penguins player pops in to serve as guest bartender.

Dining

Great food, great view:
Longtime Penguins star Ron Francis loved the **Grand Concourse** (412-261-1717) at Station Square. It's an old train station built 100 years ago next to the Monongahela River. It was turned into a restaurant 20 years ago and features succulent seafood. "The kids love it because the trains go by, and you're right on the water," Francis says. "The food is great, too." You could eat there before the game, then catch the T to the arena.

Local fare:
You could bite into a Pittsburgh classic at **Primanti Brothers** (46 18th St., 412-263-2142). Beware: They pack the sandwiches with french fries and coleslaw. Hall of Famers Mario Lemieux and Bryan Trottier, not to mention Jaromir Jagr and ex-Penguins star Joey Mullen, have been known to dig into a Primanti Brothers sandwich.

For steak:
At **Morton's of Chicago** (625 Liberty Ave., 412-261-7141),

you're likely to find a Penguin or two ripping into a filet mignon. Or head up to scenic Mt. Washington, where assistant coach Mike Eaves declares "the food is fantastic and the view can't be beat" at the **Lemont** (1114 Grandview Ave., 412-431-3100).

Lodging

For luxury:
The crown jewel of Pittsburgh hotels is located three blocks from the Mellon Arena. The **Westin William Penn** (530 William Penn Way, 412-281-7100) is the oldest hotel in the city (built in 1916) and a National Historic Landmark, complete with Baccarat crystal chandeliers. Many opposing teams stay at the Westin. Sunday through Thursday, the average cost for a room is $174. On weekends, rooms start as low as $89.

Some opposing teams opt for another hotel within walking distance of the arena, the **Marriott** (112 Washington Pl., 412-471-4000, 800-233-1234). Get some great seafood at the **Marriott's Steelhead Grill** (412-394-3474).

Other choices:
Any number of hotels—from **Red Roof Inns** to **Marriotts**— stretch from the airport all the way into downtown Pittsburgh.

Shopping & Attractions

Looking for a Jaromir Jagr sweater? How about one with Mario Lemieux's name on the back? Penguins souvenirs are readily available at the pro shop inside the Mellon Arena and at the Penguins **Locker Room Pro Shop** at the **Iceoplex at Southpointe**, the Penguins' practice facility about 25 minutes outside the city off Interstate 79 South in Canonsburg. It's a

Penguins

great place to get autographs, too. After practice, fans clog the exit gate from the players' parking lot, and the players happily pull over to sign autographs. Make sure to call Southpointe (724-745-6666) and check the practice schedule.

If it's more than a jersey you want, hit **Station Square** (412-261-9911). The popular mall, across the Monongahela River, features night clubs, restaurants, gifts shops, shoe stores, clothing outlets and specialty stores. The swanky shopping strip on Walnut Street in Shadyside atracts its share of visitors, too. **The Gap**, **Victoria's Secret**, **Ann Taylor**, the **Banana Republic** and **Starbucks Coffee** all can be found on Walnut Street.

Other local attractions include the **Carnegie Science Center** (1 Allegheny Ave., 412-237-3300), which features laser shows, interactive exhibits, and a 3-D projection screen; the **Carnegie Museum of Natural History** (4400 Forbes Ave., 412-622-3131) with its incredible dinosaur exhibit; and the interactive exhibits at the **Andy Warhol Museum** (117 Sandusky St., 412-237-8300) on Pittsburgh's North Side. For a whiff of fresh air, check out the world-famous **Phipps Conservatory** (1500 Forbes Ave., Schen-

Tom Barrasso #35

ley Park, 412-622-6914) near the University of Pittsburgh.

Favorite City on the Road

Many Penguins enjoy Montreal with its after-hours pubs and tantalizing night life. One of the players' favorite road restaurants is **Giulio Cesare** (516-334-2982) near Nassau Coliseum in Long Island. It serves the best gnocchi on the NHL circuit. When he was in town, Stu Barnes enjoyed the western road trips. "Anytime you get to see sun in the middle of the winter, that's a good thing," Barnes says.

Cool Fact:

Mario Lemieux established himself quickly by scoring on his first shift and first shot in 1984. On December 31, 1988 he scored every possible way: even strength, power play, shorthanded, penalty shot, and empty net. He also had eight points in a 1989 playoff game. Aside from winning back-to-back Stanley Cup championships, his biggest triumph came in 1993. Battling Hodgkin's disease, he flew to Philadelphia the day of his final radiation treatment and scored a goal that night. He overcame Pat LaFontaine's lead to win the scoring title and was named league MVP.

Franchise History

When the Penguins were granted a franchise on June 5, 1967, it wasn't the first time that Pittsburgh had become an NHL city. The Pittsburgh Pirates, named after the baseball team, played in the league from 1925 to 1930, then moved across state to become the Philadelphia Quakers for one disastrous season before folding and leaving Pennsylvania without NHL action for almost 40 years. While their fellow expansion team and rival the Philadelphia Flyers enjoyed early success, the Penguins suffered through many difficult seasons. Then Mario arrived. Even with Mario Lemieux in the line-up the team finished out of the playoffs five out of the next six years. With the right combination of players to support Mario, and the arrival

Penguins

Robert Lang #20

of Jaromir Jagr, the Penguins then won back-to-back Stanley Cups in 1991 and 1992 with a team that was truly popular across the league. The Pens have made the playoffs for nine straight seasons.

Famers

Most Valuable Player (Hart Trophy): Mario Lemieux, 1988, 1993, 1996; Jaromir Jagr, 1999.

Penguins

Hockey Hall of Fame:

Players: Andy Bathgate, 1978; Leo Boivin, 1986; Mario Lemieux, Bryan Trottier, 1997.

Builders: Scotty Bowman, 1991; Bob Johnson 1992.

Retired numbers: 21 Michel Briere, 66 Mario Lemieux

Alexei Kovalev #27

Records

Games played		Most points, season		Most goalie wins, career	
Jean Pronovost	753	Mario Lemieux	199	Tom Barrasso	221
Career goals		**Most goals, game**		**Most goalie wins, season**	
Mario Lemieux	613	Mario Lemieux	5	Tom Barrasso	43
Career assists		**Most assists, game**		**Most shutouts, career**	
Mario Lemieux	881	Mario Lemieux,		Tom Barrasso	21
Career points		Greg Malone,		**Most shutouts, season**	
Mario Lemieux	1,494	Ron Stackhouse	6	Tom Barrasso	7
Most goals, season		**Most points, game**		**Stanley Cups:**	
Mario Lemieux	85	Mario Lemieux	8	1991, 1992.	
Most assists, season					
Mario Lemieux	114				

P I T T S B U R G H

around the town with the
Blues

Blues

Chris Pronger #44

When expansion was an uncertain premise in 1967, the St. Louis Blues ensured it would work. By reaching the Cup final for three straight years, by signing great veterans like Jacques Plante and Glenn Hall, the Blues not only showed that the new clubs on the block were here to stay, they turned their city on to the sport for good. Though the Blues are too far removed from the major Canadian and American markets to get a lot of attention, they have a fan base that's as committed as those in New York or Philadelphia. "They love the players," says Brett Hull, the biggest star other than Wayne Gretzky to ever wear the Blue Note. "They adopt them. They bring them into their lives. It's a special feeling."

In the city of the Arch, the Blues own the twin towers: Al MacInnis and Chris Pronger, two of the best defensemen in the league. MacInnis is in the latter half of his Hall of Fame-caliber career, while Pronger is just beginning the journey that might take him to the same destination as Big Al. As 1998–99 showed, this is a team on the rise, and the two backliners are spearheading it.

If you visit St. Louis to see a game, you'll also find a city that's unique in America. Perched on the banks of the Mississippi River, it retains its heritage as a frontier town. The Tom Sawyer and the Becky Thatcher, replicas of 19th century steamboats named after Mark Twain characters, carry tourists along the river regularly. You can even find a casino and a McDonald's floating on the water.

Laclede's Landing, named to honor the French trader who founded the town in 1764, is now an official Historic District featuring old, restored buildings. The downtown, once a seedy area, has improved markedly thanks to changes like this. St. Louis is also a corporate city, and at the head of that list stands Anheuser-Busch brewers. If you take a tour of the brewing plant, you'll pay nothing and receive a little free beer as well. The refreshment will serve you well, for the city is large and requires plenty of energy to explore.

Blues

Kiel Center

Where to sit:
There isn't a bad seat in the house, from the most expensive seats near center ice to the least expensive nosebleed end seats. The club seats are wider and more comfortable, and attendants cater to your drinking and dining needs. They go for $85 and $90.

If it's all you can get:
The so-called Ceiling Fan seats in the upper rows are the least expensive seats and sell out in a hurry, so you might have to settle for sitting just below them for between $15 (mezzanine high end) to $34 (mezzanine middle). The end seats in the lower bowl where the opposing team shoots twice are the last to be sold and cost $45.

Special services:
Kiel Center has areas set aside in all price ranges for wheelchair seating.

| $90 | $75 | $70 | $60 | $45 |
| $42 | $37 | $30 | $21 | $15 |

Capacity: 19,260

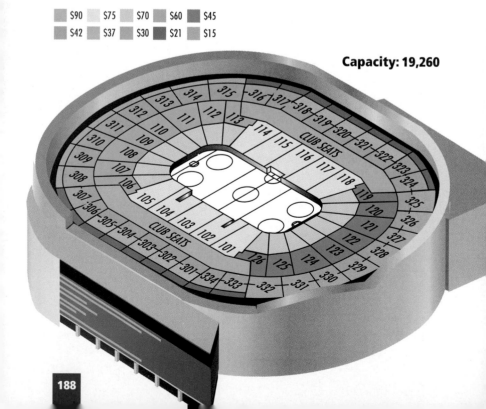

Ticket availability:
The Blues had 17 sellouts last season and averaged 95% attendance. Singles for Saturday night games sell in a heartbeat.

Parking:
There are limited spaces in the garage next to Kiel Center available at $9, but arrive early. Otherwise, there are many lots between Tucker Boulevard to the east and 18th Street and Union Station to the west. Prices range from $5 to $10.

Public transportation:
MetroLink (314-231-2345), the local commuter train, has a stop at Kiel Center, but the line is limited. You can take it from several spots downtown or from the airport.

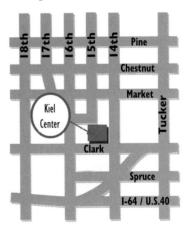

By car:
All the major interstate highways converge in the downtown area. From Illinois, cross the Poplar Street Bridge and exit at Ninth Street. Turn left onto Clark Avenue and follow it West to Kiel Center. From Highway 40 eastbound, exit at 14th Street, turn left and you're

Kiel Center

there. From eastbound I-44, northbound I-55 and eastbound I-70, take the downtown exit, proceed to Market Street (near Busch Stadium), take Market west to 14th Street, and turn left.

Cuisine:
There's something for almost every taste and palate, from the usual arena fare of burgers and hot dogs to pizza, chicken, pasta, and tacos. There also are two restaurants: the Kiel Club, for season-ticket and suite holders, and the new 14th and Clark next to the lobby for anyone with a ticket.

Home-ice advantage:
The Blues' crowd spontaneously breaks into cheers without much prompting from the scoreboard. The Blues keep that kind of stuff to a minimum—the game is the show.

Blues

Kiel Deal Opened:
10/8/94

First regular-season game:
1/26/95,
3–1 win over
Los Angeles

First goal:
Craig Johnson
of St. Louis

First playoff game:
5/7/95,
2–1 win over
Vancouver

Address:
1401 Clark Ave.,
St. Louis

For single-game tickets:
314-241-1888,
314-421-4400
or 618-222-2900

Website:
stlouisblues.com

Nightlife

Players' favorites:
Across from Union Station, **Maggie O'Brien's** (2000 Market St., 314-421-1388), a bar-restaurant with live music in the cozy back room, is favored by Blues alumni Bernie Federko, Greg Paslawski, and Rick Meagher. Players and coaches from visiting teams have also been known to frequent this spot. Blues players often show up at **Harry's** (2144 Market St., 314-421-6969), an upscale bar-restaurant that features live entertainment on weekends. The star of the game, though, will be at **Turvey's On The Green** (255 Union Blvd., 314-454-1667), where the Blues' postgame show on KMOX radio is hosted by Ken Wilson and Bernie Federko.

Blues

Getting away:
If you want to avoid the crowds near Kiel Center but stay near downtown, try **Laclede's Landing**, a bar-restaurant district just north of the Arch on the riverfront. **Planet Hollywood** (800 N. 3rd St., 314-588-1717), **Boomer's** (707 Clamorgan Alley, 314-621-8155), **Fat Tuesday** (700 N. 2nd St., 314-241-2008), **Hannegan's** (719 N. 2nd St., 314-241-8877), and **Mississippi Nights** (914 N. 1st St., 314-421-3853) cater to all tastes and styles. Players from visiting teams often show up in Laclede's Landing, or at AJ's (315 Chestnut St., 314-241-7400), the swingin' dance bar at the **Adam's Mark**. If you're feeling more adventurous,

travel 10 minutes west of downtown to **Blueberry Hill** (6504 Delmar Blvd., 314-727-0880). The St. Louis Walk of Fame, with stars and plaques honoring the city's legends, is outside Blueberry Hill, while inside, the famed Elvis Room offers fine live music.

Dining

For Italian:
The Hill, the Italian neighborhood that produced baseball legends Yogi Berra and Joe Garagiola, is home to the finest collection of Italian restaurants in St. Louis: **Dominic's** (5101 Wilson Ave., 314-231-0911), **Cunetto House of Pasta** (5453 Magnolia Ave., 314-781-1135), **Favazza's** (5201 Southwest Ave., 314-772-4454), **Gianpeppe's** (2126 Marconi St., 314-772-3303), and the upscale **Giovanni's On The Hill** (5201 Shaw Ave., 314-772-5958). During the NHL Entry Draft in St. Louis in 1996, former Blues general manager Ron Caron hosted a party for the Colorado Avalanche execs and their Stanley Cup at Dominic's. Two other popular spots on the Hill are **Bartolino's** (2524 Hampton Ave., 314-644-2266) where former Blue Doug Gilmour still dines on nearly every visit to St. Louis—even though he's been gone for over 10 years—and **Rigazzi's** (4945 Daggett Ave., 314-772-4900), home of the fishbowl beers, where former Blues' Italian heroes Paul and Gino Cavallini hung out in the late 1980s. There's a hat trick of excellent choices downtown. **Charlie**

Gitto's (207 N. 6th St., 314-436-2828) is a favorite hangout of Los Angeles Dodgers GM Tommy Lasorda, and **Kemoll's** (1 Metropolitan Sq., 314-421-0555) has family ties to KSDK sports anchor Frank Cusumano. But the best of the best is **Tony's** (410 Market St., 314-231-7007), a world-renowned five-star restaurant owned and operated by Vince Bommarito.

For steak:

If it's red meat you want, it's red meat you'll get at **Dierdorf & Hart's** (701 Market St., 314-421-1772), which is owned by football commentator Dan Dierdorf and Jim Hart, former teammates on the St. Louis Cardinals football team. St. Louis Cardinals baseball announcer Mike Shannon also has a steak place called, appropriately, **Mike Shannon's** (100 N. 7th St., 314-421-1540).

For trendy:

Look no further than the **Lynch Street Bistro** (1031 Lynch St., 314-772-5777) in the Soulard District just south of downtown, specializing in seafood. Or head to the Central West End, an entire district of trendiness with **Balaban's** (405 N. Euclid Ave., 314-361-8085), a player hangout, and **Dressel's** (419 N. Euclid Ave., 314-361-1060), an English pub.

Blues

Roman Turek #1

For ethnic:

You'll find Cajun-style seafood at the **Broadway Oyster Bar** (736 S. Broadway, 314-621-8811) just south of Busch Stadium. French cuisine can be had at **Cafe de France** (410 Olive St., 314-231-2204), while **Saleem's** (6501 Delmar Blvd., 314-721-7947) is the place to go for Lebanese food. **The Mandarin House** at Union Station (314-621-6888) offers authentic Peking and Szechuan cuisine. The **Magic Wok** (1 Maryland Plaza, 314-367-2626) is another popular destination for Chinese food in the Central West End.

Players' favorite:

If you're hoping for a player sighting among the lunchtime crowd, you'll have to travel west to Chesterfield to **Annie Gunn's** (16806 Chesterfield Airport Rd., 314-532-7684), right across Highway 40/I-64 from the Blues' practice facility, the U.S. Ice Sports Complex. It's a popular spot, so reservations are a must. Players also frequent **Carson's** (1712 S. 9th St., 314-436-2707) in the Soulard District, where the waitresses wear extra short shorts. It might not be politically correct, but this is one of the most popular lunch spots for St. Louis males.

Lodging

For luxury:

If you feel like putting on the Ritz, stay at the **Ritz-Carlton** (100 Carondelet Plaza, Clay-

ton, Mo., 314-863-6300, 800-241-3333), a mere 10 minutes west of downtown off Highway 40/I-64. The Great One, Wayne Gretzky, lived here during his three months with the team in 1996. This is a luxury hotel with all the amenities.

Close to the arena:

The **Hyatt at Union Station** (One St. Louis Union Station, 314-231-1234, 800-233-1234) is two blocks west of Kiel Center. The rehabbed train station has a variety of shops and restaurants. The beautiful hotel lobby is known for the famed whisper archway at the front door on Market Street where you can whisper sweet nothings to your loved one. For the budget-conscious, a **Hampton Inn** (2211 Market St., 314-241-3200) and a **Marriott** (2340 Market St., 314-241-9111) are also nearby.

Players' favorite:

The **Residence Inn** (1100 McMorrow Ave., 314-862-1900), which offers suites, has been the home away from home for a variety of Blues players over the last 10 years, mainly players called up from the minors or newcomers searching for permanent housing. Visiting teams often stay downtown at the **Hyatt at Union Station** or the **Adam's Mark** (315 Chestnut St., 314-241-7400).

Something special:

Downtown St. Louis features three delightful old hotels that have been lovingly renovated: **Omni Majestic** (1019 Pine St.,

Blues

314-436-2355), a high-end hotel not far from Kiel Center; **The Mayfair** (806 Saint Charles St., 314-421-2500) near the Trans World Dome; and **The Drury Inn at Union Station** (201 S. 20th St., 314-231-3900), a rehabbed railroad hotel.

Shopping & Attractions

There's plenty to do on the off days between Blues games in St. Louis, whether you want to play tourist, take in another sporting event or shop.

For shoppers, Union Station, the **Saint Louis Galleria** (I-64 & Brentwood Blvd., 314-863-6633) and **Plaza Frontenac** in Frontenac (Lindbergh

Blvd. and Clayton Rd., 314-432-0604) are among the choices to max out the credit cards.

The tourists in the crowd should start with the **Gateway Arch** (Memorial Dr. & Market St., 314-425-4465) on the riverfront. It commemorates the 19th century pioneers who traveled west using St. Louis as a jump-off point. The stainless steel arch stands 630 feet tall and was designed by Eero Saarinen. Take the tram ride to the top to get a bird's-eye view of downtown St. Louis and the muddy Mississippi River. The **Museum of Westward**

Blues

Pierre Turgeon #77

Expansion, as well as the **George B. Hartzog Visitor's Center**, are under the Arch.

West of downtown lies the beautiful **Forest Park**, site of the 1904 World's Fair. Forest Park covers 1,300 acres and includes hiking, biking, and jogging trails, two golf courses, tennis courts, as well as an outdoor ice rink and several of St. Louis' top attractions. There's the world-famous **St. Louis Zoo** (1 Government Dr., 314-781-0900) with more than 5,000 animals. There's the **St. Louis Art Museum on Art Hill** (1 Fine Arts Dr., 314-721-0072) , a popular sledding area in winter. The Museum served as the fine arts pavilion at the World's Fair and contains 30,000 works of art. There's also the popular **St. Louis Science Center** (5050 Oakland Ave., 314-289-4444), with its planetarium and IMAX theater.

The 79-acre **Missouri Botanical Garden** (4344 Shaw Blvd., 314-577-5100), southwest of downtown off I-44, was opened in 1859, and now holds Japanese, Chinese and Victorian gardens.

For sports nuts, St. Louis is also home to football's **Rams** (314-534-1111), baseball's **Cardinals** (314-421-3060), and soccer's **Ambush** (314-849-4625). The **International Bowling Museum** (111 Stadium Plaza, 314-231-6340), as well as the **Cardinals Hall of Fame Museum**, are across from Busch Stadium.

If you're into gambling, two major casinos are downtown. The **President Casino on the**

Blues

Admiral (314-622-1111) is on the Missouri side of the Mississippi River, near the Arch, while the **Casino Queen** (618-874-5000) is on the Illinois side, adjacent to a MetroLink stop.

If you're into culture, the world-renowned **St. Louis Symphony** performs from mid-September through mid-May at **Powell Symphony Hall** (718 N. Grand Blvd., 314-286-4148) in midtown, with the **Fabulous Fox Theatre** (527 N. Grand Blvd., 314-534-1678) and the **Sheldon Concert Hall** (3648 Washington Blvd., 314-533-9900) close by.

Favorite City on the Road

Something about the warm weather warms the hearts of St. Louis' Boys of Winter. They love the trips to the West Coast, where they usually take one or two extended trips a year. When the opponents are Los Angeles and Anaheim, the Blues usually set up shop at the Loews in Santa Monica. Captain Chris Pronger has a lot of friends in L.A., and he enjoys the city because there's so much to do. On a trip two years ago, former Blue Tony Twist rented rollerblades and skated to nearby Muscle Beach.

Hometowns also warm the players' hearts. Jim Campbell is partial to Boston, near his home Worcester, Mass. Turgeon, Marc Bergevin, and Pascal Rheaume are partial to Montreal, in their home province of Quebec. Goalie

Jamie McLennan calls Edmonton home. Former Blue Jamie Rivers is partial to Ottawa, where he gets to see family and friends, while Craig Conroy, an enthusiastic sort who always wears a smile, seems to like every place he travels. And finally, since country western music seems to be the music of choice in the Blues' locker room, particularly with boot-stomping tough guy Kelly Chase, the stop in Nashville this season will be a welcome respite.

Cool Fact

Being the son of fiery Hall of Famer Bobby Hull probably hurt Brett Hull early in his career. He was never able to satisfy the Calgary Flames, who thought he was unmotivated. But his 1988 trade to St. Louis for Rick Wamsley and Rob Ramage ended up being one of the most lopsided trades in NHL history. In Hull's first full six seasons in St. Louis, he reeled off 41, 72, 86, 70, 54, and 57 goals.

Franchise History

St. Louis was one of six cities awarded franchises on June 5, 1967. In its early years the Blues enjoyed the most success of those expansion teams, making it to the Stanley Cup Finals in the team's first three seasons, only to be swept aside four straight games each time. Although they have not since returned to the Finals, the Blues have remained a remarkably consistent team, failing to

make the playoffs only three times in their history. St. Louis has also had the distinction of seeing its famous Blue Note worn by some of the greatest hockey players of all time, including Wayne Gretzky, Brett Hull, Doug Gilmour, Glenn Anderson, Scott Stevens, Al MacInnis, Phil Housley, Barclay Plager, not to mention goalies Glenn Hall, Jacques Plante, Curtis Joseph and Grant Fuhr.

Blues

Famers

Most Valuable Player (Hart Trophy): Brett Hull, 1991.

Al MacInnis #2

Hockey Hall of Fame:

Players: Doug Harvey, 1973; Dickie Moore, 1974; Glenn Hall, 1975; Jacques Plante, 1978; Guy Lapointe, 1993; Peter Stastny, 1998, Wayne Gretzky, 1999.

Builders: Emile Francis, 1982; Scotty Bowman, 1991; Al Arbour, 1996.

Retired numbers: 3 Bob Gassoff, 8 Barclay Plager, 11 Brian Sutter, 24 Bernie Federko

S T

L O U I S

Blues

Pavol Demitra #38

Records

Games played		Most points, season		Most goalie wins, career	
Bernie Federko	927	Brett Hull	131	Mike Liut	152
Career goals		**Most goals, game**		**Most goalie wins, season**	
Brett Hull	527	Red Berenson	6	Curtis Joseph	36
Career assists		**Most assists, game**		**Most shutouts, career**	
Bernie Federko	721	Brian Sutter,		Glenn Hall	16
Career points		Bernie Federko,		**Most shutouts, season**	
Bernie Federko	1,073	Adam Oates	5	Glenn Hall	8
Most goals, season		**Most points, game**		**Stanley Cups:**	
Brett Hull	86	Red Berenson,		None	
Most assists, season		Garry Unger	7		
Adam Oates	90				

196

around the town with the
Sharks

Sharks

Gary Suter #20

Despite a shuffle of five coaches in seven seasons and a player roster with more turnovers than the cast of "Baywatch," the Sharks have increased their appeal to sports fans in San Jose. Does it seem ludicrous that a team could go eight years without finishing above .500 and still manage to record 118 consecutive sellouts in the process? Bay Area residents have so fallen in love with hockey that they gave their team a standing ovation after a 20-win season in 1995–96.

Before the Sharks began play in 1991–92, the Bay Area's pro sports action was always in San Francisco or Oakland. But the Sharks' arrival has rearranged the sports landscape: San Jose is now a player and the citizens of Silicon Valley have locked on to the Sharks with fierce pride. The devotion deepened in the team's third season, when the franchise left its temporary home in the dilapidated Cow Palace near San Francisco and moved into the downtown San Jose Arena. In their first season inside the "Shark Tank," the Sharks slipped into the playoffs. They then stunned the top-seeded Detroit Red Wings in the first round, thanks to the crafty play of two old Russians, Igor Larionov and Sergei Makarov, and a lovable little Latvian goalie named Arturs Irbe, whose personal mantra of "Like Wall" became a rallying cry among fans.

Silicon Valley's high-tech economy might have made San Jose—with its manageable downtown, mountain views, and up to 300 days of sunshine—a city for the millennium. But Sharks Fever helped downtown San Jose emerge as a viable option for nightlife. And even though the team slid back to Palookaville, fans' dedication never wavered. The 1995–96 season ended with a 6–0 loss to the Calgary Flames, yet fans rose as one and offered a standing ovation that left players puzzled. "The fans are for us no matter what," Irbe said then. "It is kind of crazy

Sharks because we don't deserve

it." But players take it to heart. When Jeff Friesen missed three games because of a contract impasse in 1997–98, one of his first reactions was "I hope this doesn't affect my relationship with the fans."

ESPN hockey analyst Bill Clement ranked San Jose Arena, which sits near the palm trees along the edge of Guadalupe River Park, second among his favorite arenas, behind only the old Maple Leaf Gardens in Toronto. "It's not just a spectator sport, it's a participatory event in the Shark Tank, so it's real exciting," Clement said.

Imagine how exciting it will be when the team finally has a Stanley Cup contender.

San Jose Arena

Where to sit:

The best seats in the "Shark Tank" are roughly 20 rows up in Section 101 or the first several rows of Section 201, which is in the upper bowl. From this vantage point, you are at center ice, above the benches for both teams.

■ $83	■ $73	■ $54	■ $49
■ $37	■ $32	■ $25	■ $17

Capacity: 17,483

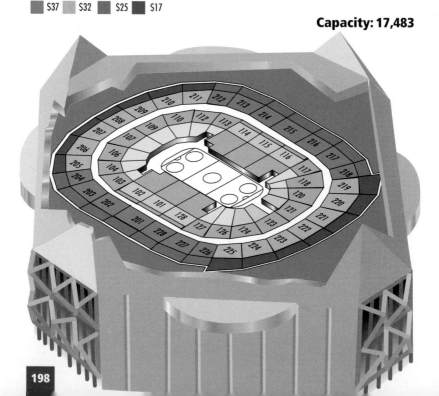

If it's all you can get:

The incline of the bowls is steep enough at the Tank that even seats high in the second bowl have somewhat of a "perch perspective."

Special services:

The Sharks offer seating to persons with disabilities on a full-season, partial-season, and single-game basis. Listening devices for the hearing-impaired are available at information booths.

Ticket availability:

Tough but not impossible. If the box office has nothing, check the classified ads in the San Jose Mercury News or haggle with a scalper. Scalping is legal in California as long as the

San Jose Arena

scalper charges face value.

Parking:

The lots immediately outside the arena charge as much as $10. Lot prices drop as you move away from the arena. Metered street parking downtown is free after 6 p.m.

Public transportation:

In California? Ha! Light Rail, a modern cable car system, is a convenient option in the downtown area and to certain segments of the city, but it is woefully lacking for the general population. An even smaller minority of people opt for the CalTrain, a commuter rail service that extends north to Palo Alto and San Francisco. Both trains have stops across the street from the Arena.

By car:

From freeway 101, get on 880, then take The Alameda exit. Proceed east on The Alameda, which after a half-mile curls left and becomes Santa Clara Street. If you're coming from Guadalupe Parkway (Route 87), either the Santa Clara Street or the Julian Street exits will lead to the Arena. From

Sharks

In "the Tank"

Opened:
9/8/93

First regular-season game:
10/14/93,
2–1 loss to Calgary

First goal:
Kip Miller of
San Jose

First playoff game:
4/22/94,
3–2 loss to Detroit

Address:
525 W. Santa Clara St.,
San Jose

For single-game tickets:
408-998-TIXS

Website:
sj-sharks.com

680 or 280, take Bird Street exit and turn north.

Cuisine:
Like all new arenas of the '90s, the Tank goes out of its way to offer something for everyone, and some picnic tables to boot.

Home-ice advantage:
The fan intensity is incredible. The Sharks could score midway through the third period to cut their deficit to 7–2 and the **Sharks** crowd reaction would be as if they announced beer was free for the rest of the night.

Nightlife

For after the game:
Henry's World Famous Hi-Life (301 Saint John St., 408-295-5414), two blocks from the Arena, is widely regarded as Sharks Central for post-game get-togethers of players and fans. Henry's should also rate high on the dining list for a pre-game meal. It specializes in steak and barbecue. Jeff Friesen and some of the younger Sharks have been spotted at **The Flying Pig Pub** (78 S. 1st St., 408-298-6710). Complete with a well-stocked jukebox, a fireplace, and a smoking patio, the Pig offers a party-like atmosphere, especially on weekends. Pub grub is available until 10 p.m., and if you drop in for dinner, the three-way, four-way, or five-way chili is recommended.

For a quiet drink:
The **Hedley Club** at the **De Anza Hotel** (233 W. Santa Clara St., 408-286-1000) allows you to relax in art deco surroundings, from the handpainted ceiling to the sculpted archways to the marble-and-cherrywood bar. The live jazz music and piano make a pleasant accompaniment to quiet conversation.

To spot players:
The **Mission Ale House** (97 E. Santa Clara St., 408-292-4058) has a back room that features a pool table and furniture and gives it the feel of a respectable frat house. Owen Nolan has been known to enjoy a game of pool here, and it is also a regular spot for visiting NHL players in quest of a post-game beer.

For live music:
Toons Piano Bar (52 E. Santa Clara St., 408-292-7464) appeals to a younger crowd. One-stop shopping is available at the **Agenda** (399 S. 1st St., 408-287-3991), which offers three levels of entertainment: jazz lounge, dance club, and restaurant.

Dining

For Italian:
Several Sharks have said **Bella Mia** (58 S. 1st St., 408-280-1993) is the place to take your date, and who are we to argue? Their pasta dishes and salads are delicious, and their desserts are huge. Many Sharks like to grab a bite before the game at **Original Joe's** (301 S. 1st St., 408-292-7030), a San Jose landmark for its hearty but not fancy Italian food. It's also a good postgame spot for fans because it serves dinner until 1 a.m.

Food and beer:

The garlic fries are a superb set-up to the entrees at **Gordon Biersch** (33 E. San Fernando St., 408-294-6785), a brewpub that also has several establishments across southern California. The restaurant offers a marvelous blend of California and international cuisines. Its beers are good but not great. Meanwhile, the beers at **Tied-House** (65 N. San Pedro St., 408-295-2739), have won medals at recent Great American Beer Festivals. A big-screen TV provides a nice view of the Sharks game if you can't snag tickets. The food is good. Locals are still waiting for them to combine their brewing forces with the Gordon Biersch kitchen to get the best of both worlds.

For seafood:

People have been coming to **Lou's Village** (1465 W. San Carlos St., 408-293-4570) for more than 50 years for its Maine lobster, clam chowder, and other seafood dishes. Another bonus: the restaurant provides a bus shuttle to the Tank for games, so you can avoid parking hassles.

Lodging

Close and classy:

The **De Anza Hotel** is a five-minute walk from the Tank, and many NHL teams stay there. The hotel is rated four stars because of its elegance. The penthouse suite features a fireplace, two balconies, a jacuzzi, steamroom, and wet bar. All rooms are attractively appointed and provide terry cloth bathrobes for guests. A fine Italian restaurant, **La Pastaia**, is inside, and the bar is a sight to behold.

For luxury:

Other NHL teams opt for the **Fairmont** (170 S. Market St., 408-998-1900, 800-527-4727), which overlooks the fountains of scenic Plaza de Cesar Chavez. The Fairmont has quality dining at the **Pagoda Chinese Restaurant** and the new and highly touted **The Grill on the Alley**. This is

Sharks

Mike Ricci #18

where NHL players and corporate bigwigs stayed during the 1997 All-Star Game, so expect to pay accordingly.

Close to the airport:

The **Doubletree** (2050 Gateway Pl., 408-453-4000, 800-547-8010) is on the doorstep of San Jose International Airport. It is a drive of 10–15 minutes to the Arena via Guadalupe Parkway. The rooms are spacious and comfortable, and the hotel has an espresso bar, a sushi bar, a nightclub, a quieter bar (called the **Quiet Bar**), and a restaurant featuring American cuisine and California wines.

Shopping & Attractions

San Jose tried to establish a shopping district near the Fairmont, but it didn't stick. So until the city tries again, your best bet is to head to the suburbs. Or better yet try Gilroy, a 30-minute drive on 101 South. It's famous for two things: being the garlic capital of the world (garlic ice cream is available during its annual summer Garlic Festival) and being home to a massive outlet shopping complex. If you're looking for Sharks' merchandise, the **Sharks Store** is on the ground floor of the arena and open during the day. In addition to carrying the latest lines of hockey fashion and accessories, the Sharks Store also offers used equipment, such as broken sticks and game-worn jerseys.

What's a trip to Silicon Valley without learning how a microchip actually works? The **Tech Museum of Innovation** (145 W. San Carlos St., 408-279-7150) is a peek at the

Mike Vernon #29

future as much as it is a collection of the past. Even longtime residents of the area are startled when told that San Jose is home to the **American Museum of Quilts** (110 Paseo de San Antonio, 408-971-0323) and the **Egyptian Museum and Planetarium** (1600 Park Ave., 408-947-3636), which is complete with mummies.

Favorite City on the Road

Chicago is definitely their kind of town. Coach Darryl Sutter was a Blackhawks draft pick, captain, assistant coach, and coach. Murray Craven, Bryan Marchment, and Stephane Matteau all played for the Blackhawks. Tony Granato is a native of nearby Downers Grove, Ill., and the story has often been told of how his parents' first date was a Blackhawks game at the late, lamented Chicago Stadium. Dinner at **Gino and Georgetti's steakhouse** is often on the itinerary. Toss in the fact that they have won at least one game in Chicago for five consecutive seasons and it's no wonder why the Sharks love that toddlin' town.

Cool Fact

Sharks coach Darryl Sutter has a reputation of being tough as nails. How tough? He cracked his skull and broke his shoulder in a Feb. 23, 1997, accident at his Alberta farm. He managed to get back to his house, spend 10 days in the hospital, and was back at work on his farm by mid-March. During a meeting

at Sutter's farm that summer, GM Dean Lombardi came away convinced that he should hire the former Chicago Blackhawks coach. "I remember sitting there with him, not even talking hockey, and it was just, 'This guy is a man's man, and if I'm going to war, it's going to be with this guy,'" Lombardi said.

Franchise History

Hockey is not new to the Bay Area. Minor league teams have played here since the 1930s, and in the 1967 NHL

Owen Nolan #11

expansion a franchise was granted to the Oakland Seals, which after struggling on the ice and at the gate for nine seasons left the state. The NHL approved San Jose for an expansion franchise on May 9, 1990. The prospects for NHL hockey in the Bay Area had dramatically changed in the 15 years since the Seals departed. San Jose fans quickly embraced their new team, especially when the Sharks made an unexpected playoff run in only their third season, upsetting number one seed in the Western Conference, the Detroit Red Wings. The Sharks then extended the Toronto Maple Leafs to seven games before finally losing. The franchise suffered some setbacks in subsequent seasons, but has made steady progress towards becoming a Stanley Cup contender.

Sharks

Jeff Friesen #39

Famers

Most Valuable Player (Hart Trophy): None
Hockey Hall of Fame: None
Retired numbers: None

Records

Games played		Most assists, season		Most goalie wins, career	
Jeff Friesen	366	Kelly Kisio	52	Arturs Irbe	57
Career goals		**Most points, season**		**Most goalie wins, season**	
Jeff Friesen	111	Kelly Kisio	78	Mike Vernon,	
Career assists		**Most goals, game**		Arturs Irbe	30
Jeff Friesen	142	Owen Nolan	4	**Most shutouts, career**	
Career points		**Most assists, game**		Mike Vernon	9
Jeff Friesen	253	Several players tied	4	**Most shutouts, season**	
Most goals, season		**Most points, game**		Mike Vernon	5
Owen Nolan,		Owen Nolan,		**Stanley Cups:**	
Jeff Friesen	31	Marco Sturm	5	None	

TAMPA BAY

Tampa Bay
LIGHTNING

around the town with the Lightning

Darcy Tucker #16

"Everyone said hockey would never work in Florida," said Phil Esposito after Tampa landed a franchise. "But I always believed. I never gave up faith." The Lightning have had some rough times, and Esposito is no longer managing the team he created, but hockey is certainly alive in the state. Now, with a completely new ownership and management, the team looks to bring back its fans and the winning ways it enjoyed in 1995–96.

There is a market for hockey in Tampa, as well as a host of other attractions. The area has steadily become more popular over the years to the point where it is a prime tourist destination.

If nature is your fascination, this is the place to be. At Crystal River, the wildlife refuge is a sanctuary for manatee, which hang out there throughout the hockey season. In Homosassa Springs, the state wildlife park holds the spectacular Spring of 10,000 Fish, which you study through a floating glass observatory. The highlight of Tampa's Florida Aquarium is the replica of a coral reef that fills an entire section. There are plenty of opportunities to explore nature on your own, too. Though Sarasota and Clearwater are crowded, the Manatee Coast and Caladesi Island State Park are quiet and unspoiled. Caladesi, off Dunedin, is one of the few undisturbed barrier islands in the region. For an experience that lets you stay in your car, simply drive across the Sunshine Skyway bridge in St. Petersburg and look down on the bay. The view is incredible.

With some promising youngsters like Pavel Kubina, Vincent Lecavalier and Dan Cloutier, the Lightning hope to turn a few eyes towards the Ice Palace as well.

Ice Palace

Where to sit:

The club seats in the latest round of arenas are hard to beat and the Ice Palace club seats are no different. You get private parking, waiter service, and a pretty comfortable seat. The club level is a little high (Level 4) and there are only 3,000 seats, but you also get a chance to enjoy a private bar/restaurant available only to club seat holders.

If it's all you can get:

There isn't a bad seat in the Ice Palace, but if you're looking for a cheap yet innovative way to watch a game, do as most scouts do: sit high in the corners. Former general manager Phil Esposito swore he'd rather sit there than anywhere else.

Special services:

Call 813-301-6500 for information.

Ticket availability:

As the team rebuilds, tickets are generally available. The Ice Palace holds 19,758 for hockey and, surprisingly, most of the available seats on a game-by-game basis are the cheaper, upper-level tickets. Scalping is illegal in Tampa, but then again, it hasn't been a seller's market for scalpers in Tampa. Over the past two seasons, unfortunately, the only time the Lightning comes close to a sell-out is when transplants to Florida line up to see either their former hometown New York Rangers, Boston Bruins, Pittsburgh Penguins, Philadelphia Flyers, or Detroit Red Wings. And even then, tickets

$125	$72	$60	$59
$44	$29	$21	$16

Capacity: 19,758

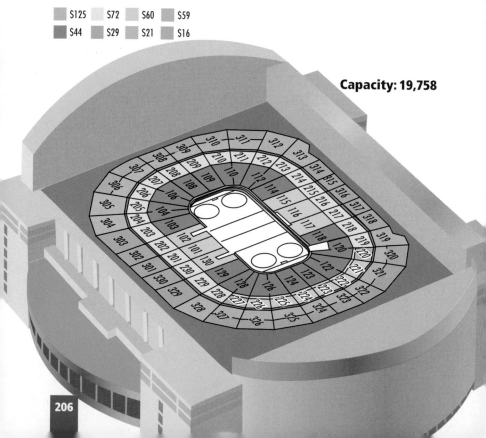

Ice Palace

service drops you off at the Ice Palace. Call 813-254-4278 for information.

were available through the opening faceoff.

Parking:
Official parking spots are $6, but your best bet is to find a private lot near the arena and hoof it. As it is, the city of Tampa owns most of the lots near the arena and you end up dishing out $6 anyway. There's a parking garage (also $6) that holds 1,500 cars, but half are reserved for club-seat holders. There are 10,000 spots available within three miles of the Ice Palace and a shuttle runs to those on the outer edge of the radius. The garage is nice when the weather is rough, but it's murder getting out after a game. The outer lots are your best bet.

By car:
The Ice Palace is at the corner of Channelside Drive and Morgan Street in Tampa. From Tampa International Airport, take I-275 north to exit 26 (Downtown East). Go south on Jefferson/Pierce to Whiting Street. Go west on Whiting Street to Morgan Street. Go south on Morgan Street to Channelside Drive.

Cuisine:
The Palace Club restaurant offers you fine dining and an upscale buffet.

Home-ice advantage:
Not yet. The Lightning averaged the lowest attendance in the league last year. The fans were quite vocal when the team made the playoffs in '96 (just ask the Flyers' Eric Lindros), so when the Lightning start winning again, the Palace should develop some energy.

Nightlife

For after the game:
Let traffic clear out and walk across the street to **Newks Cafe** (514 Channelside Dr., 813-307-6395). Newks is an indoor-outdoor bar and grill that's hopping two hours before the game and two hours after. A live band plays on game nights on the outside deck. And keep your eye out after the game. It's common to see more than a visiting player or two in

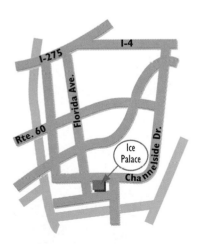

Public transportation:
Route 8 of the HARTline bus

addition to several Lightning players. Most Lightning players, though, choose to stay in-house and visit the club level inside the Ice Palace for a quiet drink and a sandwich. Other options within a five-minute walk from the Ice Palace include a pair of sports bars: **Hat Tricks** (107 S. Franklin St., 813-225-4288) and **Beef O'Brady's** (2819 S. Macdill Ave., 813-835-9464).

For a quiet drink:
During the Esposito years, Phil and Tony could usually be seen at **Bella's** (1413 S. Howard Ave., 813-254-3355). Here, you can order a half-priced calzone or pizza that will be as scrumptious as anything outside Sicily. Bella's is a late-night restaurant, never rowdy, always chic and classy.

Best pub:
Isn't it funny that the little holes in the wall are where all the hip people go? Go off the beaten path and find a little dive called **Red Dog Bar & Grill** (3311 W. Bay to Bay Blvd., 813-835-4347). Check your attitude at the door and enjoy everything a good pub should offer: cold beer, loud music from the coolest jukebox in town, and a variety of games such as pool tables, air hockey and darts.

To hear live music:
The younger Lightning players take a walk on the wild side by visiting **Ybor City**, located just a few miles from downtown Tampa. Ybor's 7th Avenue is legendary, offering everything from Gothic clubs to the jazz scene to authentic Cuban restaurants. Each club offers something different and all are enjoyable. Ybor gets ridiculously packed on the weekends, but going just to people-watch is well worth the trip. Seventh Avenue is closed to traffic on the weekends and the streets resemble the French Quarter on New Year's Eve. It's an experience not to be missed and you're bound to catch any type of music you want to hear.

To meet the opposite sex:
Occasionally you can catch one

Chris Gratton #77

of the single Lightning players drifting over to Hyde Park at a bar/grill called **Mangroves** (208 S. Howard Ave., 813-258-3302). And few places in this world are better to meet all kinds of people than Ybor City, especially on Friday and Saturday nights.

Dining

For steak:

We're not talking about the best steak in town—but the best in the world. Players and coaches around the league swear by **Bern's Steak House** (1208 S. Howard Ave., 813-251-2421). Check it out: the place raises its own cattle! It's pricey and you'll want to dress up and make a reservation, but you won't ever forget the place. If you don't think you can afford the dinner, then eat somewhere cheaper and hit Bern's dessert bar afterward. You can also get great steaks at **Ruth's Chris Steak House** (1700 N. West Shore Blvd., 813-282-1118) or **Shula's Steak House** (4860 W. Kennedy Blvd., 813-286-4366). Shula's puts a certificate on the wall if anyone can eat its giant steak in a specified amount of time. Look for the certificate bearing the name of the Stars' Mike Keane.

Best grouper sandwich:

You must try the **Hurricane Seafood Restaurant** (807 Gulf Way 727-360-9558) on St. Petersburg Beach. The place, once a little one-story shack that has turned into a three-story building, is legendary in these parts. It still has the deck

that faces the Gulf of Mexico and a fantastic view from anywhere inside as well. The best part? Shorts, sandals and a T-shirt are not only acceptable, but encouraged. So when you get here, jump in your rental car and ask the first local you see how to get to "the Hurricane." Believe us, anyone who has lived in Florida for a week can tell you how to get there.

Local cuisine:

There are 1,001 authentic Cuban restaurants in town and everyone around Tampa has a favorite. If you are traveling with someone who wants Cuban, but you'd rather not, try **Carmine's** (1802 E. 7th Ave., 813-248-3834) in Ybor City. It's reasonably priced and offers a wide variety. Try the steak milanesa or the baked ziti—it's the best in the city.

For barbecue:

There's an old house on the corner of Gandy and Bayshore in Tampa called **Kojak's House of Ribs** (2808 W. Gandy Blvd., 813-837-3774) that looks as if it's been transported from the middle of North Carolina. It doesn't look like much from

Lightning

Ice Palace Items
Opened:
10/20/96

First regular-season game:
10/20/96, 5–2 win over New York Rangers

First goal:
Brian Bradley of Tampa Bay

Address:
401 Channelside Dr., Tampa

For single-game tickets:
813-287-8844 or 813-301-6600

Website:
tampabaylightning.com

the outside—a dirt parking lot, an old wooden outside deck with picnic tables and a creaky screen door—but are you looking for a good-looking place or good ribs?

Lodging

For luxury:

The team plays in Tampa, but two of the most luxurious hotels in all of Florida are in St. Petersburg. If you're a beach person, there's no better place than the **Don Cesar Beach Resort and Spa** (3400 Gulf Blvd., 727-360-1881, 800-282-1116) located on St. Petersburg Beach. The huge pink resort is nestled against the Gulf of Mexico and offers all the luxuries of a five-star hotel. If you rather would look at water than swim in it, try the **Renaissance Vinoy Resort** (501 5th Ave. NE, 727-894-1000, 800-468-3571) in downtown St. Petersburg. The hotel overlooks Tampa Bay and is just a scenic five-minute walk from The Pier in St. Petersburg, the site of many shops, restaurants, and museums. Both hotels are just a 25-minute drive from the Ice Palace. The rooms are expensive, but call early and you have a good chance for a season special.

Close to the arena:

There are several hotels in downtown Tampa, including the **Marriott Westshore** (1001 N. West Shore Blvd., 813-287-2555), the **Hyatt Tampa** (2 Tampa City Center, 813-225-1234), the **Hyatt Westshore**

(6200 W. Courtney Campbell Causeway, 813-874-1234), and the **Wyndham West Shore** (4860 W. Kennedy Blvd., 813-286-4400). The closest hotel to the Ice Palace is the **Wyndham Harbour Island Hotel** (725 S. Harbour Island Blvd., 813-229-5000, 800-822-4200), a swanky and convenient place where most of the visiting teams stay. A two-minute walk to the Ice Palace, it's located on a tiny island along with some intriguing shops and dining spots.

Hit the beach:

What's the point of going to Florida if you don't get a tan and return as the envy of all your co-workers back up north? There's a zillion places to stay along Florida's Gulf Coast that still put you within a 40-minute

Vincent Lecavalier #4

drive of a Lightning game.

Shopping & Attractions

Hyde Park, just on the outskirts of downtown, offers a few upscale shops and dining spots and is a good way to spend a nice afternoon. But Florida has to be the mall capital of the world. There are eight major malls in Pinellas and Hillsborough Counties and that's where most of the people go. After all, they're air-conditioned, something you can't beat on a typical Florida day.

If you're a hockey fan, and the spouse and kids are bugging you about taking a family vacation, there's no better winter getaway in the league than Tampa Bay. Here's how you do it: fly into Tampa, spend a night and catch a Lightning game at the Ice Palace. The next morning, get up and make the 80-minute drive to Orlando and **Walt Disney World** (407-WDISNEY). Take a few days and visit the Magic Kingdom, Disney/MGM Studios, Epcot Center and the new Animal Kingdom. Also right there is **Universal Studios** (407-363-8000) and **Sea World** (407-351-3600). Visit all of them while staying in one of the many Disney resorts. Then make the short drive back to Tampa, catch another Lightning game before giving into the family again with a day's visit to **Busch Gardens** in Tampa (3605 E. Bougainvillea Ave., 813-987-5209). Busch Gardens exhibits one of the most impressive African animal kingdoms in the country, as

well as rides and rollercoasters in a state-of-the-art theme park. Mix in a round or two or golf, a trip to the beach and another Lightning game and you have a vacation that everyone can enjoy.

Favorite City on the Road

No offense to Motown, but not many hockey players pick Detroit as their favorite NHL city. But former Tampa Bay's Brent Peterson does. Why? Maybe it has something to do with the fact that he went to Michigan Tech. (Plus, Detroit gets a thumbs up for good hockey and a fantastic restaurant called Fishbone's.)

In the NHL, familiarity breeds love. That's why it's not surprising that assistant coach John Cullen lists Toronto as his favorite NHL city and Boston, where he played college hockey, as his second choice.

For several Lightning players Washington has become the newest NHL hotspot. For years, the Capitals played in Landover, Md., and visiting teams usually stayed in Greenbelt. Talk about nothing to do. It was the one spot in the NHL where curfews were never broken. Now the Caps have moved to the MCI Center, down the street from Bill Clinton's place. If you're an intellect like ex-Lightning Cory Cross, you love the museums and historical landmarks. If you're ex-Lightning Rob Zamuner, you love the tours of the White House (especially the special ones

given to NHL celebrities). And if you're like practically every player in hockey, you love club-hopping in Georgetown. A little some-thin' for everyone.

Cool Fact

Vincent Lecavalier, top pick in the 1998 draft, was described in juniors as the best prospect out of Quebec since Mario Lemieux. Former owner Art Williams said he had the potential to be the "Michael Jordan of the NHL." The Lightning hockey brass are being more reserved and will bring him along slowly, but they were keenly interested in him. They traded Bryan Marchment to San Jose in March to ensure they had a chance to pick Lecavalier in June.

Franchise History

Andrei Zyuzin #30   Tampa Bay was granted a franchise on December 16, 1991, and began play in the 1992–93 season. Although the Lightning have reached the playoffs only once, they made it a memorable event, taking a lead in the opening series against the Philadelphia Flyers before losing in six games. In game four the Lightning set an all-time NHL attendance record of 28,183.

Famers

Most Valuable Player (Hart Trophy): None
Hockey Hall of Fame: None
Retired numbers: None

Records

Games played		Most points, season		Most goalie wins, season	
Rob Zamuner	475	Brian Bradley	86		
Career goals		**Most goals, game**		Daren Puppa	29
Brian Bradley	111	Chris Kontos	4	**Most shutouts, career**	
Career assists		**Most assists, game**		Daren Puppa 12	
Brian Bradley	189	Joe Reekie,		**Most shutouts, season**	
Career points		Marc Bureau	4	Daren Puppa	5
Brian Bradley	300	**Most points, game**		**Stanley Cups:**	
Most goals, season		Doug Crossman	6	None	
Brian Bradley	42	**Most goalie wins, career**			
Most assists, season					
Brian Bradley	56	Daren Puppa	76		

The "T A M P A B A Y" text appears vertically along the right margin.

T O R O N T O

around the town with the
Maple Leafs

Bryan Berard #34

Armed with the most loyal fans in hockey, the Maple Leafs survived long dry spells until they bloomed again in 1998–99. The team that couldn't score was suddenly scoring; the team that couldn't skate was skating rings around opponents. It was a joyful renaissance and a memorable way to debut the new Air Canada Centre.

In the Leafs' glory years—through the late 1960s—staid Toronto reflected the character of its team. While Montreal won Cups with firewagon hockey, elan, and emotional fans, the conservative Leafs finished first just twice in 60 years, winning their share of titles with great defense and hard work. The spotless Gardens galleries were a sea of bland suits and ties and well-heeled ladies, most of whom would applaud politely rather than passionately. You couldn't buy a beer at the game, Sunday sports matches were outlawed for years, and fans were expected to be as dignified as Queen Elizabeth II, whose portrait dominated the south end of the Gardens. Season-ticket holders even received curt letters from management urging them to keep a proper dress code. When ushers told screaming teens to sit down during concerts by Elvis and the Beatles, they sat.

But "Hogtown," Canada's largest city, learned to swing in the late 1960s. Unfortunately, it was about the same time that the hockey team stopped collecting silver. Confident in its role as the nation's economic engine, roused by an influx of diverse culture, and eager to show it could compete with American rivals such as New York and Chicago, Toronto became adventurous and let down its collective hair. The same streets that had rolled up on the weekends boasted 5,000 restaurants and nightclubs by the 1990s, representing 100 different cultures. A few years ago, last call for alcohol was moved back to 2 a.m., ending a decades-long debate. Clearly, Toronto is living up to its name, a Huron Indian word for "meeting place."

As Toronto has changed, so too have the Leafs. They found success last season by playing attacking, high-risk hockey. The fans enjoyed it: not only in Toronto, but across Canada, where the Leafs are more popular than any other club. The city was so excited by the Leafs' semi-final finish in 1999 that they held a parade, but president Ken Dryden says the next time a parade happens, it will only be for a champion.

Air Canada Centre

Where to sit:

There isn't a bad seat in the house with the last row of the purples closer to the ice than a comparable seat in the Gardens. A sports bar overlooks the ice at the upper level. The most luxurious seats are the 1,500 seats in the Platinum club. They're in the first nine rows and feature in-your-seat service and access to special lounges. They will fetch $115 Cdn. each.

Special services:

1% of the seats are specially priced for the disabled.

Ticket availability:

A hike in prices has made no difference: the Leafs are still the toughest ticket in Canada and one of the toughest in the NHL. Single-game tickets can be bought well in advance, however. You can find scalpers

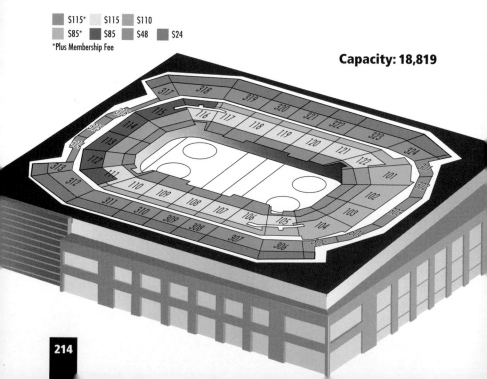

| $115* | $115 | $110 |
| $85* | $85 | $48 | $24 |

*Plus Membership Fee

Capacity: 18,819

advertising tickets in the classifieds or brazenly standing near the arena.

Parking:
There are 13,000 parking spaces within a 10-minute walk of the Centre, as well as 15 major hotels. Some lots will jack prices on game nights.

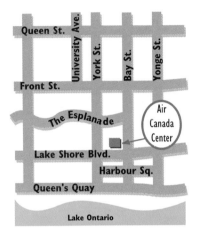

Public transportation:
To get to Air Canada Centre by TTC/GO train, get off at Union Station, exit on Bay Street and walk south two minutes. The Bay Street bus runs through the hotel and financial district and stops at the door. A direct underground link between Union Station and the arena is near completion.

Air Canada Centre

By car:
Exit Gardiner at Yonge St., go one block west along Lake Shore Blvd.

Cuisine:
The food court is built along a theme, resembling Toronto's St. Lawrence Market, which features a wide variety of ethnic food.

Home-ice advantage:
The Gardens had a uniquely intimate feel that can't be duplicated. On the other hand, this is still Toronto, where the fans back their team no matter what happens. They are loud and knowledgeable.

Nightlife

For after the game:
Superb food and drink are found at **Wayne Gretzky's** (99 Blue Jays Way, 416-348-0099), stocked with memorabilia of the Great One's career. There is lots of great people-watching on the terrace of the **Hard Rock Cafe** (283 Yonge St., 416-362 3636). Visiting teams, player agents and other hockey intelligentsia frequent **The Madison** (14 Madison Ave., 416-927-1722), the city's best pub.

Maple Leafs	
At the ACC Opened:	2/20/99
First regular-season game:	2/20/99, 3-2 win over Montréal
First playoff game:	4/22/99, 3-0 win loss to Philadelphia
First goal:	Todd Warriner of Toronto
Address:	40 Bay St., Toronto
Box Office Phone:	416-872-5000
Website:	torontomapleleafs.com

Located on a sidestreet right next to busy Bloor Street, the

Madison has two floors and a basement. You can have a private talk in a basement booth, go upstairs to play pool among the crowds or go out on the deck if it's warm. The food is solid and there are televisions scattered throughout the spacious building. More than anything, the place has a unique mood that will draw you back again and again. The **Pump House** (3395 American Dr., 905-671-3721) is a favorite Mississauga stop for the players living in the Western suburbs.

For a quiet drink:

Ex-Leaf Rob Zettler recommends **C'est What** (67 Front St. East, 416-867-9499), open late with eclectic music. Nearby is the **Down Under** (49 Wellington St. East, 416-362-6452), beneath Toronto's picturesque and historic Flatiron Building. Also try the **Acme Bar and Grill** (86 John St., 416-340-9700), **Scotland Yard** (56 Esplanade, 416-364-6572), and the pizzas at **Rockit** (120 Church St., 416-947-9555). English style pubs near the Gardens include the **Artful Dodger** (12 Isabella St., 416-964-9511).

To hear live music:

Mats Sundin often checks out The **Phoenix Club** (410 Sherbourne St., 416-323-1251). **Montana Cafe** (145 John St., 416-595-5949) is a good place to catch local blues legend Paul James. **Bamboo** (312 Queen St. West, 416-593-5771) is a great

summer spot and the gateway to vibrant Queen St. West.

To meet the opposite sex:

Al Frisco's (133 John St., 416-595-8201) and **Alice Fazooli's** (294 Adelaide St. West, 416-979-1910) have great food and lounges, part of a large concentration of restaurants and bars that border the Air Canada Centre and SkyDome. Also try **Crocodile Rock** (240 Adelaide St. West, 416-599-9751) and Vinnie's (22 Duncan St., 416-979-5565).

Dining

Player favorites:

The Kit Kat Italian Bar and Grill (297 King St. West, 416-977-4461) serves big portions and the kitchen is built around a

Sergei Berezin #94

huge leafy tree. It's considered lucky to kiss the tree, which Kris King did two seasons ago before scoring a rare goal the next night. **Centro Grill and Wine Bar** (2472 Yonge St., 416-483-2211) is well worth leaving the downtown core, according to Tie Domi and King. Retired Leaf Nick Kypreos loves the nouveau Thai food at **Shark City** (117 Eglinton Ave. East, 416-488-7899). "The food is good and spicy, there's ample wine, and a cigar bar," Kypreos says, "and afterwards, I usually kick Mats Sundin's butt on the pool tables downstairs."

Best ethnic:

Players say the best way to enjoy the cornucopia of restaurants in Toronto is to experience them in the distinct neighborhoods where they flourish. Start at the St. Lawrence Market area (Jarvis St. and Front St. East), where you can get everything from pizza, tangy barbecued chicken, or schnitzel on the run to the big deli sandwiches at the renowned **Shopsy's** (33 Yonge St., 416-365-3333). Lively Greektown, in the East End, is a short drive or TTC ride from downtown. Among the gems are the **Pantheon** (407 Danforth Ave., 416-778-1929) with its excellent dips, and the trendy **Pan** (516 Danforth Ave., 416-466-8158). Chinatown West (Dundas St. West between Bay and Spadina) has every conceivable Asian cuisine.

With three huge and distinct Italian neighborhoods in Toronto, you can't go wrong with their charming cafes and

traditional fare. For a taste of the Caribbean, there's **The Real Jerk** (709 Queen St. East, 416-463-6055). The top Cajun house is **Southern Accent** (595 Markham St., 416-536-3211). A French delight is **Le Papillon** (16 Church St., 416-363-0838). If you like Indian food stay on the streetcar east past the Gardens and get off at the Indian Bazaar, concentrated between Greenwood and Coxwell on Gerrard Street East. Other enclaves with outstanding local food are Portugal Village, Little Poland, and Koreatown, all in the West End.

Maple Leafs

Best steaks:

Barberian's (7 Elm St., 416-597-0335) has been a team favorite for three decades.

Family restaurants:

King takes his brood to **Movenpick** (133 Yorkville, 416-926-9545). For breakfast, former Leaf Rob Zettler loaded up at **The Senator** (249 Victoria St., 416-364-7517). The **Golden Griddle** (45 Carlton St., 416-977-5044) draws big crowds during Sunday junior hockey games across the street at the Gardens.

Lodging

For luxury:

The **Royal York** (100 Front St. West, 416-368-2511), opposite Union Station, is the city's most regal hotel, where the Original Six teams came by train and stayed when playing the Leafs. "If it was good enough for Queen Elizabeth, it's good enough for King Nick," ex-winger Nick Kypreos

says. Kris King likes its plush carpets, chandeliers, and spiral staircases. It will likely become a popular stop again for teams visiting the Air Canada Centre. Some of the more well-to-do clubs still make use of the **King Edward** (37 King St. East, 416-863-9700) near historic St. Lawrence Market. The **Crowne Plaza Toronto Centre** (225 Front St. West, 416-597-1400) adjoins the Convention Centre, which is in turn a short walk from the Leafs arena.

Player favorite:

Almost all of the Leafs have been to the **Westin Harbour Castle** (1 Harbour Sq., 416-869-1600), either with visiting clubs or for team functions. King likes the long, lavishly decorated corridor and Rob Zettler enjoyed the view of Lake Ontario and the boats, which putter around the docks near the hotel or in and around the Toronto Islands. It'll be an even more popular stop now that the Air Canada Centre is just a few blocks away.

Other options:

The moderately priced **Days Inn Downtown** (30 Carlton, 416-977-6655) is literally on the other side of the wall of the Gardens and has a pleasant street-level restaurant. There was once a plan for the Leafs to buy the hotel, demolish the wall and expand the Gardens to a 20,000-seat arena that would

run east-west as its original blueprints called for. Two other downtown establishments are **Sutton Place** (955 Bay St., 416-924-9221), where Zettler appreciated the fine service, and the **Delta Chelsea** (33 Gerrard St. West, 416-595-1975), which is handy to Yonge Street and a favorite of King's. A recent addition is the **Marriott** (525 Bay St., 416-597-9200), attached to the downtown indoor mall and the PATH system of underground shopping and sightseeing.

Mats Sundin #3

Shopping & Attractions

It's not the incredible number of world-class sites that make Toronto such a tourist favorite, but that you can get to almost all of them downtown by underground. PATH is six miles of interconnected passageways in the downtown core and home to more than 1,000 retail stores below ground. The theatre district is now considered the third most important for live performances in the English-speaking world. **Nathan Phillips Square** at City Hall has an ice rink in the winter. **The Beaches**, a 15-minute ride east on the 501 streetcar, brings you to an eclectic group of shops, restaurants, and fine old homes, centered around Kew Beach and just a block from the famous boardwalk. Fashionable **Yorkville** is just to the north of the Gardens. The one-time bastion of flower power is now the most chic shopping district in the city. **Queen Street West**, dominated by the ultra-cool CITY-TV building, has a great blend of shops and is home to many dance clubs. **The Annex**, which borders the beautiful University of Toronto campus, is a great walking and shopping area.

You'll be able to walk from the Air Canada Centre through Union Station to the **Hockey Hall of Fame** (30 Yonge St., 416-360-7735). The old stained-glass domed bank building contains the Bell Great Hall and the World of Hockey exhibit.

People have been picnicking on the Toronto Islands since the 1800s and a ferry boat ride for a couple of dollars affords an amazing view of the skyline. The ferry terminal is at the foot of **Bay Street**. The Islands have bike paths, an amusement park, and bathing areas. **CN Tower** (301 Front St. West, 416-868-6937), with its glass elevators and bird's-eye view is the city's best observation post.

Ontario Place (955 Lakeshore Blvd. West, 416-314-9900), home of the Molson Amphitheatre and the Cinesphere movie house, is a chain of man-made islands with an innovative children's activity village. Adults will get more out of **Harborfront** (235 Queen's Quay W., 416-973-3000), which has several upscale stores, several restaurants, and a bustling antique market.

Maple Leafs

Favorite City on the Road

Perhaps it's because it's also a great city by a Great Lake—Chicago is still the No. 1 choice of most Leafs. "You go along that (Magnificent Mile) and you feel like a million bucks," Tie Domi says. "We love staying at the **Drake Hotel**. It all just feels so old, so comfortable." Unfortunately, the Leafs changed conferences in 1998-99 and they will visit Chicago just once every two years.

Mats Sundin is very much at ease in Vancouver. The Leafs stay at the **Westin Bayshore** and like to stroll **Stanley Park** after practice and dine at **Joe Forte's** or **The Cannery**. Now that they are back in the East, many Leafs have expressed a desire to rediscover New York.

About a quarter of the team played there for either the Rangers, Islanders, and Devils. "I've played there and I've played in Winnipeg," Domi notes. "As far as I'm concerned, people are as nice in both places."

Cool Fact

The Maple Leafs have two of the top playing-with-pain playoff legends. Bobby Baun scored in overtime of Game 6 of the 1964 Finals despite breaking his leg earlier in the game. He then played in a 4–0 win in Game 7 in excruciating pain. Only after that game did he consent to an X-ray. Thirty years later, Doug Gilmour managed 28 points in 18 playoff games despite an injury that required his foot "to be frozen every time he put his skates on," then-teammate Ken Baumgartner said. Gilmour had surgery right after the season.

Franchise History

Toronto is a charter member of the National Hockey League, awarded a franchise on November 22, 1917. With 13 Stanley Cup Championships to their credit, the Maple Leafs are the rival of the Montreal Canadiens in accomplishment and legacy. Toronto was known as the Arenas when it won the first Stanley Cup in the league's inaugural season. The franchise then promptly withdrew from the league and returned a year

later as the St. Patricks. It was not until 1927 that the team became known as the Toronto Maple Leafs and its famous blue and white uniform colors replaced the green and white of the St. Pats. Meanwhile Foster Hewitt had pioneered the use of radio to broadcast Toronto games, creating a mass following for the team and prompting owner Conn Smythe to build legendary Maple Leaf Gardens. What was called "Smythe's folly" turned out to be Symthe's vision. Playing to overflow crowds in the Garden, the Leafs would boast powerhouse clubs in both the 1940s and early 1960s, hoisting the Stanley Cup ten times in that span. Legends such as Johnny Bower, King Clancy, Tim Horton, Charlie Conacher and Syl Apps have proudly worn the Toronto colors.

Famers

Most Valuable Player (Hart Trophy): Walter "Babe" Pratt, 1944; Walter "Babe" Pratt, 1945; Ted Kennedy, 1955

**Hockey Hall of Fame:
Players:** King Clancy, 1958; Jack Adams, 1959; Syl Apps, Charlie Conacher, Clarence "Hap" Day, George Hainsworth, 1961; Harry Cameron, Rusty Crawford, Reg Noble, David "Sweeney" Schriner, 1962; Joe Primeau, 1963; Red Horner, Syd Howe, 1965; Max Bentley, Ted Kennedy, Walter "Babe" Pratt, 1966; Turk Broda, 1967; Red Kelly, 1969; Cecil "Babe" Dye, 1970; Harvey Jackson, Terry Sawchuk, 1971; Harry Holmes,

T
O
R
O
N
T
O

1972; Dickie Moore, 1974; George Armstrong, Ace Bailey, Gord Drillon, Pierre Pilote, 1975; Johnny Bower, 1976; Tim Horton, 1977; Andy Bathgate, Jacques Plante, Marcel Pronovost, 1978; Harry Lumley, 1980; Allan Stanley, Frank Mahovlich, 1981; Norm Ullman, 1982; Bernie Parent, 1984; Gerry Cheevers, Bert Olmstead, 1985; Leo Boivin, Dave Keon, 1986; Darryl Sittler, 1989; Fern Flaman, 1990; Bob Pulford, 1991; Lanny McDonald, 1992; Harry Watson, 1994; Borje Salming, 1996.

Builders: Conn Smythe, 1958; Frank Selke, 1960; Foster Hewitt, 1965; Harold Ballard, 1977; J.P. Bickell, 1978; Punch Imlach, 1984; Norman "Bud" Poile, 1990.

Retired numbers: 5 Bill Barilko, 6 Ace Bailey

Honored numbers: 1 Turk Broda, Johnny Bower, 7 Francis "King" Clancy, Tim Horton, 9 Ted Kennedy, Charlie Conacher, 10 Syl Apps, George Armstrong

Maple Leafs

Jonas Hoglund #14

Records

Games played
George Armstrong 1,187

Career goals
Darryl Sittler 389

Career assists
Borje Salming 620

Career points
Darryl Sittler 916

Most goals, season
Rick Vaive 54

Most assists, season
Doug Gilmour 95

Most points, season
Doug Gilmour 127

Most goals, game
Corb Denneny,
Darryl Sittler 6

Most assists, game
Walter "Babe" Pratt,
Doug Gilmour 6

Most points, game
Darryl Sittler 10

Most goalie wins, career
Turk Broda 302

Most goalie wins, season
Curtis Joseph 35

Most shutouts, career
Turk Broda 62

Most shutouts, season
Harry Lumley 13

Stanley Cups:
1918, 1922, 1932, 1942, 1945, 1947, 1948, 1949, 1951, 1962, 1963, 1964, 1967.

Canucks

Mark Messier #11

around the town with the
Canucks

Vancouver hardly seems like a Canadian hockey city. With its warm Pacific climate and its abundance of leisure activities, the town feels more like a resort. Yet if you turn on local sports radio, you'll hear them talking about the Canucks in July. The team is undergoing a wide rebuilding program, but attendance in 1998–99 averaged close to 16,000. That's all you need to know that the Canucks hold a firm place in Vancouver's heart.

If you were to pick one city in Canada to see a game in, Vancouver would be the right choice. It is stunningly beautiful in places—it even has its own wilderness area, Stanley Park, which holds the top-flight Vancouver Aquarium. Speaking of flight, Stanley's Prospect Point is home to cormorants and herons. Appropriately, the park is named after Lord Stanley, the same man who donated the Cup to hockey. From the park to the University of B.C., the shore is almost entirely composed of beaches, so you can take your pick. Some have lifeguards, others street performers and artists.

Vancouver is very much a collection of distinct neighborhoods. Chinatown dates back to the mid-1800s, and its architecture is patterned after that of Canton. In Yaletown, once a warehouse district, high-quality restaurants and art galleries now flourish. Kitsilano is a fascinating, quiet place with mansions and upscale shops leading down to a popular beach, while downtown is characterized by old landmarks like the Marine Building, not to mention Robson Square, the site of many speeches and protests. Vancouver may seem laid-back, but protests are common in the area, which has a reputation for civil dissent unequaled in other parts of Canada.

For a taste of the mountains, look no further than North Vancouver and Lynn Canyon Park, a rainforest with waterfalls and a suspension bridge over the canyon. It's this variety and beauty that has convinced people like actor Robert Redford and basketballer Hakeem Olajuwon to buy homes here. It is an exciting home for hockey players too, even when their team is rebuilding.

General Motors Place

Where to sit:
Waiter service is available in the club seats, but these are available only to season-ticket holders. As with most arenas, it's best to sit in the upper seats of the lower bowl. Try to avoid sitting too low in the corners or your view of the other end will be distorted by the glass.

If it's all you can get:

Canucks

There are no bad seats in the house. The building is steep and seats are closer to the ice than in some new arenas, so sitting high up isn't a problem.

Special services:
There are spots for 80 wheelchairs. For help, call the ticket information office at 604-899-4625.

Ticket availability:
Because the team is rebuilding, attendance is off lately, so it's not hard to find tickets. The exception is games against Montreal and Toronto, teams

$100	$74	$65	$56.50
$37	$36.20	$27.25	$51
$65 Restaurant View Seats	♿		

Capacity: 18,422

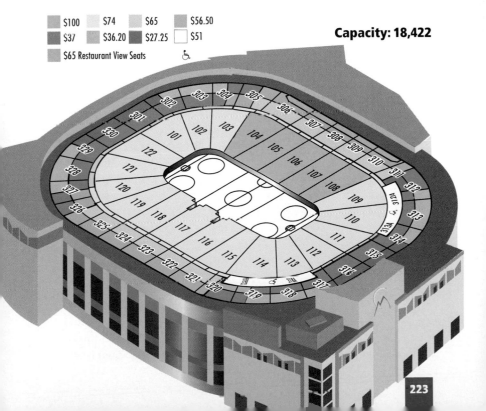

223

which have a lot of local fans after watching decades of Hockey Night in Canada before the Canucks came to town.

General Motors Place

Canucks

Parking:
There are 565 on-site parking spots with an additional 14,000 within a 15-minute walk.

Public transportation:
SkyTrain, Vancouver's above-ground subway, lets fans off at the door at the Stadium stop. You can use a transfer for city buses.

By car:
From the airport, go over the Arthur Lane Bridge, take the Marine East exit and turn left on Cambie. Follow Cambie four miles and cross the Cambie Street Bridge. GM Place will be on your right.

Cuisine:
On the concourse levels, it's the usual between-periods fare: pizza, burgers, smokies, Starbucks coffee, beer, soft drinks. There are three restaurants, including the Orca Bay Grille,

which has 110 seats with a view.

Home-ice advantage:
As the team rebuilds, expect the fans to return to their vocal ways.

Nightlife

Downtown Vancouver—which consists of Gastown, the West End, Coal Harbour, False Creek and Yaletown neighbour-hoods—is home to about 150,000 people, so there's a vibrant, safe downtown that's filled with bars and nightclubs catering to every taste.

For after the game:
If standing elbow-to-elbow, chatting up the opposite sex is how you want to spend the night, check out the **Shark Club** (180 Georgia St., 604-687-4275) at the Sandman Inn or **The Roxy** (932 Granville St., 604-331-7999). Both are pop-ular postgame hangouts for players, with The Roxy particu-larly popular with visiting teams. Expect house bands doing covers. **Richards on Richards** (1036 Richards St., 604-687-6794) has been a post-game spot for years and, yes, you're likely to spot a player or two.

Sonar (66 Water St., 604-683-6695) in Gastown is a

good place to dance to progressive house, dub, and tribal tunes. **Mars** (1320 Richards St., 604-662-7707) has a garden and a tight sound system.

For watching a game:

If you can't get inside GM Place, there are several good places to watch the game. **Courtnalls Sports Grill** (118 Robson, 604-683-7060) is run by NHLers Geoff and Russ. The walls are lined with autographed memorabilia and the TV plays lots of sports. Donald Brashear lives nearby and stops in for an occasional beer after games.

For a quiet drink:

Bar None (1222 Hamilton St., 604-689-7000) has a hectic singles bar upstairs and a more sedate cigar bar downstairs. Rumor has it Mark Messier has his own cigar locker there. There are plenty of good brew pubs. Ex-Canuck Jamie Huscroft likes the Yaletown area and its **Yaletown Brewing** Co. (1111 Mainland, 604-681-2739). "We go down there, walk around a bit, have some lunch. It's nice there—pretty casual." Former Canuck Steve Staios likes **Fred's Uptown Tavern** (1006 Granville, 604-605-4350). "It's busy but more relaxed. It's not a dance club. It's more my style."

Dining

Vancouver is a city of widely diverse dining options and it's not surprising that the Canucks—veterans and rookies alike—have had fun sampling the city's options.

Platinum-plus plates:

There are lots of places where you might see a Canuck or an actor working on one of the many movies or television shows being shot at "Hollywood North." **Mangiamo** (1116 Mainland, 604-687-1116) in Yaletown near GM Place is, as the name would indicate, an Italian trattoria. It's a popular haunt of Mark Messier because he can eat there in relative peace. It has an extensive Old World wine list. Try the quail and pasta. Nearby **Century Grill** (1095 Hamilton Street, 604-688-8088) is also a favorite of the Canucks "Millionaires' Row"— Alexander Mogilny and Messier. It features great steaks, big drinks, and an oyster bar. **Cardero's** (1583 Coal Harbour Quay, 604-669-7666), near the Westin Bayshore, is a little more laid back but gets top marks for the view and the fish. Ex-coach Mike Keenan is a fan. Players also like **Joe Fortes** (777 Thurlow St., 604-669-1940),

Canucks	
Inside "the Garage" Opened:	9/17/95
First regular-season game:	10/9/95, 5–3 loss to Detroit
First goal:	Steve Yzerman of Detroit
First playoff game:	4/20/96, 4–0 loss to Colorado
Address:	800 Griffiths Way, Vancouver
For single-game tickets:	800-663-9311 in Vancouver or 250-386-7600
Website:	canucks.com

an upscale place downtown. It's popular with stockbrokers and the upwardly mobile. Visiting players tend to dine here frequently. "It has a nice patio outside in the summer," says ex-Canuck Jyrki Lumme.

Canucks

Best ethnic:

Sushi restaurants are everywhere. From the higher-end **Tojos** (777 Broadway, 604-872-8050) to the takeout bento box places that line Robson Street, there are plenty of options. Ex-Canuck Steve Staios and forward Todd Bertuzzi gave a big thumb's up to **Miko Sushi** (1335 Robson, 604-681-0339). As for Italian food, Lumme likes **Chianti** (1850 4th St., 604-738-8411), a reasonably-priced establishment that provides big plates of tasty pasta.

Burgers and fries:

Players like to hang out at the **Cactus Club Cafe** (1136 Robson, 604-687-3278), a noisy fun-filled place known for its red-hot chicken wings. It's a great people-watching place, either from the streetside tables or the bar. Ex-Canuck Scott Walker calls it a hangout and will likely bring a few Predators along when Nashville comes to town. Former Canuck Bryan McCabe agrees: "It's where we used to hang out and go for lunch a lot. We sat outside when it was nice, had a bite to eat and watched people." After practice Staios liked **Sophie's Cosmic Cafe** (2095 4th St., 604-732-6810) in Kitsilano. "It's a little bit different and the portions are big," he says.

Hit the decks:

One of the best things about Vancouver dining is the number of restaurants that have outside decks where diners can eat and take in at the view. **Bridges** (1696 Duranleau, 604-687-4400) on Granville Island has a superb view as does **Monk McQueen's** (601 Stamps Landing, 604-877-1351) on False Creek. Monk's runs a bus service to games.

Steve Kariya #18

Lodging

Closest to the arena:

General Motors Place is located in the middle of Vancouver's downtown, so it's an easy and safe half-hour walk from most hotels. A good pick would be the **Georgian Court** (773 Beatty St., 604-682-5555), across the street from the B.C. Place football stadium and about a three-minute walk from GM Place. It houses a nice bar and the William Tell, one of the city's finer restaurants. If you're on a lower budget, check out the **Sandman Inn** (180 Georgia St., 604-681-2211). It's part of a chain and is right next to GM Place. It's also home to the Shark Club, one of Vancouver's trendier bars.

For luxury:

There are plenty of plush digs around Vancouver. Most of them are situated where the views are. The top choice is the **Pan Pacific** (999 Canada Pl., 604-662-8111), a 504-room hotel right on the waterfront. It's distinctive because of its roof, which has a big white canopy sail. Originally the site of the Canada pavilion at the Expo '86 World's Fair, it offers spectacular views of the water and mountains and the cruise ships that dock right outside. President Clinton stayed there for the Pacific Rim Summit. Right across the street is the **Waterfront** (900 Canada Pl., 604-691-1991). It's also nice and a little less costly. Further along the shore, closer to the Lions Gate Bridge and Stanley Park, sits the **Westin Bayshore** (1601 Georgia St., 604-682-3377). It's another establishment where you open the curtains to a spectacular view. The Bayshore has a nice outdoor pool.

Canucks

Where the boys are:

Two seasons ago, 13 teams stayed at the Pan Pacific, 11 at the Bayshore and one—Montreal—at the Waterfront. Some Canucks live at the **Rosedale on Robson** (838 Hamilton St. 604-689-8033), an apartment-hotel that's just a five-minute walk from GM Place. There's a good upscale deli there called Rosey's.

Something different:

The Sylvia (1154 Gilford St., 604-681-9321), a forgotten relic, is further away from the arena in the middle of the concrete residential area just a block away from Stanley Park. Built in 1912, it's right on the water, and covered in ivy like the fence at Wrigley Field. It's an older, funkier, cheaper alternative to the big new hotels in the heart of the downtown. The Syl also has a distinctive bar with great water views. Actor Errol Flynn is said to have died in the company of a young woman while in the midst of a binge at the Sylvia.

Shopping & Attractions

This one's a bit of a no-brainer. All the players enjoy strolling Robson Street. "I like to go down Robson Street, walk around and shop," says Ex-

Canuck Peter Zezel. Robson is a trendy street lined with boutiques, restaurants, and coffee bars and crowded with shoppers, gawkers, and buskers.

Canucks

There are other places. The **Pacific Centre** is a decent-sized indoor mall downtown. If you're into antiques, Granville Street between 6th and 16th is good, as is Main Street south of 26th. Vancouver has the third-largest North American Chinatown after New York and San Francisco. **Gastown** is a touristy but fun area which is a good place to buy those "I visited Vancouver" souvenirs.

Vancouver's main attraction is its beauty. It's not unusual to see a player or two rollerblading along the **Sea Wall**, a 5.5-mile pathway that surrounds beautiful Stanley Park. If you wish to stray farther from the city, take a Skyride up **Grouse Mountain** for a panoramic view of Vancouver and its environs. Vancouver also offers excellent museums. The **Museum of Anthropology** (6393 Marine Dr., 604-822-3825) at the University of British Columbia has an extensive collection on Native North American artifacts, including a spectacular display of totem poles.

Those with ample time should try skiing in **Whistler**, a 90-minute drive, bus ride or train ride from downtown. Be sure to plan ahead. Several U.S. ski magazines have listed Whistler as the best ski resort in North America, so it gets crowded.

Favorite City on the Road

Mark Messier, who won a Stanley Cup with the New York Rangers in 1994, finds it a thrill to return to that city. Jyrki Lumme, who played for Vancouver for nine seasons before signing with Phoenix, concurs. "That would be the most popular spot for most of the guys," he says. "When we get an extra road day off, it's nice when it's in New York."

Toronto and Ottawa are popular because so many players come from Ontario. Players also like Chicago because it's such a great hockey city.

Cool Fact

Pavel Bure, the most dynamic scorer in Canucks history, almost wasn't. In 1990, NHL President John Ziegler voided the Canucks' choice of the Russian winger in 1989, citing rules governing drafting of Europeans, and said he would have to go back into the 1990 draft. Ziegler reversed himself a month later, citing new evidence from Russia. Bure won rookie-of-the-year in 1991–92, scored 60 goals each of the following two seasons, and put together a 16-game point-scoring streak in the 1994 playoffs to help lead the Canucks to the Finals.

Franchise History

Winning a Stanley Cup is not new to the city of Vancouver. In 1915, before the National Hockey League was formed, the Vancouver Millionaires of

VANCOUVER

the Pacific Coast Hockey Association won the Cup. The trophy has not made the rounds of Vancouver since, although the Vancouver Canucks have had a chance in the finals on two occasions. Vancouver was granted an NHL franchise on May 22, 1970. The first ten years of the team's existence were marked by a failure to make the playoffs, but in 1982 the Canucks assembled a contender that lost to the powerhouse New York Islanders in the Finals. Although it looked as if the franchise had turned the corner, it would be another 12 years before the Canucks would again return to the Finals, this time losing to another New York team, the Rangers.

Canucks

Markus Naslund #19

Famers

Most Valuable Player (Hart Trophy): None
    Hockey Hall of Fame:
    Builders: John "Jake" Milford, 1984; Norman "Bud" Poile, 1990; Frank A. Griffiths, 1993.
    Retired numbers: 12 Stan Smyl

Records

Games played			Most points, season			Most goalie wins,		
Stan Smyl	896		Pavel Bure	110		season		
Career goals			**Most goals, game**			Kirk McLean		38
Stan Smyl	262		Several players	4		**Most shutouts, career**		
Career assists			**Most assists, game**			Kirk McLean		20
Stan Smyl	411		Patrik Sundstrom	6		**Most shutouts, season**		
Career points			**Most points, game**			Gary Smith,		
Stan Smyl	673		Patrik Sundstrom	7		Garth Snow		6
Most goals, season			**Most goalie wins,**			**Stanley Cups:**		
Pavel Bure	60		career			None.		
Most assists, season			Kirk McLean	211				
Andre Boudrias	62							

Capitals

Andrei Nikolishin #13

around the town with the Capitals

Mention a power play in Washington and hockey isn't necessarily the first thing that comes to mind.

By its political nature, Washington is a city that reveres winners. That's why the three-time Super Bowl champion Redskins are the city's premier team. And it's also why the Capitals, who have tasted more playoff heartbreak than success, were merely a blip on the suburban radar.

But all that's changing. The Capitals moved from the out-dated US Airways Arena in isolated Landover, Md., to the sparkling MCI Center in the heart of the bustling nation's capital. They brought in the flashy management team of general manger George McPhee and coach Ron Wilson. And they reached the Stanley Cup Finals for the first time in their history before falling in four games to the Detroit Red Wings juggernaut in 1998.

"This is a great sports market," McPhee says. "All you have to do is provide some hope and the fans will respond."

They did—eventually. Many suburbanites didn't follow the team downtown and midweek regular-season games were sparsely attended. Mindful of the team's playoff past, fans didn't buy out postseason games as quickly as in other hockey-crazed cities. But in the '98 playoffs master motivator Wilson kept pushing the right buttons, the Capitals kept advancing, and Washingtonians began talking about Olie the Goalie more than the Speaker of the House.

Even the First Fan got into the action. President Clinton was spotted in then-owner Abe Pollin's box during Game 2 of the Eastern Conference finals. His impression as the first sitting president to attend a hockey game: "It's more exciting in person than it is watching it on TV."

That's a high-powered recommendation to go to a game. And the MCI Center is a great place to visit. In addition to great sightlines, it has a national sports gallery and a sporting goods store with 12 TV monitors.

That's not to say the MCI Center will ever rival the White House, Washington Monument or Lincoln Memorial as tourist must-sees. And attendance did drop when the Capitals slipped to non-playoff status in 1998–99. But new owner,

America Online exec Ted Leonsis, promises to make following the Capitals as interactive and high-tech as his company. If he succeeds in re-establishing a winning tradition in the city that backs winners, a hockey game at the MCI Center might become a place to see or be seen.

Capitals

MCI Center

Where to sit:
The best view is at the club level, which enables the fan to hear the whoosh of skates on ice. Unfortunately, there are only 3,000 of these seats and few are available on game day.

If it's all you can get:
There isn't a bad seat in the house, although some say watching a game from the top

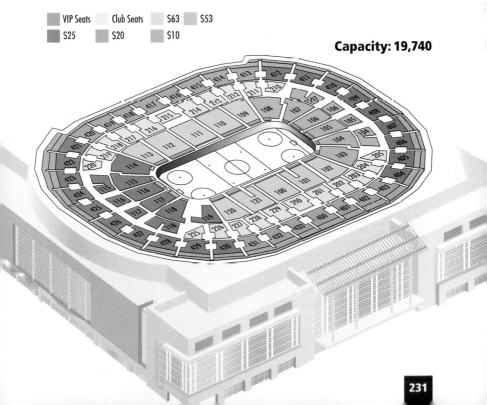

| ■ VIP Seats | ■ Club Seats | ■ $63 | ■ $53 |
| ■ $25 | ■ $20 | ■ $10 | |

Capacity: 19,740

of the high 400 sections is akin to viewing an army of ants fighting over a crumb. If nothing else, the high seats offer a great vantage point from which to see a play develop. A lot of Flyers, Penguins, and Rangers fans make the trip when their teams are in **Capitals** town, and this is where they usually sit.

Special services:
Accessible seating is available on all levels, and reachable by elevator. Call the Accessible Seating and Services office at 202-661-5065. Those wishing to use TTY can dial 202-661-5066.

Ticket availability:
There are 19,740 seats for hockey. Few games sell out, and tickets are usually available at the box office. Scalping is illegal in Washington.

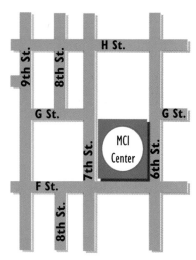

Parking:
The 500 spaces beneath the MCI Center are reserved. There are 7,000 parking spaces in lots and garages within a 10-minute walk of the arena. Expect to pay between $15 and $20, and note that most lots close an hour after the game. There are very few spots on the street within a 4-block radius.

Public transportation:
The subway is the way to go. Take the Metro to Gallery Place station on the Red, Yellow and Green lines. If on a Blue or Orange Line stop, transfer to the Red Line at Metro Center. Gallery Place is steps from the front entrance of the MCI Center.

By car:
Signs throughout downtown Washington lead you to the MCI Center, located in the heart of the Chinatown district at 7th and F Sts. NW. From Baltimore, Philadelphia, or New York, follow I-95 toward Richmond on the Capital Beltway and then take Exit 22 onto the Baltimore-Washington Parkway. Continue to New York Avenue and make a left on 7th Street.

Cuisine:
The MCI Center has 24 concession stands that offer everything from Buffalo wings to pizza to deli sandwiches to Chinese food.

MCI Center

Home-ice advantage:
Many visiting teams find themselves in awe of the sightseeing. But sometimes, this hurts the Caps. A few teams have won after being inspired by the Vietnam Veteran Memorial.

Nightlife

For after the game:
This is conservative Washington, so why not be different? **Cafe Atlantico** (405 8th St. NW, 202-393-0812) is the home of new Latin cooking, some of which will be prepared right at your table. You can order such items as quesadillas, Argentine breaded steak and Brazilian stew, all at a very decent price. One spot that's always full of people is **Cashion's Eat Place** (1819 Columbia Rd. NW, 202-797-1819). The mood is very relaxed, and they serve old-fashioned, home-style food. Try the seafood dishes and the roast chicken. Afterwards, make sure you have a dessert made by their top-flight chef.

For a quiet drink:
Former Cap Kelly Miller and some of his over-30 teammates like the **District Chophouse** (509 7th St. NW, 202-347-3434), which offers more than fine food. The restaurant has an upscale atmosphere in which one can choose from many micro-brews; it's a favorite of some of the team's more laid-back players. The drinking crowd at the **Capital Grille** (601 Pennsylvania Ave. NW, 202-737-6200) prefers suits to jeans and enjoys soft chairs instead of bar stools. Located in the shadow of the Capitol, the steakhouse is a short subway ride from the arena and often attracts high-ranking team officials before and after the game.

Best pub:
You won't find the Capitals walking across the street to **The Rock** (717 6th St. NW, 202-842-7625), but that doesn't mean you shouldn't. It's a sports bar for the fan who wants to grab a beer after the game and maybe watch a bit of SportsCenter before heading home. If you must wear a tie here, at least loosen it. It's a great place to watch the game if you can't get a ticket. Live music is the order of the day at **Nightclub 930** (815 V St. NW, 202-265-0930), which specializes in alternative rock.

Dining

For Italian:
Want to eat the dinner of (Eastern Conference) champions? Then try **That's Amore** (5225 Wisconsin Ave., 202-237-7800). Chef Gennaro Ferrigno

---

Capitals "Phone Booth" Facts

Opened:
12/2/97

First regular-season game:
12/5/97, 3–2 win over Florida

First goal:
Steve Washburn of Florida

First playoff game:
4/22/98, 3–1 win over Boston

Address:
601 F St. NW, Washington

For single-game tickets:
202-432-SEAT, 703-573-SEAT or 410-481-SEAT

Website:
washingtoncaps.com

---

cooked the team's pre-game meal for most home playoff games at MCI Center and provided meal-service for the team's charter in 1998. He also followed them to Detroit for the Stanley Cup Finals. Was it a coincidence that the team got the farthest it ever did in the playoffs? You decide. The chain has six restaurants in the Baltimore-Washington area. Designed to look like a Neapolitan mother's dining room, the restaurants serve up southern Italian cuisine—pasta,

Capitals

seafood, veal, and more—plus a vast array of wines imported from Italy. Capitals defenseman Joe Reekie recommended the Steak Vesuvio in the commercial he did.

For steak:

The Palm (1225 19th St. NW, 202-293-9091) is a short subway ride away in the Dupont Circle area. It is arguably one of the classiest restaurant-bars in the city and is priced accordingly. It's known for its steak, lobsters and Italian dishes, and is where the city's powerbrokers

Olaf Kolzig #37

gather. Get there early because seating is limited. Kelly Miller often went to the **District Chophouse** with teammates for a steak or a thick lamb chop after the game. It's housed in an old bank building and is very convenient to the MCI Center, less than two blocks away.

Best ethnic:
Given that the arena is in the heart of Chinatown, there are numerous Chinese restaurants to choose from. **Hunan Chinatown** (624 H St. NW, 202-783-5858) is considered by many to be the closest to the real thing. The General Tso's chicken comes recommended. Also, the Adams Morgan section of the city (north of Florida Avenue between Rock Creek Park and 16th Street) has nearly every type of ethnic food imaginable. Left wing Chris Simon often heads up there after games.

I ate in D.C.:
Also check out the **Hard Rock Cafe** (999 E St. NW, 202-737-7625) and **Planet Hollywood** (1101 Pennsylvania Ave. NW, 202-783-7827). The food isn't sensational, but the T-shirts and souvenirs they sell will let everyone know you spent time in the nation's capital.

Lodging

Washington hotels tend to fill up quickly and get pricey during tourist season, which begins in March and April, so it's best to plan ahead.

Team favorite:
The **Grand Hyatt** (1000 H St.

NW, 202-582-1234) offers rich accommodations and is within walking distance of the MCI Center. This is the site team officials recommend to out-of-town guests. Ex-Capital Esa Tikkanen lived here during the 1998 playoff run and the NHL used it as its headquarters hotel during the 1998 Stanley Cup Finals.

Most luxurious:
For a hotel that is a cut above the rest, check out the **Renaissance Mayflower** (1127 Connecticut Ave. NW, 202-347-3000), which has a classy interior, luxurious rooms, and a wonderful restaurant. It's also the hotel for most visiting NHL teams. Guests may take the Metro to the MCI Center from there.

If you're a tourist:
Hilton (1001 16th St. NW, 202-393-1000) is a subway ride away from the MCI Center and within walking distance of the White House and Washington Monument. It also features a quaint bar with soft chairs, the better to unwind after a game.

If you want those Marriott points, there's the **Marriott** (1331 Pennsylvania Ave. NW, 202-393-2000) or the **Washington Marriott** (1221 22nd St. NW, 202-872-1500, 800-228-9290). They are well appointed but less expensive than the Mayflower and Grand Hyatt.

Shopping & Attractions

Union Station (50 Massachusetts Ave. NE, 202-371-9441)

has three stories of shops inside a converted train shed. It's two stops down the Red Line from the arena. Or you can stroll down M Street and Wisconsin Avenue in Georgetown to find trendy shops and even trendier restaurants. If your taste goes to the upscale, try **White Flint Mall** (11301 Rockville Pk., Kensington, MD, 301-468-5777), with stores like **Bloomingdale's** and **Lord & Taylor's** and a free shuttle from the White Flint stop on the Red Line. The **Fashion Centre** (1100 S. Hayes St., Arlington, VA, 703-415-2400), off the Pentagon City Metro stop on the Blue Line, is anchored by **Macy's** and **Nordstrom's** and has three stories of shops arranged around a sunny atrium. For sports souvenirs, check out **Modell's Sporting Goods** in the MCI Center. It has a full line of Capitals merchandise as well as other NBA, NHL, NFL, and MLB teams.

Sightseeing: The MCI Center's downtown location makes it convenient to all the wonderful museums and monuments that make the city a worldwide attraction. Your choices are many, so plan a long trip. A good walker can see the **Washington Monument** (tickets are available at the 15th Street kiosk), **Vietnam Veterans Memorial**, **Lincoln Memorial**, **FDR Memorial**, and the **Jefferson Memorial**, which is beautifully framed by cherry blossoms in early spring. Tours are offered at the **White House** (1600 Pennsylvania Ave., tickets also required), and the **Smithsonian Institution's** museums, between

Constitution and Independence Ave. and 14th and 3rd St., are world famous. The **National Air and Space Museum**, with its rockets and IMAX theater, is popular with kids, as are the dinosaur and gemstone exhibits at the **National Museum of Natural History**.

Favorite City on the Road

"I like going to the Canadian cities," says left wing Chris Simon, who was born in Wawa, Ontario. "It's my favorite place to play because of the atmosphere, especially Montreal. I love the city; it's got great food and a great nightlife."

Jan Bulis was a huge Toronto fan until Maple Leaf Gardens closed. Now, South Florida gets his vote.

Steve Konowalchuk loves Vancouver. "I have a lot of family out in that area and spent a lot of time there growing up as a kid," he says.

Cool Fact

The Capitals hold the dubious distinction of blowing 3-games-to-1 playoff leads three times. The most frustrating loss came in 1987, when they lost Game 7 at home to the New York Islanders in four overtimes. When new coach Ron Wilson entered the 1998 playoffs, he talked about the team's need for "exorcising demons." The Capitals tempted fate by taking 3–1 leads in their first three series and held on to reach the Stanley Cup Finals for the first time.

Capitals

WASHINGTON

Franchise History

Granted a franchise on June 11, 1974, the Washington Capitals suffered through the first eight years of its existence without going to the playoffs. When the Philadelphia Flyers came to visit the Capital Centre, their rowdy fans renamed the arena "Spectrum South" and created something of a home ice disadvantage for the Caps. A turning point in the fortunes of the team can be traced to one date: September 10, 1982. That's when general manager David Poile sent Rick Green and Ryan Walter to Montreal for Doug Jarvis, Craig Laughlin, Brian Engblom and Rod Langway. The ex-Canadiens, in particular Rod Langway, brought a winning spirit that had been lacking in the club. In the spring of 1983, for the first time in franchise history, the Washington Capitals made the playoffs. They would go on to earn post-season berths for 14 consecutive years. After missing the playoffs in 1997, the Capitals bounced back the next season to make their finest showing by advancing all the way to the Stanley Cup Finals.

Capitals

Peter Bondra #12

Famers

Most Valuable Player (Hart Trophy): None
Hockey Hall of Fame: None
Retired numbers: 5 Rod Langway, 7 Yvon Labre

Records

Games played		Most points, season		Most goalie wins, season	
Kelly Miller	940	Dennis Maruk	136	Jim Carey	35
Career goals		**Most goals, game**		**Most shutouts, career**	
Mike Gartner	397	Bengt Gustafsson,		Jim Carey	14
Career assists		Peter Bondra	5	**Most shutouts, season**	
Michal Pivonka	418	**Most assists, game**		Jim Carey	9
Career point		Mike Ridley	6	**Stanley Cups:**	
Mike Gartner	789	**Most points, game**		None	
Most goals, season		Dino Ciccarelli	7		
Dennis Maruk	60	**Most goalie wins, career**			
Most assists, season					
Dennis Maruk	76	Don Beaupre	128		

237

Photo Credits

Bruce Bennett Studios: v, 33, 72, 76, 77, 78, 79, 80, 94, 162, 193, 197, 205, 208

C. Andersen/BBS: 9, 12, 14, 56, 82, 84, 86, 88, 204, 213, 216, 218, 229

Bruce Bennett/BBS: 23, 26, 48, 111, 114, 135, 144, 149, 155, 163, 169, 178, 184, 201, 203

H. DiRocco/BBS: 93, 95

J. Giamundo/BBS: 16, 32, 36, 55, 147, 152, 154, 158, 222

J.Leary/BBS: 15, 29, 30, 102, 146, 175

Scott Levy/BBS: 230

D. MacMillian/BBS: 40, 44, 47, 64, 70, 71, 89, 103, 106, 107, 171, 177

A. Marlin/BBS: 20, 22, 137, 185

Jim McIsaac/BBS: 39, 51, 52, 54, 62, 118, 130, 134, 136, 138, 170, 186, 187, 191, 195, 196, 210, 212, 221, 234

Lisa Meyer/BBS: 69, 237

Layne Murdoch/BBS: 63

National Hockey League® Clubs: 11, 18, 25, 35, 42, 50, 58, 66, 74, 83, 91, 98, 105, 114, 124, 132, 140, 150, 157, 165, 173, 180, 189, 199, 207, 215, 224, 232

A. Pichette/BBS: 38, 60, 68, 100, 117, 120, 121, 161

L. Redkoles/BBS: 96, 166

W. Roberts/BBS: 109, 110, 202

J. Russell/BBS: 122, 127, 128, 129

Brian Winkler/BBS: 18, 142, 145, 182, 226